THE FINAL FOREST
WILLIAM DIETRICH

▲▲▲▲▲▲▲

THE BATTLE FOR
THE LAST GREAT TREES OF
THE PACIFIC NORTHWEST

▲▲▲▲▲▲▲

SIMON & SCHUSTER
New York London Toronto Sydney Tokyo Singapore

SIMON & SCHUSTER
Simon & Schuster Building
Rockefeller Center
1230 Avenue of the Americas
New York, New York 10020

Designed by Pei Loi Koay
Map by Christine E. Cox
Manufactured in the United States of America

1   3   5   7   9   10   8   6   4   2

Library of Congress Cataloging-in-Publication Data
Dietrich, William, date.
The final forest / William Dietrich.
p.   cm.
1. Old growth forests—Northwest, Pacific.   2. Forest
conservation—Northwest, Pacific.   3. Logging—Northwest, Pacific.
4. Forest ecology—Northwest, Pacific.   I. Title.
SD387.043D53   1992   91-46646
333.75′09795—dc20   CIP

ISBN: 0-671-72967-5

ACKNOWLEDGMENTS

▲▲▲▲▲▲▲▲

This book was made possible by the patience and trust of the extraordinary people who fill its pages. I thank them for their time, help, and eloquence. I particularly appreciated the warmth and honesty of so many people in Forks, Washington.

Absolutely essential was the aid and resources of the Seattle, King County, University of Washington, Forks, *Seattle Times*, and *Oregonian* libraries. Also invaluable was information provided by the College of Forestry at the University of Washington, the Wilderness Society, the Sierra Club Legal Defense Fund, the Plum Creek Timber Company, and Weyerhaeuser.

A special thanks to my own employer, the *Seattle Times*, for giving me the time and support needed to complete this book, to agent Kris Dahl for her advice and encouragement, to editors Alice Mayhew, Eric Steel, and their staff at Simon & Schuster for their superb guidance and support, and to David Shipley and Tim Egan of *The New York Times* for helping provide the opportunity to write this book.

Finally I want to express my love and appreciation to my wife, Holly, and daughters, Lisa and Heidi, for their support and sacrifices.

To My Wife, Holly.

▲▲▲▲▲▲▲

CONTENTS

▲▲▲▲▲▲▲

Believe one who knows. You will find something greater in woods than in books. Trees and stones will teach you that which you can never learn from masters.

St. Bernard of Clairvaux, 1145

Do you think I was born in the woods to be afraid of an owl?

Jonathan Swift, 1738

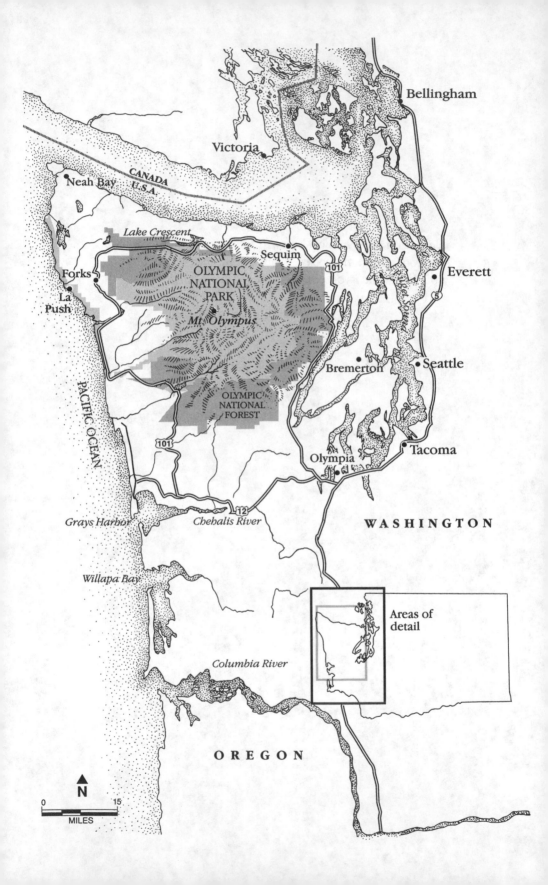

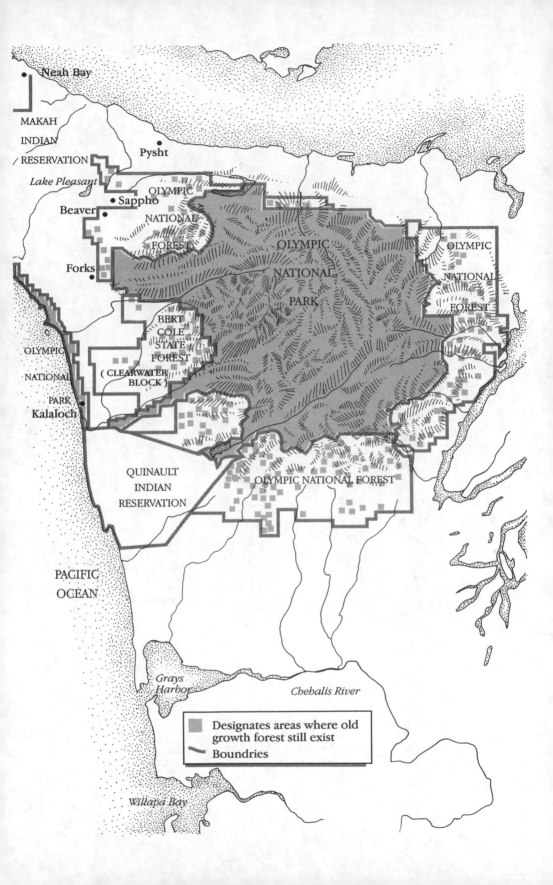

Neah Bay

MAKAH

INDIAN

/ RESERVATION

Lake Pleasant

OLYMPIC

Pysht

Beaver

Sappho

NATIONAL

FOREST

Forks

OLYMPIC

NATIONAL

PARK

OLYMPIC

NATIONAL

FOREST

BERT
COLE
STATE
FOREST

OLYMPIC

(CLEARWATER
BLOCK)

NATIONAL

PARK
Kalaloch

QUINAULT
INDIAN
RESERVATION

OLYMPIC NATIONAL FOREST

PACIFIC
OCEAN

Grays
Harbor

Chehalis River

Designates areas where old
growth forest still exist
Boundries

Willapa Bay

INTRODUCTION
THE LAST CORNER

▲▲▲▲▲▲▲

If it were more ordinary country, less lovely and less hard, maybe the love and the outrage would not be so keen.

But there is a quality about the forested mountains of the Olympic Peninsula, that very northwestern corner of the continental United States, that gets a grip on the mind and heart.

The traditional assumption is that the Pacific Northwest's moody skies keep newcomers away, but I think it is partly the clouds that draw people to this corner: the way they brood over the mountain tops, or mist the base and seem to cut the Olympic range loose from its connection to the earth.

The Olympic Mountains form a ring on the Peninsula like a sawtooth wall. You can stand on the steep sidewalks of downtown Seattle— the skyscrapers next to streets where just a bit more than a century ago fat virgin timber was skidded down to the crude sawmills on Elliott Bay—and study the mountains for a reminder of what once must have been here. The metropolis sprawls nearly one hundred miles along Puget Sound. Its new urban dwellers look to the forested mountains for memory.

The Peninsula is best introduced from the deck of a Washington State ferry, the boat's metal vibrating underfoot and a brisk wind blowing across the prow of the vessel from the gray waters of Puget Sound. From there, America's fourth corner can look like a place more imagined than real. Sometimes you'll board the ferry to get closer to the mountains and a trick of the air will make them seem to recede out of reach.

In the ferry's fluorescent-lit, linoleum-tiled interior, tourists can study maps of the Olympic Peninsula. The more you study it, the more remarkable the geography seems. It is the kind of improbable, compact landscape a child might draw for a fantasy kingdom.

I am reminded of a castle, with a moat. The Peninsula is about 6,200 square miles in size—about halfway between the size of Connecticut and Massachusetts—and is surrounded on three sides by water: almost four, if you want to count the Chehalis River to the south. Making up the saltwater portion of this castle moat is the Pacific Ocean to the west, the broad Strait of Juan de Fuca to the north, and the fjord of Hood Canal and its neighboring Puget Sound on the east. Its ramparts are the Olympic Mountains, and its central keep is glacier-clad Mount Olympus.

Most mountain ranges arrange themselves in a line, giving clues to the geologic forces underneath. The Olympics, sitting atop some of the most complicated plate tectonics in the western hemisphere, are a circular fortress, the interior of the range hidden by the outlying peaks. A proper castle would have an engineered symmetry of wall and tower, gate and courtyard. The Olympics are less tidy. Crests of rock and ice run hither and yon with no discernible logic. "There is no regularity about their formation, but jumbled up in the utmost confusion," Army Lieutenant Joseph P. O'Neil reported in 1885 after getting a glimpse of the range from a foothill after ten days thrashing through thick forest. O'Neil had hoped to lead the first party into the unexplored mountains. Unfortunately, his Indian guide deserted when told their destination, a mule toppled off a cliff and carried with it critical supplies, and a private got lost in the trees and disappeared, never to be found again. The country is still a bit like that.

The wildest ocean coastline left in the Lower Forty-eight is on this peninsula. So are the wettest valleys and some of the greatest weather extremes. Annual rainfall ranges from an estimated two hundred inches a year on the Peninsula's western mountain slopes to seventeen inches just thirty miles away in the mountains' rain shadow at Sequim. The climate difference between the dense rain forest and the wind-swept alpine ridges, just twenty miles apart, is similar to moving 1,500 miles northward toward the Pole. The mix produces some of the most varied ecology and biggest trees in the world. Down in the Queets River drainage is the world's largest Douglas fir. Up in the Quinault is the world's largest western hemlock and yellow cedar. On the remote Bailey Range of the Olympics is the world's largest subalpine fir.

Of course the very biggest trees are probably gone, cut generations ago, logged when the stupendous nature of the forest was so commonplace as to make it unremarkable. The present world's-record Douglas fir in total volume is 221 feet with its top broken off, but the tallest conifer ever found in the United States was a nineteenth-century fir measuring 385 feet before it was cut down. There is an historic photo of a fallen giant in Canada claimed to have exceeded 400 feet. The current record-holding western red cedar is twenty-one feet in diameter, but there is an 1899 newspaper photo of a cedar near Snoqualmie Falls, in what is now virtually a suburb of Seattle, that was forty feet in diameter.

The castle's battlements climb, ridge snaking up to crest, until they peak at grandly named Mount Olympus, 7,980 feet high, its jagged hump draped in ice. Rivers gush out of the heart of these mountains in radial fashion like the spokes of a wheel, and in several places glaciers push blue-green snouts of ice down toward the shadowy valleys.

There is aboriginal poetry in the names of the rivers the tribes gave: Elwha and Sol Duc, Hamma Hamma and Duckabush, Humptulips and Quillayute, Skokomish and Wynoochee. The romance of this landscape rubbed off on its pioneer explorers as well. There are names around the Peninsula worthy of a pirate's treasure map: Destruction Island, Octopus Mountain, Gray Wolf Pass, and Dead Man's Hill. And names to evoke the landscape: a Mount Olympus and an Enchanted Valley, a Hurricane Ridge and a Storm King mountain. When the clouds wrapped around Storm King, the settlers learned, wet weather was coming.

This impression of grandiose improbability is reinforced when one looks up from the ferry map and studies the mountains themselves. Depending on the air and its ability to magnify or color the light, the Olympics change. They loom large one day and fade another. When ocean weather fronts routinely lay a lid of cloud across the populated Puget Sound basin, the Olympics can disappear for weeks. When the weather clears and they rematerialize—particularly in winter, when covered in glistening white—the effect of their sugared skyline can be startling, as if adding a third dimension to a land flattened by those clouds.

Sometimes the Olympics stand up on the horizon with sobering solidity, every crag and crevice picked out by a morning sun with the precision of a dental drill. I remember one late-summer dawn from the ferry when the mountains towered over Puget Sound like cathedral buttresses, nearly snowless and hard as iron. A full moon hung above them like a communion wafer.

More common is their insubstantiality. From Seattle, cloud and light often turn the Olympics into a range of shifting blue shadow, the valleys seeming to lead back into an ethereal gloom as mysterious as the mouths of caverns. No one who sees them like that—crowned by interior storms and with a spectral allure—can argue the decision of British Captain John Meares to name the highest peak Olympus when he spotted it from the sea in 1788. "If that not be the home wherein dwell the Gods," he wrote, "it is beautiful enough to be."

Just over a century after Meares's naming, in the year 1889 when Washington became a state, the Olympic Mountains remained one of the last places in the nation that was unexplored. Seattle already had 40,000 people, and Tacoma 36,000. Just twenty-five miles away across Puget Sound was a range that remained unknown. Settlers had hacked out homesteads on the Peninsula's coast and penetrated a bit up its river valleys from the sea, but the interior had defied penetration. It was fortified with a forest as big and dense as anything ever seen. There were trees so big that a few eccentrics roofed hollow stumps and made a home there.

According to pioneer accounts, no Indians professed to have penetrated the interior. Their reluctance was attributed to fear of fierce natives, evil spirits, or past disasters. In 1888, Territorial Governor Eugene Semple penned an article advocating the Peninsula's exploration. "It is a land of mystery," he wrote, "awe-inspiring in its mighty constituents and wonder-making in its unknown expanse of canyon and ridge. . . . Red men and white men have gone all around this section, as bushmen go around a jungle in which a man-eating tiger is concealed, but the interior is incognito."

Semple cited Indian legends, which held that the interior of the Olympics was a large, temperate valley that had once been inhabited by a peaceful race. They were supposedly driven out by a catastrophic earthquake caused by Seatco, chief of the evil spirits.

Newspapermen were even more imaginative. The *Seattle Press* reported on October 23, 1889, that the Indians believed a fierce tribe still occupied the interior. The writer added that the common theory of pioneers was that rivers on the interior slopes of the mountains fed a great lake hidden behind the visible peaks, which had a subterranean outlet to the ocean. A New York newspaper went further, postulating that the inhabitants of the center were cannibals.

That winter, the *Seattle Press* decided to sponsor a six-man exploring party to cross the Olympic Mountains as a publicity stunt. A group was assembled, given a ton of supplies, Winchester repeating rifles, bandoleers of ammunition, and a ration of whiskey they drank up before going more than a few miles. They were landed in Port Angeles on the Peninsula's northern coast in December, the beginning of the heavy snow season. Despite the snow and the warnings of locals, they proceeded up the Elwha River, hoping to reach the interior valley when spring broke and fearing that if they did not set out a rumored rival exploring party would beat them to glory. Entering the range at its northeast corner, the Press Expedition emerged at the southwest in May 1890. It had taken them six months to travel about sixty miles as the crow flies. Their clothes were in tatters, virtually all their supplies were consumed or lost, and at one point they were so hungry that in two days they devoured a bear they had shot, greedily drinking cups of its melted grease. They found no cannibals and no broad valley, just rugged peaks and monstrously vegetated canyons.

"There is something much like exploring a dark rat hole in this following a stream in these woods, and enclosed by such hills as these," wrote Captain Charles Adams Barnes, an expedition member, of the Quinault River Valley. "One can only see a few yards in any direction near the ground, and overhead the foliage shuts out even the sky. One cannot get a sight of the mountains or hills. At long intervals on approaching the river the most that can be seen is just sufficient to enable one, by tracing the specks of light through the branches of the trees, to expect that the gap continues a little further in the given direction."

Barnes was struggling through one of the densest parts of America's final great forest, a wet coastal strip that extends more than 1,500 miles from the high redwoods of northern California to the thick Sitka spruce of southeast Alaska. California could boast the tallest and oldest groves. The redwoods routinely lived 2,000 years and some giant sequoia reached three millennia. Southern Oregon had the most varied ecology. Alaska displayed the most rugged, grandest terrain of peak and fjord. But temperature and rainfall combined in the coastal mountains of northwestern Oregon, southwestern Washington, and the west slope of the Olympics to produce the thickest, richest, most swiftly growing forest of all. By the time the Press Expedition struggled through the Olympic Mountains, loggers had been whittling at the edges of this conifer empire for two generations, and seemed to have scarcely made a mark.

At first the trees simply proved daunting to the primitive technology available. In 1850, British Captain Richard Hinderwell stopped at Olympic Peninsula's Discovery Bay to cut trees for masts and spars. One of the biggest problems confronting his ship's carpenter, William Bolton, was finding Douglas fir small enough to fit the specifications of two-foot-thick butts. It took the ship's crew and a band of hired Clallam Indians four months to cut seventeen spars. The trees were so dense it was difficult to find room to let them fall over. It was even worse trying to move them to the water. Four-inch-thick hawsers snapped trying to drag the trees across the rough, log-strewn ground.

The forest's unbroken gloom could prove psychologically taxing as well. Charles Nordhoff wrote about the forest for *Harper's New Monthly Magazine* after a February 1874 visit to Astoria at the mouth of the Columbia River. He remarked on "the dreary continuity of shade. . . . It had, I confess, a gloomy, depressing influence. The fresh, lovely green of the evergreen foliage, the wonderful arrowy straightness of the trees, their picturesque attitude where they cover the headlands and reach down to the very water's edge, all did not make up for their weight upon my sensibilities."

The forest was an obstacle. "And off we bounded into the woods at the rate of three to four miles an hour," wrote Samuel Bowles of a stage journey through Washington Territory in 1865 that concluded a trek across the United States. "These are the finest forest we have yet met, the trees larger and taller and standing thicker; so thick and tall that the ground they occupy could not hold them cut and corded as wood; and the undergrowth of shrub and flower and vine and fern, almost tropical in its luxuriance and impenetrable for its closeness. Washington Territory must have more timber and ferns and blackberries and snakes to the square mile than any other state or territory of the Union. We occasionally strike a narrow prairie or threadlike valley; perhaps once in 10 miles a clearing of an acre or two, rugged and rough in its half-redemption from primitive forest; but for the most part it was a continuous ride through the forests, so unpeopled and untouched that the very spirit of Solitude reigned supreme, and made us feel its presence as never upon ocean or plain."

In such a place, logging became a necessary first step for progress. The vast virgin forest that had stretched from the Atlantic Seaboard to west of the Mississippi was mostly gone. After 250 years of pioneer settlement, this forest was the last great place to be conquered. The scale of the harvest was heroic. Here were trees as tall as thirty-story buildings and ten or fifteen feet in diameter. Many were growing before

Columbus arrived; some went back a thousand years. A single log could fill a logging truck and a family could picnic on its stump. An acre typically held five to seven times the amount of wood as an acre of Eastern white pine forest. Farmers could not simply yank out these stumps; rather, they dug a pit underneath and built fires that would eat for months, burning the tree's butt away from its roots. It was an outsized kind of place, and the challenge was to bring it down to human scale.

"It was strangely like war," Northwest historian Murray Morgan wrote of the first logging of the Olympic Peninsula in his 1955 book, *The Last Wilderness*. "They attacked the forest as if it were an enemy to be pushed back from the beachheads, driven into the hills, broken into patches, and wiped out. Many operators thought they were not only making lumber but liberating the land from the trees, making room for the farmers. They advertised the cut-over areas for sale as farmland, and they found takers, for the price was low and the dream of a bit of land of one's own was almost universal. They were called stump ranchers, these hopeful people who came from everywhere to farm this new-won land. They grubbed at the great roots; they fought the encroaching salal and alder and huckleberry, and the spikey, insinuating, indestructible blackberry vines. They raised a few crops and gave up, nearly all of them, though many wasted as much as a lifetime trying to grow truck and grain on land that, it finally became clear, was meant only to grow trees."

The homestead instinct failed in most of the great forest. The land went to either the government or the big timber companies. A 1913 report by the U.S. Bureau of Corporations indicated 70.7 percent of the private timberland in western Oregon was owned by only sixty-eight individuals.

History came late to the Olympic Peninsula, however. Last to be explored, last to be farmed, last to be logged. Oh, there were trees there, wood in greater volume than any place on earth. "Taken as a whole this is the most heavily forested region in Washington and, with few exceptions, the most heavily forested region of the country," a 1902 government survey concluded of the western Peninsula. But out in the West End there were no harbors and few roads. Logging was scarcely feasible until the wood demands of World War I pushed a railroad out near the tiny farm hamlet of Forks, so-named because it was built on an Indian prairie about where the Calawah and the Bogachiel and the Sol Duc and the Quillayute Rivers all ran together.

The boom years of Forks—the years when the town's population would double and a man could get hired onto a logging crew just by standing on a street corner—would not come until the 1970s.

By that time, the wild and unruly forest of giant trees and silver snags and behemoth mossy logs and secret rot—the titanic Northwest wood that even farsighted timber tycoon Frederick Weyerhaeuser had once judged to be inexhaustible—was mostly gone. It had been replaced by a younger, trimmer, smaller, plainer industrial forest. Either that or wastelands of broken slash, so thick that new trees could not regrow. By that time, when Forks was booming, a debate had started on what was disappearing and what was taking its place.

The Olympic Peninsula was no stranger to this debate. Way back in 1897, President Grover Cleveland had taken the first step toward averting a feared "timber famine" by setting aside national timber reserves, including two-thirds of the Peninsula. Land use there has been contested ever since.

Responding to timber industry protests, President William McKinley reduced the size of Cleveland's Olympic reserve by a third. In 1909, President Theodore Roosevelt took the opposite tack again, setting aside the heart of the Olympic Range as a 620,000-acre National Monument. In 1915, President Woodrow Wilson cut the monument's size to 328,000 acres in hopes of spurring manganese prospecting to feed war industries. In 1935, a bill was introduced in Congress to create a 728,360-acre national park. Local residents, hoping to persuade President Franklin Roosevelt that such a park was too big, drove him halfway around the peninsula in 1937, from Lake Crescent in the north, through Forks, to Aberdeen and Hoquiam in the south. The drive was in large part through a tunnel of trees: so many trees that to many inhabitants the idea of setting such a great number aside was lunacy. If Roosevelt was impressed, it was not in the way his hosts had hoped. He completed his visit by announcing his support for the park. Additions would eventually swell its size to nearly a million acres.

The Olympic Peninsula thus developed into a microcosm of the land-use pattern throughout the Pacific Northwest that was to spark one of the bitterest ecological and economic debates in the nation's history. The lines between exploitation and preservation were drawn not just figuratively but literally, right across the Olympic map.

The Peninsula became in essence a donut. Olympic National Park, where logging is prohibited, is the donut hole, occupying the highest mountains in the middle. Olympic National Forest, part of it wilderness and part open to logging, circles much of the park in a second ring. State and private lands, heavily cut, circles this national forest, and salt water in turn circles that. The more land that was set aside, the more frantically the timber industry cut. Unlike Solomon and the baby, Congress not only proposed cutting the forest in two, but allowed it. The best place to see the absurd juxtaposition of this dual desire is on the Olympic coastline. There, a mile-wide strip of old-growth spruce and cedar preserved as part of the national park follows the beaches, mist streaming off the breakers and hanging in the belt of trees like campfire smoke. The shore seems unchanged since the explorers coasted by. This primeval forest ends a mile eastward as if shaven with a razor, the timber industry ensuring that the belt will not widen. To the east everything is cut in a rolling panorama of stumps and shorter, regrowing trees.

By the 1980s, the Olympic "castle" looked besieged. Most of the grand virgin old growth that so awed and depressed the pioneers was gone in the foothills between the water and the mountains. Replacing it was patchwork mosaic, green and brown, of recent clearcuts and regrowing timber, most of it still too young to be harvested again. To the timber industry, the mosaic was proof that trees were indeed a renewable resource. But environmentalists had coined the term "ancient forest" for the virgin remnants, scattered in patches here and there like a shattered regiment. Most of the ancients that were left were bunched up near the park boundary like fugitives seeking refuge in the castle keep. The transformation of the landscape, most of it accomplished in less than fifty years, is remarkable.

Not a few are proud of the change. To their view a stagnant forest has been replaced with a growing one. Much of the nation is housed with their wood. When the housed say too much wood was cut, loggers perceive hypocrisy and betrayal.

Others see not just a changed landscape but a disappearing ecosystem. It is not just that the big trees are gone, but that they are being replaced with a human-designed forest that is smaller, simpler, more uniform, and absent many species. They perceive erosion and sterility.

I grew up camping and hiking in the Olympics, but I was introduced to the controversy truly when I became a newspaper reporter. In time, the arguments became familiar and it was clear there were merits to all sides. What remained mysterious to me was how so many good people could love the forest so fiercely in such completely different ways. What experiences led people to take such competing views? And I was curious about just how the established view of the forest, promulgated by scientists and government, had seemed to shift so rapidly against logging.

That people see the forest differently is not entirely surprising. Just as the mountains can seem concrete at one time and insubstantial another, the forest can seem to mutate in mood and character. If it can be inspiring, it can also be overpowering, even suffocating. So thick and high are the trees that it can be difficult to see one hundred yards. It is easy to lose direction. Leaving established trails is only for the experienced, but so thick are the fallen logs and fecund underbrush that few are tempted. Cross-country travel in these forests can be a misery.

In appearance, the forest can indeed be majestic. When sunlight filters through the overhead canopy in shafts of illumination, the effect can be as inspiring as window-stained light in a Gothic cathedral.

More commonly there is cloud or fog, however, and the forest takes on a darker, brooding weight. In valley bottoms the very air seems to take on a green hue, and one has the sensation of being at the bottom of an aquarium.

Science has, unconsciously perhaps, reflected these different impressions. Forestry science developed to mold, defend, and justify the great harvest, and then more recently began to question it. The story of the struggle over America's final forest is in part the story of how science gave legitimacy to new points of view.

People have also brought new eyes into the forest, depending on where they came from and how they lived and what they cared for. The forest is the same, and yet different to each individual who looks at it. It is not uncommon for the landscape to inspire a mixture of fear and love and longing and greed.

Any big tree, for example, is a kind of time capsule, the accumulated biological memory of one hundred thousand days and nights, of snow and wind and rain. It is the rare person who remains unaffected by this aura of deep time, the wonder of things so big and so old. But trees are also mortal. They are inevitably dying in their core, succumbing to decay, ripe to be victimized by fire and storm. Each tree can be worth thousands of dollars, even tens of thousands, if harvested at its peak. To many who live in the dim woods, who work until their bodies ache, who sometimes see their friends and relatives killed by this forest, and who see it grow back up in riotous rankness in the cold rain, it is madness to ignore this economic gift.

Yet it was not the trees themselves that finally brought this conflict to a political boil. It was of all things a bird, so rare that few in the Pacific Northwest have ever seen one, and so conveniently trusting in responding to human calls that it made it possible for scientists to count and quantify its decline. The northern spotted owl came to symbolize the struggle between conquering nature and worshipping it.

In 1885 Lieutenant O'Neil, having failed to penetrate the Olympic vastness but able to at least look into the mountains, their flanks cloaked in dark timber, proved prophetic. The day will come, he wrote, when people "will glory in their wealth and beauty."

Wealth and beauty. This book is a glimpse of those twin desires of the human heart, and of the struggle to constantly remake our troubled relationships to the ancient earth.

1

THE CUTTER

▲▲▲▲▲▲▲

It is six A.M. and still dark this late September morning when the loggers begin crowding into Jerry's saw shop. Although the fir and hemlock in back of the store are still just silhouettes against the fading stars, the town of Forks is awake and moving with men on their way to the woods. At this hour it is still too gloomy for a logger to read the twin yellow banners that hang over the street at either end of the half-mile-long business strip: THIS COMMUNITY SUPPORTS TIMBER, TIMBER SUPPORTS THIS COMMUNITY. But there is no need to. That banner expresses bedrock sentiment. Timber is what is making the darkness before dawn hum. Highway 101 that runs past the front of the logging supply store is a steady stream of commuting pickups, their headlights blowing through occasional pockets of fog. Of course five and six A.M. isn't even early. In midsummer, when the days are really long, a log truck driver can be up at two A.M. to eat breakfast and get first load.

The self-proclaimed "Logging Capital of the World," Forks is neither as rough nor raggedy-ass as it once was, just a plain little timber community with about 3,000 people, 120 inches of rain, and a chewed-up forest where conifers grow back like weeds. The people here call their part of the Olympic Peninsula, "The West End." The term signifies not only its location on the compass, but its sense of isolation and independence. "Forks against the world," is how the town's activists wryly put it. This is a community that proclaimed a "James Watt Appreciation Day" in 1983 when the controversial interior secretary was pushed into resignation by polls showing Americans opposed his policies three to one. That erected a cross topped by spotted owls. That posted reader-board signs with defiant messages that sometimes irked the tourists driving through: JUST SAY NO TO THE BIGGEST LAND GRAB IN HISTORY, for example.

Forks's identity is so tied to harvesting the forest around it that it has gained a notoriety for resisting proposals for change. There is a big fight now over the last old trees, so nonsensical to most people in this town that they can't quite believe the scrap has gotten as far as it has. It is as if there isn't already a huge Olympic National Park a few ridges away, locking up whole valleys of trees forever. It is as if out here, in this worked-over country, there is really that much to fight over. A veteran cutter like Larry Suslick, who has thirty years in the woods, sees a bit of irony in having this fight now, after most of the big trees are gone. "When I started here, this whole peninsula was one, vast, huge forest," he recalled. "They're too late. They're fighting over the few little trees they call old growth, and half don't even know what real old growth is."

Maybe so. But the woods are shutting down over an owl few loggers claim to have ever seen. That may just be the beginning. There is also excitement about a sea bird, a marbled murrelet, so elusive it took scientists years to actually find a nest in the big old trees on the Peninsula to prove what they had long claimed must be there. There's the pileated woodpecker, which pecks at the insects that invade the dead and dying trees found in ancient forests. And Vaux's swift, called a chimney swift back East, which in this part of the country likes to nest in the hollow snags.

"Tweety birds"—that's what Jim Bleck of the state's Department of Natural Resources calls these symbols of this strange, disruptive debate. Every month, it seems, the biologists have some new idea of what to do for the tweety birds. Bleck figures state government in Washington is giving up $40,000 in good timber for every acre of trees it leaves alongside streams; and $45,000 to leave occasional snags and other wildlife habitat scattered on one hundred clearcut acres. "To me, that's a lot of money."

Bleck, who helps administer timber sales in the Forks area, doesn't necessarily disagree with the state's decisions. By and large, he approves the reforms that have swept over logging the past generation. But change is being heaped upon change. First the experts wanted logs hauled out of streams to clean them up. Now they want them left in, even *put* in, if you can believe that, to improve fish habitat. What will they want next week? "Scientists are fickle," he said. "They're like the wind, blowing every which way. They've got us chasing our tail."

One saw shop in Forks has already folded, and the owner of the last one, Jerry Leppell, just hopes he doesn't follow suit. Leppell figures his business was worth half a million dollars a couple of years ago, when timber was riding high. Now, with every suburbanite and his cousin in America trying to rein in logging, he thinks he'd be lucky to have a buyer pay $75,000 for the repair shop and store.

The saw shop is modern, but homey. There is a double-barreled wood stove made out of two fifty-five-gallon drums stacked on top each other, and a coffee pot, serve yourself. There is a Pepsi machine inside, Coke outside, take your pick. There is rough-sawn wood on the walls that sport mounted bison, deer, and bear heads. Under the main counter are posters that read, ENDANGERED SPECIES, picturing a trio of loggers, one of them a child. Back in the repair shop, where the carcasses of worn chainsaws are broken open to show their metal bones, there are more posters with scantily clad models touting the advantages of Stihl or Husqvarna chainsaws. A workaday chainsaw costs $900 and the loggers who actually cut down the trees—known as cutters or fallers or bushelers—are expected to bring their own to the job. A good cutter will wear out two of them per year.

Half of Jerry's business is servicing these saws. There is a pile of logs outside the shop door, their tops slit with a hundred cuts from the testing of repaired machines. Inside are displayed the rugged items loggers need: different lengths of saw bars the chain revolves around (up to sixty inches long in memory of the biggest trees and the deepest cuts), extra chains, shovels, axes, and mauls. There are the round silver mallets used by "shake rats" to split out bolts of cedar that will be sawn into shakes for American roofs. There are pipe wrenches for field repairs and come-alongs for winches, leather tool belts and bright plastic wedges pounded into a saw cut to help direct a tree's fall. The plastic is replacing the old steel variety because it is lighter. Still, a cutter can find himself lugging 60 or 70 pounds up and down the steep tree country.

All around the shop there are gas cans and engine lubricants and spray paints to mark trees due for cutting or survival. There are spools of thick steel cable and fine sharpening files for chainsaw teeth. There are the hobnail logging boots spelled "caulks" but pronounced "corks" that let loggers stride along the tops of wet logs without slipping into the dense underbrush below. There are gloves and rugged jeans and rain gear and rip-resistant pin-striped shirts called "Hickorys" for their toughness, even though there is no hickory in these Pacific Northwest woods. There are sweatshirts emblazoned with sayings that reflect the tense undercurrent of economic fear:

MY FAMILY IS SUPPORTED BY TIMBER DOLLARS.

SUPPORT YOUR LOCAL SPOTTED OWL: FROM A ROPE.

IF WE'D KICKED THE SHIT OUT OF THE PRESERVATIONISTS, WE WOULDN'T HAVE THIS PROBLEM TODAY.

Russ Poppe, twenty-nine, ambles in: a tall, rangy, friendly looking man with a toothy smile and the spare, sinewy look of one who truly earns his keep. His workday clothes are typical, part of what almost seems a uniform in timber country: billed cap, dirt-stained jeans with the bottoms cut high, or stagged off, to avoid catching branches and dirt, worn suspenders, a ragged flannel shirt, and the scuffed running shoes he drives to the logging site in so he won't pock the floor of his pickup with his caulks. If Poppe was to conform fully to the Forks stereotype he would have a snoose can and drive a Ford: back in the boom years of the 1970s you could buy a Ford in Forks's only auto dealership about as cheap as anywhere on earth, so everyone had Fords. Now you see Dodge and Chevy, even Mazda and Toyota.

The suspenders are usually deliberately dirty, a mark of hard work. Sometimes they sport a worn saying, such as a neutral FORKS LOGGER or, more belligerently, SAVE A LOGGER and SHOOT AN OWL. Suspenders out here are a necessity. Belts don't work in the woods: there is too much stooping and twisting and reaching and scrambling going on for it to make any sense to cinch yourself in at the waist.

Inside Jerry's there is the usual morning banter of men meeting briefly who have worked shoulder to shoulder on other crews, the words less important than the acknowledgment of each other's presence. The talk is barbed a bit by their uncertain future and the recognition of how controversial their work has become.

"Ready to kill more trees?" Russ jibes with one of the saw shop men.

Out in Russ's idling yellow pickup, Joe Helvey waits to go. He was able to sign on for work today because Russ's usual cutting partner has gone to Mexico for vacation. Cutters like to work in pairs: enough company for safety, not so much you get in each other's way. Once Russ had worked for Helvey, forty-five. Now, after Helvey's sawmill failed in Montana, the older man is back on the Pacific coast, getting work where he can.

A logger named Steve spots Joe Helvey and walks over to the pickup to say hello. Joe cranks down the window of the overheated cab to talk and let in the slight chill of early autumn. Steve joshes that Joe has signed on for a rough job. "S'posed to be scary," he relates.

"S'posed to be steep, and s'posed to be pretty rough," Helvey agrees.

Poppe and Helvey are doing the cutting on a blown-down twenty-acre quadrangle of timber in the foothills of the Olympic Mountains. It is a snarled, dangerous mess. The blowdown occurred after the U.S. Forest Service clearcut a fan-shaped bite of trees on the slope. Clearcutting—taking down every tree on a swathe of land—has been the practiced method of logging in this region for two generations. It is cheap, efficient, and leaves a clearing so barren that it gives the most desired tree to replant, Douglas fir, a chance to outgrow its shade-tolerant competitors. However, clearcutting also opens gaps in the forest as potentially calamitous to the neighboring ranks of shallow-rooted conifers as cracking the shield wall of a Roman legion. As the Northwest's forests have become increasingly fragmented by clearcutting, more and more miles of "edge" are exposed to the wind. In this case, the wind took a straight shot at the hillside from the restless North Pacific out on the horizon, striking the next draw full of trees and promptly knocking most of them over. Some had been growing two or three centuries. Now the government wants the downed trees salvaged before they decay, along with most of the survivors still standing. Just to complicate things, however, some of the biologists have spray-painted big blue W's on the bark of a few trees they want left for wildlife. Of course, what will happen to those wildlife trees or the next rank of unprotected trees, when the next big winter storm hits, no one professes to know.

Poppe had looked at the site in early summer and turned it down. The hillside is steep. The wind created a chaotic tangle of trunks and branches. The downed logs must be bucked, or cut into correct length, to fit on logging trucks and produce dimension lumber. Bucking can be even more hazardous than falling standing trees. When sawed into length, the downed logs have a tendency to lose their grip on the slope and careen downhill. The surviving trees must also come down. Some are half-rotten, and others hung up and leaning from the weight of fallen logs around them. The roots that exploded out of the ground in the storm created craters of dirt and broken sandstone, walled on one side by the upturned root ball. Other sections of the site are thick with sword fern, blackberry bramble, thistle, and fireweed.

Twice Poppe told the man who won the Forest Service bid for this mess, Rick Hurn, that he didn't want the job. Hurn persisted. It looked worse from the logging road on top than it really was, Hurn assured. He called several times, an indication he was having difficulty finding a good cutter. Finally Poppe, afraid his refusal could cost him future jobs in what promised to be a lean winter, reluctantly agreed.

"For $300 a day, a man will do just about anything," Steve jokes to Joe. The figure is a deliberate exaggeration—good cutters only earn half or a third that—but the meaning is clear. The woods are being locked up by the preservationists. A man can't afford to be too choosy. Take work where it comes.

"It's going to be a tough winter," says Steve.

Poppe emerges from the saw shop and we start up the Calawah River drainage, the brilliant stars fading now. He explains his trade. Poppe is a cutter, and thus at the top of the logger's pyramid in the way fighter pilots are atop the flier's pyramid. Of course falling trees are only the first part of logging. The logs then have to be dragged, or yarded, to a flat clearing called a landing, using steel cables pulled by massive engines. Then they must be trimmed of any branches, loaded on trucks, graded, and then taken to the mill. The chokers who go into the clearcuts to loop steel cables around the logs have one of the roughest and lowest-paying jobs. "Worst job in the world," said Bleck. "How'd you like to get up in the dark, at four or five in the morning, drive an hour, get out all stiff, look two thousand feet down the hill, and then scramble down there and start choking logs? If the sun ain't blazing, and if it ain't one hundred twenty degrees, it's pissing rain."

The truck drivers work some of the longest hours. The hook tenders, who set a network of supportive steel cables to brace the steel spar tower that is used to haul up the logs, need to have a common-sense judgment equal in calculation to an engineer's. The shovel operator who maneuvers the mechanical pincers that load the logs onto the truck sets the pace for the whole operation. The siderod that runs the show is a jack of all trades, supervisor and mechanic. But before any of them arrive at the logging site it is the cutters who go into the lonely woods. Theirs is the job that is the most dangerous, the most solitary, the most dramatic, and in some ways the most skilled.

There are a thousand ways to die in the woods, and everybody knows people who have. Lyle Nelson, the man who taught Poppe how to cut, was killed when a cedar tree dropped by a companion tipped the wrong way and fell on him. A cutter like Larry Suslick considers himself lucky after a quarter century in the woods with only a broken knee, torn muscles, and blows on the head and side from falling or rolling wood. He watched a lot of friends die; Forks can turn out for logger funerals two or three times a year. "There was one final blow that made me decide to get out," Suslick recalled. "There was a guy working for me who got hit on the neck and paralyzed from the neck down. Looking at him, laying there in the woods, knowing there was nothing we could do for him . . . well, it was time to just physically back away from it." Suslick took a shop maintenance job with the state Department of Natural Resources.

The danger has been there as long as anyone can remember. One historical study concluded that between 1870 and 1910, the life expectancy of a man starting logging was on average only seven years. Safety has improved since then but even today, loggers figure there is a one in three chance they will be killed or seriously injured during a career in the woods.

There is almost a spookiness about the randomness of calamity in the forest. I talked a bit to a young logger named Dewey Rasmussen, his restless energy still burning in what had become a broken body. One of six sons of a man who worked for Weyerhaeuser, he was the only one to follow his father into logging.

Rasmussen's passion was to climb old-growth trees. He would strap metal spurs to his ankles and loop a climbing rope up to sixty feet long around the massive trunks. He hitched the rope upward as he climbed, using a chainsaw to cut branches out of his way. The purpose of his climbing was to attach a steel cable to the upper part of a tree. Tension could then be applied so that when the tree was cut, it would fall uphill instead of down, building less momentum and thus being less likely to crack or break when it hit the ground. A generation ago, trees were so plentiful and cheap around Forks that the expense of sending Rasmussen up a tree would have been unthinkable. But wood prices skyrocketed fivefold in the late 1980s and preserving the soundness of a log became cost effective.

It was a daredevil job, climbing up these giant beanstalks. The climbing rope has a steel center to help guard against accidentally sawing through it. Then there is the problem, one hundred feet up, of getting the thick cable that dangled from one hip around the thick trees. Rasmussen would tie heavy fishing weights onto the cable's end and begin swinging it in an increasing arc. When the weighted cable had enough momentum he would snap his arm to hurl it in a circle around the tree's girth. Aim was crucial. He had to take care that the whizzing end that whipped around the trunk came near enough to grab, but not so near it would hit the climber on the head. Rasmussen loved this job: the heights, the danger, the skill. "I couldn't believe they were paying me to do it," he said. "It was a like a sport."

Rasmussen got so good he entered spar-climbing contests at summer logging shows. As an amateur he wasn't beaten for five years, and was considering turning professional. A good climber can earn $25,000 or $30,000 in prizes during a summer of logging exhibition shows around the United States. Dewey's arms and chest and stomach were so strong that he liked to grasp a metal pole on the stairway of his Forks home and hold himself out horizontally, like a flag.

But on May 9, 1989, an eight-foot-thick cedar no one had yet touched went over as Rasmussen's crew worked in the woods. There was no warning except the growl and squeal it made. Rasmussen was on the ground and scrambled too late. A few hundred tons of wood clipped him, breaking his back. The doctors in Port Angeles, who had seen this kind of thing too many times before, put steel rods in Rasmussen's back and pieced him back together enough so he could walk. His logging career was over.

The old energy is still there: Dewey and his wife Dana have converted some cabins into a small motel in Forks and his restless mind tackles other projects. He has drawn up plans for a commercially producible rocking horse. He has invented a mushroom-cleaning machine. But he wishes he were back in the woods. "I just like being outside," he said.

Given such dangers, one has to wonder what draws men to this job. Poppe explains that the cutter is his own boss. There is no second-guessing, no nagging supervision. A cutter makes his own decisions at each tree, earning more if he calls it right, risking his life if he guesses wrong. Most of the time a cutter works alone, at his own pace, one man at one tree. All he has to answer for is how much wood he's laid down, how well, at the end of the day. He sights the tree, peering up its trunk to judge its curve and twist and lean. He looks for weak branches, called widow-makers, that could fall on him with the force of a hurled spear. He judges the rot that can cause a tree to kick or pivot prematurely when cut. A good cutter likes to boast he can fall a tree so accurately that it will hit precisely enough to drive a stake into the ground. But every tree is a bit of a mystery until it's cut. This danger, this challenge, is what makes men fall in love with a hard, dirty, dangerous job.

"It was exciting," recalled Suslick, a bit wistfully. "It took your all, and you had to be on the ball to survive."

Cutters also work the shortest hours, because the job is so exhausting and the misjudgment that comes from exhaustion can be so dangerous and expensive. Fall a log in the wrong spot—busting it across a stump, or sending it careening downhill—and you can drop its value by hundreds or even thousands of dollars.

Accordingly, the cutter eats a mammoth breakfast—"pancakes and eggs, pretty well every day," said Poppe—goes to work by daybreak, and doesn't pause for lunch, quitting by early afternoon.

The slope of fallen tree trunks they leave behind in six hours of work can look like a scene out of World War I. But to cutters, a sheaf of trees laid over carefully like scythed wheat, nestled in a matting of broken boughs, can be the signature of a peculiar, dying artistry.

We leave the main highway for a Forest Service road that winds up the Calawah River, and then leave that paved road for a gravel logging road winding up into these hills. Poppe explains the business end of his trade. He is an independent contractor who gets paid by how much of the tree he falls makes it to the mill. If the tree is so broken or rotten that it is left on the logging site, he earns nothing for falling it. If he turns some of the trees into splinters, wasting wood, he earns nothing for that, either. His usual pay is about $15 per thousand board feet, though rates can run as low as $10 and as high as $40, depending on the site and wood prices and the hunger of the cutter. A board foot is a unit of wood a foot square and an inch thick and is the commonest form of quantification in forests that defy easy calculation. There are perhaps 13,000 board feet of framing lumber in an average house and 7,000 board feet of plywood or similar panels.

Cutters who fell on this kind of agreement are called "bushelers," and most prefer it because the harder and more skillfully they work, the more they get paid. There is justice in that. The idea of good pay for hard, honest work is the foundation of self-esteem in Forks. It is a place where productivity is tangible. It can be eyed from a logging landing. If a man doesn't want to work, or if he tries to skate by, he'll find himself by noontime walking back down the logging road, trying to hitch a ride with a log truck to town. From this $15 a thousand, Poppe must pay for his help, his truck, his saw, his industrial insurance. "It's a pretty good living for a guy with no education," he said. But even in good times, it is not a way to get rich.

The logging road climbs in switchbacks through a mosaic of "managed" forest. The forest has been turned into patches, each patch of different height, marking when it was cut. A log truck driver named

Jimmy Albin will later take me up in his 1956 Piper Cub to see this pattern on its broadest scale: the thickly forested valleys of the national park, the raw clearcut ridgetops just outside the park boundary, and the rolling hills of green where millions of trees have been planted on earlier clearcuts and are coming back in a new kind of forest, the merit of which is bitterly debated.

A Pacific Northwest clearcut is one of the most startling manifestations of resource consumption in the world. A mature coastal conifer forest is like a dense, high-pile carpet of dark green. In the drier country of the mountainous West where the trees are less thick, logging is sometimes done selectively, with a quarter or third of the pines left behind to seed and shelter the next crop. This kind of selective logging has long been considered uneconomical in wetter country, where it is difficult to fall and snake individual trees out of a stand because of the closeness of the trunks and the abundant tangle of decaying logs on the ground. Once clearcutting was discovered to be economic, a host of scientific arguments were offered to justify its ruthless appearance. Yet it remains a visible shock. The forest looks not so much harvested as destroyed, so vivid is the contrast between the evergreen trees and the brown dirt and wood of a cut.

Earlier in the century there was almost no replanting and the clearcuts lingered for long, ugly years, bleeding dirt and growing up in brush and low-value alder. Today the ground is too valuable not to replant, and state and federal law requires it anyway. The timber industry and government set out about 2.3 billion seedlings across the United States each year, 170 million of them in Washington State alone. But still, there is a five- to ten-year period before the brown completely fuzzes with the new green. Even when it does, the forest looks funny. It is patchy, made up of clumps of trees growing on old clearcuts. Each clump is of uniform age and height, but the clumps together are of varied heights, stepping up and down, as if the forest had been assembled from different pieces. An industrial forest tends to have sounder wood, smaller trees, and less variety of wildlife. There is a curiously tidy, shrunken, and sterile feel about managed stands.

Poppe's truck switchbacks up through this brave new national forest: the raw new clearcuts, young groves regrown from logging, scrawny places that are remnants of fire and wind, and surviving pockets of once-vast old-growth stands of virgin timber. There is towering Douglas fir, the most valued structural wood in the world; spruce, which ounce for ounce is the strongest wood in the world and was once used for airplane frames; decay-resistant and long-lived cedar; and the ubiq-uitous hemlock, fast-seeding and fast-growing, once dismissed as worthless and now, in the shrunken forest, used for paper, lumber, and finish wood.

As striking as the clearcuts is the fecundity of the land. Time and again in Forks, people will point to former burns and clearcuts now with trees that are a hundred or more feet high. "Trees grow back," they point out, with just a touch of exasperation. Buy a backyard here and try to have them *not* grow back.

In the pale predawn light, which reduces the landscape to silhou-ettes, some of the clearcut stumps of the old-growth trees—deliberately blackened by fire set to consume excess debris and open the soil to planting—look like tombstones studding the hill of an old cemetery. It looks, this quiet early morning, a bit like a graveyard of giants.

It is old growth, the titanic virgin forest in this corner of the world, that captures the imagination. In a grove several centuries old the trees are like the pillars of a cool temple. The web of foliage overhead, shot through with sunlight, spangles the air with gold and green.

Ironically, it is old growth that captures the imagination of fallers as well. Their age and girth and the crash of their fall adds drama to a cutter's work. Their volume of wood makes them lucrative to cut. Above all, their value and unpredictability calls for skill. "I'd rather cut in old growth," sayd Joe Helvey in the pickup as he and Russ Poppe and I near the day's salvage site. "It's a lot more of a challenge. It's an accomplishment when you can lay it out and save it out to the berries at the end."

Regrown trees, called second growth, are more boring, he explains. Of uniform dimension and soundness, too frequently they fall over without challenge. On ground that is not too steep, trundling machines called fellerbunchers can snip off the smaller ones with giant scissors. Besides, the modest trees can prove exhausting. On a big tree, a faller can lay the weight of his fifteen- to twenty-pound chainsaw in the cut as the blade pivots, resting his arms. On smaller ones the cut goes too fast and the saw is held up by muscle power alone most of the day, turning arms leaden. It is monotonous, it is fast, it is hard, and it is too easy for the mind to slack off. That's the kind of situation where a man can get hurt. Get lax around any tree, and it can kill you.

We've climbed in the pickup far above the valley of the Calawah now. Fog hangs in the hollows of the landscape. Up high the air is crystalline, sweet with the smell of the woods. It is a landscape constantly in transition, as heavily worked as an Iowa cornfield. As we pull to a stop the rising sun is lighting a clearcut opposite, across the deep canyon. The cut is big, at its widest perhaps a half-mile brown swathe across the green forest.

There's a story, possibly apocryphal, about President Jimmy Carter's flight across the foothills of southwest Washington to view the devastation caused by the eruption of Mount St. Helens. Peering down at the shaven hills, the president expressed horror at the destruction below him. State officials who were his guide had to gently explain that the helicopter had not reached the volcano blast area yet, that what Carter was seeing was clearcut logging.

This fresh clearcut exhibits some reform. It runs down the mountainside to a line of sheltering trees marking a stream on the canyon bottom.

I ask Poppe what he thinks about leaving those trees along the creek. A decade or two earlier they would have been cut, the stream bed torn, and the water exposed to heat and muddy in the sun. "I don't have any problem with that," Poppe said. "Leaving those trees is a good forest practice."

Other changes are also visible. These logs are not being dragged uphill to the waiting trucks, but are suspended from a steel cable stretched across the valley. Dangling like a gondola, they spare the ground.

The clearcut also seems tidier than those of a generation ago: almost everything of any size is being yarded and trucked away. In the old days the clearcut would have been strewn with casually discarded wood, and in fact so much slash would be left behind it would probably have to be burned after logging to expose the soil to seed and discourage lightning-set wildfire. The deliberate burn would in turn send a polluted haze across miles of sky. Afterward the toasted ground would be planted with new seedlings of a single tree species, such as Douglas fir. Foresters for Washington's Department of Natural Resources (which environmentalists like to ridicule as the Department of Nothing Remaining) coined a self-deprecatory saying for the common logging practice: "Cut it down, burn it black, bring it back."

But logs are too valuable to leave anymore: even the scrawniest pecker poles can be chipped for pulp. Tom Maloney, a wood materials scientist at Washington State University, has calculated the industry today gets 15 million tons of product annually out of material burned as waste thirty years ago. As a result, this new clearcut looks picked clean. There is a fresh irony in that. Now some scientists think clearcuts have gotten too tidy. They want not only standing trees left behind, but logs too. Food for bugs. Shelter for the birds.

A glance over the edge explains Poppe's reluctance to take this job. The mountain falls away to the wooded canyon bottom as if in a dreadful hurry to get down to thicker air. Just moving on such a pitch is an act of conscious balance. The wind knocked most of the conifers into a matchstick jumble, the survivors that still stand grizzling the slope like missed whiskers. To get to their work the two cutters will have to descend half a mile along the edge of the blowdown, breaking their own trail through the weeds of the adjacent clearcut. At the bottom of the tangle they begin cutting, working upward. "Gravity is always your worst enemy in a place like this," Poppe explains. A faller starts low and works upward so if trees break away and plunge downhill, they won't squash the loggers or become snarled in the work still to come.

The cutters pull on their caulks. Where possible they will use the logs as elevated sidewalks above the brush, the hobnails of these boots lending traction. They pull on steel hats as well. Beyond that, there is not too much to carry today. Because Poppe and his partner have already started this job, the chainsaws and wedges and axes are already down in the tangle, left over the weekend. Poppe and Helvey hoist gasoline, saw oil, and jugs of water out of the back of the pickup and we start down.

Poppe and Helvey drop down the slope with an easy lope. I follow a bit clumsily in my hiking boots, trying to pick out footholds but periodically sliding down the loose dirt. Poppe points out the Douglas fir seedlings planted in the clearcut. They are a few inches high, lost in the grass and fireweed this first year. Their tips are covered with plastic netting to discourage browsing deer.

It is cool this early fall morning, but I'm sweating by the time we reach the bottom. Poppe is not. He simply looks preoccupied at deciding where next to saw in this tangle, and how to break in Joe, his new partner. He has little doubt of Helvey's skill, but partners accustomed to each other's habits can adopt a wordless kind of communication like that seen in a long marriage. Russ and Joe still have to feel each other out.

I ask Poppe if he's ever considered a safer, easier job. "Sure have," he replies. "I just don't know what it is."

He tries to explain the feeling that brings him down into a patch of woods that looks like it's been hit by an artillery barrage. "It sure feels good to work up a good sweat for six hours and then go home and be tired. It feels good to step in that shower and know you've done a good day's work. I don't know if another job would be as satisfying. Not one that would have the physical and the mental stimulation."

The men work their way across the slope's tangle to a mammoth hemlock, laid out across the hillside the previous week. I follow as best I can, sometimes balancing on logs, sometimes slipping off and dropping several feet into the tangle, a couple of times dropping on my butt and sliding a moment before being arrested by the underbrush. The problem I am illustrating, the cutters explain when I struggle up to them, is gravity.

"People think loggers are stupid," says Poppe matter-of-factly. "They don't know that out here, every move you make you've got to be thinking. In a blowdown, it's a domino effect. This tree is going to hit that log, and that log is going to hit that log, and that log is going to hit that rock. There's just a lot of variables. You've got to know what a tree is going to do before it does it."

They thread the sharp chain onto the jutting four-foot-long arms of their saws and feed the beasts gas and oil. Pointing the blade down and away from himself while standing on a stump, Helvey pulls the motor rope with a jerk. Once, twice. He is rewarded with the cough and snarl of the motor. Experimentally, he dips the tip of the chain arm into the stump, sending up a little spout of sawdust. Satisfied, he lifts plastic muffs over his ears. A lot of old-time loggers are half-deaf by the time they come out of the woods.

The men start bucking the downed tree, working together. The saws bite through the wood astonishingly fast, spewing out sawdust like a fountain. The cutters' concern about physics is soon illustrated. With a crack, a section of log suspended above the brush breaks free and sits down on the slope with a force of several tons, the weight so powerful it yanks Helvey's saw down with it, the motor quivering in the air. Helvey pries it loose.

With this warm-up completed, they begin moving apart, Helvey bucking to the left, Poppe falling standing trees to the right. There is little talk. Each man has cut a small forest of trees, and once they get into the rhythm of the day's work the distance between them deliberately widens as they work across the slope. This means there is less chance of them sending a tree or log into each other. At their advice, I stay well upslope.

They move with a deliberate grace, a paced economy of motion and effort as interesting to watch as an athlete snaring a ball or a dancer extending her body. Helvey strides along a log with the forty-inch arm of his chainsaw out front clipping off inch-thick branches, seemingly as casual as a child pushing a wheeled toy. Trailing behind him, unreeling from a coil on his belt like a strand of web from a spider, is a metal tape. "I think this'll be a twenty-four and a thirty," he says at the beginning to Poppe, suggesting the mill lengths to which a log can be bucked. At the right intervals, he marks the bark with the tip of his chainsaw. Then he comes back to buck it. Straddling his cut as he stands on the log's back, the chainsaw whining between his legs, sawdust flying, he looks like he could castrate himself with a false move. Each log falls away with a solid crack.

Then on to the next tree. Helvey shuts down the saw motor and balances it on his shoulder like a musket, his arm draped around the saw blade that is pointed forward. He strides down the trunk like a model, planting one foot in front of the other, scanning the tangle like a chess board to plot his next move and whip the threat of gravity.

Poppe is down in a small draw, falling standing timber. From a distance he is lost in the vegetation and all one hears is the periodic snort and howl of the chainsaw. Finally there will be a crack and the top of a tree will tremble. Then it will go over in a smooth arc, seeming to suck a hole in the air in its wake. The trees always crash with a boom, the noise like a cannon shot that reverberates across the canyon with a marvelous echo. The noise is followed by quiet, as if the forest gives a moment of silence to what was once there, and then, quite quickly, the chirping of birds starts up again.

At one point the men release a precariously balanced root ball from a log and it goes cartwheeling down hill, throwing off a spray of rocks and dirt. It bangs into trees, the loggers wincing, the sound rattling off the hillsides like maniacal applause. This time the moment of silence is followed by whoops of exclamation from the loggers in the big clearcut across the canyon. It reminds me of every bunch of kids who have ever rolled a rock down into a canyon to watch it bounce. Poppe shakes his head. Gravity.

The loggers look diminutive in this landscape, like insects scrambling through a field of wheat. They bring to mind the industrious chutzpah of ants that carry bundles three times their size through a landscape of colossal scale. Poppe works his way around the butt of a massive cedar tree, eight feet in diameter and perhaps 150 to 200 feet high. The ground is so steep that the downslope side of the trunk is about four feet lower than the upslope. The geometry of this situation dominates Poppe's decision making. The momentum and force of a downhill fall is so titanic it can break even a sound tree into splinters. Unfortunately it is almost impossible, without using hydraulic jacks or a steel cable attached to the top of the tree, to make most trunks fall uphill. The tug of gravity and the gradual sloughing of ground gives most trees a slight downhill lean. A compromise is made between desire and physics: most of the trees are aimed to fall sideways across the slope. Ideally they will fall to be cradled between stumps and standing trees, braking any tendency to roll downhill.

Each trunk is cut twice: an undercut in the direction the faller wants the tree to topple, and then a backcut on the opposite side, slightly higher, to saw the tree through. Because the ground is so steep, Poppe can't reach high enough on the downslope side of this tree to make the two cuts match. To boost himself higher, he makes a springboard. A narrow slot is sawn in the side of the tree to be fallen, and the springboard—a short, rough, makeshift plank sawn off a nearby log—is wedged into it, twisted until it is firm. Old-time loggers armed only with axes and handsaws used springboards all the time to elevate themselves above the swollen butt of a tree, giving them less distance to saw through and avoiding the thick pitch and gnarly fibers at the bottom. The rotting hulks of such turn-of-the-century stumps can still be found throughout these woods, the springboard holes clearly visible in their flanks. Timber baron Frederick Weyerhaeuser hated this waste: his last words reportedly were a whispered, "Cut 'em low, boys, cut 'em low."

Poppe clambers up onto this narrow board, hoisting his chainsaw with him, and stands, teetering a moment on his caulk boots. The demand for balance here is extraordinary. The springboard's flex explains its name. The buzzing chainsaw, weighing fifteen to twenty pounds and held at arm's length, can tip a logger over. A loss of footing here means a fall into a thicket of broken branches, vines, and nettles on a slope so precipitous that Poppe, if not impaled or cut by his own saw, would keep tumbling through the mess until he fetched up against a log or stump. From this perch he has to cut a bite out of the tree nearly four feet deep to its core, the center of the cut marking precisely which direction he wants the tree to fall.

Not only must this slice be centered correctly, but it must also be level. Poppe sights along the perpendicular handles, motor housing, and arm of his saw to ensure this, as if he were sighting a gun. A tilt to the cut will tilt the tree, spilling it downhill. This is why a good cutter can entertain half a dozen different job offers in the early spring and a bad cutter can wipe out a contractor's profit margin. In the old days, when there were more trees and cheaper wood, salaried cutters for timber giants like Weyerhaeuser would sometimes deliberately break a big tree across a stump so they wouldn't have to bother bucking it, and to hell with the wasted splinters. Today, the pressure is always on to save the wood, save the wood.

Planted on his ludicrously narrow board, Poppe bends to his work. A plume of sawdust spits out, raining downhill. A horizontal cut is made into the tree, and then a lower incision comes up diagonally to meet it in what is known as a Humboldt cut. The carved mouth that results seldom opens of its own accord because the tree tends to settle on its wound a bit. So Helvey, on hand to help with this monster, hands up an ax to Poppe. A couple whacks with the butt end of the ax and the wedge pops out. The cut leaves a mouth in the cedar tree opened in an expression of mute surprise.

The tree is now cut halfway through, leaning a bit more in the direction of its intended fall. Poppe leaps down from his springboard and moves to the upslope side. Now he must make a single straight cut to meet the top of the mouth he has carved. Ideally, in a sound tree, a strip of wood across its center a few inches wide will be left between the two cuts as a hinge. The trunk will pivot on that as it goes over. That hinge and the fact the tree is falling into the open wedge will, the logger hopes, keep the tree from twisting as it falls, or, even worse, kicking back at the faller.

Poppe takes his time. This tree is several centuries old, and it will come down in less than half an hour. It is old enough and its top broken and scraggly enough to indicate it is probably rotten inside, and thus doubly dangerous. A young, healthy tree is likely to fall with some predictability. But an old-growth tree past its prime may have developed rot in its core. A cut through the outer shell of healthy bark and cambium can reveal a heart of wood powder. The resulting weakness can send the tree over before the cutter has time or wit to scramble out of the way.

His saw bites in. Poppe pauses occasionally to ensure his cuts are lining up. The cedar has a sweet, pungent odor, but the smells of sawdust and dirt are unromantic to loggers, many of whom suffer respiratory problems if they survive their first couple decades in the woods.

As Poppe's saw bites toward the core of the old cedar, there is an ominous crack. His head jerks up and the saw is yanked out. He scrambles in a quick retreat uphill, eying the top of the trunk for signs of its intentions. There is another crack and another, a succession of internal snaps of woody tendons like a chain of firecrackers. The effect is eerie. The tree is not moving and yet from its interior are coming all these pops and bangs, as if there was a strange machine inside its bark. This tree is so rotten it has started to disintegrate before the cut is adequately completed.

Finally the cedar begins to lean. Momentum multiplies on momentum. At the base of the tree, cracks race ten and twenty feet high up the bark as the weak wood loses cohesion. The tree swings a bit, as if considering whether to fall as intended or launch itself straight downhill. To Poppe's dismay, it twists further as if to choose the latter. The fall accelerates. Finally the tree hits the steep slope with a boom that shakes the earth, and it smashes into giant slabs. A cloud of dust and detritus thrown up by its fall dissipates like fog before sunlight.

Poppe is dissatisfied. He had given it a good lay. The impatience of the tree to fall made it jump downhill.

He turns to a younger, six-foot-diameter hemlock, its boughs draped with moss from a lifetime in fog and rain. The pattern is repeated, though the smaller size of this tree and a slightly less severe slope makes a springboard unnecessary. Again one is impressed with the brute grace of this work, the bend of back and the strain of arms. Poppe looks around for the best place to lay it down. There is a spot between a stump and a wildlife tree, perhaps fifteen feet wide, that would be perfect. This tree is sounder at its core, and Poppe's aim proves accurate. The tree waits patiently until the saw makes its last bite and Poppe pulls the chain arm out. Then the hemlock goes over with the power of solid weight, moss fluttering from some of the upper boughs like green scarves. It clips the branches of the wildlife tree and there is a spray of moss and bark and needles, like the midair explosion of an antiaircraft shell. Cones fly like shrapnel. Then the tree is down as if falling into bed.

"That one fell just where I wanted it," Poppe says with satisfaction.

There is a terrible beauty in this. The fall of a great tree is as instinctively satisfying as a Fourth of July fireworks explosion. Human survival has hinged on manipulation of the environment, and few manipulations are as dramatic as falling big trees. It seems extraordinary that two men with motorized handsaws can change a centuries-old landscape so profoundly, so quickly.

But there is a new idea afoot, a new uneasiness, blowing through these woods. It is the notion that we have converted the earth too thoroughly, harnessed it too tightly, and that some of this forest needs to be left alone so that we can still learn from the wisdom of evolution. This is an idea that has come from Outside, from urban communities remote from Forks. It threatens not just the livelihood of men such as these cutters, but more importantly their sense of purpose. Nothing is more bewildering, nothing hurts more, than that this work of courage and skill is now perceived as villainy.

Poppe, breathing hard, takes a break to talk about what he does. His grandfather was a logger. His father was a manager for Crown Zellerbach timber in Cathlamet, a small pulp and paper town on the Columbia River about 150 miles to the south. Poppe's father had hoped his son might go to forestry school and get on the paperwork side of logging. But Poppe had a wife and child to support upon graduation from high school. The best money was in the woods. "It was more out of necessity than desire" that he became a logger, he said.

Now it is threatened. This kind of timber job, cutting trees centuries old, is an increasing rarity. Most old-growth trees have been put off limits while scientists try to figure out how much "ancient forest" need survive to ensure the survival of its ecosystem. The allowable cut on Olympic National Forest has plunged 90 percent in a decade, much of the decline bunched into the last two years. Logging on adjacent state of Washington land has declined 50 to 60 percent. The private lands are also short of trees: the biggest local landowner, ITT-Rayonier, has seen its annual cut plunge from 200 million board feet in the 1970s to 80 million now and perhaps down to 40 million in a few years. The number of logging contracts around Forks is down by two-thirds.

Maybe things will balance out. Certainly some logging will go on. But Poppe has a small farm in the Bogachiel River Valley and has begun buying pack horses. He is thinking maybe he could be a back-country guide to tourists if logging fades out.

"I like to feel I'm as environmentally sensitive as the next guy," said Poppe. "On the other hand, I don't like to see my way of life eliminated. Environmentalists have some idealistic notion of the way the world ought to be, and as long as it don't affect their pocketbook, it's okay. Well, it would be real romantic to think the world can be some kind of paradise, but paper and lumber is going to be needed. The way I feel, if it ain't natural, it ain't good. It ain't natural to make things out of synthetics. Wood is natural. This is the most natural alternative we have, plus it's renewable."

Poppe understands some of the alarm of urbanites who come to these woods. He said he hates to see the new clearcuts along Highway 101, sawn in panic before some new round of regulation forbids their harvest. He says the industry has overcut these forests the past five years. He approves of leaving strips of trees along streams to preserve water quality. He thinks there is a lot of work that could be done in these woods to correct old mistakes, to rehabilitate forest streams.

"That kind of work would be a good alternative for a logger," he muses. "None of us wants a handout."

What Poppe can't understand is the hysteric sweep of proposals to curb logging, the drastic cutbacks, the urban callousness toward thousands of timber families. A few years ago, the timber industry was helping lead the Northwest out of a severe recession. Now it is the bad guy, reviled on national television. Loggers have flailed out almost blindly at this shift, holding rallies with hundreds of logging trucks. They called for a boycott of Burger King because the fast-food chain used salad dressing sold by Paul Newman, the actor who had narrated a critical Audubon Society special on public television. Peninsula loggers petitioned the U.S. Fish and Wildlife Department to be declared an endangered species. Dead spotted owls have been nailed to signs on Olympic National Park. Where do people think their houses come from? Their newspapers? Their toilet paper? The fibers in their clothes? Why do they scorn the rugged, artful grace of fallers like Poppe and Helvey?

Poppe considers the environmentalists a bit too self-righteous, as if they had invented love for the outdoors with their weekend hikes. Well, these loggers live in the woods and work in the woods and play in the woods. They are out in the chill rain and the hot sun. They see deer while driving to the logging job in the morning and eagles on the way home. They fish, they hunt, they hike. These forests are to them a mosaic of memory a city dweller can't imagine, a hundred places cut and regrown. To them, a clearcut isn't an end. It is a beginning.

What Poppe resents is the image of callousness, as if loggers didn't care about the forest they harvest. He recalls an incident in which he deliberately cut around a grove of trees sheltering baby elk, at least sparing them until the elk left. And another when he cut a tree and near its top found a nest of baby flying squirrels, miraculously alive after the tree's crashing fall. He watched as the mother took the tiny creatures and bounded up a nearby cedar tree.

Poppe spared that cedar for a month, cutting all around it to give the squirrels time to either move entirely out of the clearcut or grow big enough to survive. Finally the cedar had to come down too. It was thousands of dollars, just standing there. But he had tried to give the tiny creatures every chance.

The talk seems to make Poppe gloomy, and he quits for the day shortly after noon, clambering back up the slope with Joe. "I just don't want to leave Forks," he says, trying to explain how his allegiance to this hard, dangerous life is evidence not of his indifference to the forest, but his love for it. "Forks is good people."

Months later, a Weyerhaeuser employee named Bob Hoffman will put some of these sentiments in a plaintive song and sing them on the steps of the federal courthouse in Seattle where a federal judge is about to shut down most remaining national forest timber harvests:

> *What about my family, what about our home?*
> *Wildlife and timber, it's the only life I've known.*
> *I'm just one man, living off the land.*
> *It's more than what I do;*
> *It's who I am.*

2

THE BIOLOGIST

▲▲▲▲▲▲▲

Summer's dusk is pleasant and soft in the Pacific Northwest. At that latitude the light lingers, a long, blue twilight seemingly reluctant to give up the landscape. The forest gently shadows, and while its details become less distinct to human eyes, it doesn't rest: a night shift of wild creatures begins to stir. Those seeking to fully understand the forest must listen to its nocturnal cycle, just as a city can't be explained without understanding the work that goes on at night.

In the summer of 1968, a twenty-year-old Oregon State University student named Eric Forsman relaxed each evening by taking in this cool transition. His box seat for dusk's theater was the porch of a lonely guard station near Box Canyon, in Oregon's Willamette National Forest. The solitude of the place fit him. "I've always liked wild places—just getting away from people," he would later remark. Forsman was a wildlife biology student who had landed a summer Forest Service job patrolling the woods for fire. The guard station where he lived was a cabin on the edge of a clearing, tucked into a fringe of old-growth trees. Forsman liked to listen to the forest talk.

One evening, something happened off Forsman's porch that, like so many events in the final forest debate, seemed so serendipitous as to be eerily predestined. An owl hooted from the trees.

"I heard a kind of barking sound," Forsman recounted. It was a queer noise: ow-ow-ow-ow-ow. "I thought it was a dog." But that made no sense. A dog out here? No, there was a different familiarity to this noise. He listened again. Ow-ow-ow-ow. "Finally it occurred to me, because I had read a lot about owls, that it was probably a spotted owl."

Intrigued, Forsman—who had been interested in owls since childhood—decided to imitate the call. He hooted back.

Determining the origins of a big new idea, such as the notion of preserving more Northwest virgin forest not just because of its beauty, but because of its ecological significance, is never simple. Shifts in human thinking sometimes seem to explode into the media and legislative chambers like a shell launched from an unseen cannon. Yet any such change is in effect a tapestry, a completed paradigm made up of a thousand threads contributed by smaller events that have happened years, even decades before. Forsman's decision to reply to that owl is one of those threads.

The owl answered. Man and bird hooted to each other for a bit, and then something occurred that astonished the young biologist. The owl fluttered down into the yard of the guard station and stared at Forsman. The bird seemed to have no fear of humans, just curiosity at this creature that could imitate its call. This northern spotted owl was small and less fierce looking than many birds of prey, with a rounded head and black staring eyes and brown plumage spotted with white. Some would later describe it as cute, others as disappointingly unremarkable in appearance. It was the most tame wild creature Forsman had ever seen, almost unique in its willingness not to flee when approached. The quality seemed even more contradictory because the bird was reportedly so rare. In the Pacific Northwest's entire history there were only twenty-five accounts of the spotted owl having been observed, and now one had flown in as if to strike up a conversation. It was a bit as if a unicorn or Bigfoot had popped out of the woods and stood for inspection. The perfect ecological representative had landed in front of one of the few people who could recognize its significance. Two decades after this chance meeting, the Pacific Northwest's biggest industry was rocked to its foundations by this friendly little bird.

Forsman knew enough to be immediately excited. The spotted owl inhabited deep, dense forest where people seldom ventured, and almost nothing was known about it.

The wildlife student already was familiar with other owls. One of six children who grew up on a small farm outside of Eugene, Oregon, Forsman had spent half his boyhood days hunting and fishing. The first time he saw an owl up close, at age ten or twelve, was when a great horned owl flew into the family's yard. The excited children called up a neighbor. "Jerry, come get your gun and shoot this thing!" The neighbor did, the bird's body flopping lifelessly onto the ground. "We all felt terrible afterward," Forsman said.

The close-up look at the dead owl made the youth more interested in live ones. He began to look for owls. "Birds that hunted at night intrigued me," he said. The very elusiveness of night predators challenged his curiosity. He became a particular fan of great horned owls. When he went to OSU in 1966 he met Dick Reynolds, another wildlife biology student who was studying goshawks. The two fed each other's interest in raptors, or birds of prey.

Two decades after Forsman's first encounter with the spotted owl—after the owl had made the cover of *Time* magazine and its picture had been posted at an editor's meeting at *The New York Times*—Northwesterners would still express disbelief that a bird few people had ever seen could have taken on so much legal and political significance. An eagle or a bear or an elk seemed natural to play center stage in an environmental dispute, but an obscure owl? It seemed less grand, somehow. Yet Forsman argues that the region's preoccupation with owls is not unprecedented. "To people in general, owls hold a certain familiarity," he said. "If you go back in history, clear back to Egypt, owls are a symbolic group of animals."

Snowy owls have been found drawn in prehistoric caves in France. Athena, the Greek goddess of wisdom, was portrayed as having an owl as a companion. Early tales of Merlin describe him as having an owl on his shoulder. The Kirwa Indians believed their medicine men changed to owls after death. The image of the owl as elderly and sage is a common one in children's literature. A popular poem by A. A. Milne, author of Winnie-the-Pooh books, illustrates:

> A *wise old owl sat in an oak,*
> *The more he saw the less he spoke,*
> *The less he spoke the more he heard,*
> *Why can't we all be like that wise old bird?*

This association with wisdom is matched with one of darkness, however. Owls are a staple character of Halloween, their hoots long associated with death. The Chinese called owl cries "digging the grave," and in two of Shakespeare's plays, owl cries forecast the demise of key characters. The specter of owls may even have turned a battle. The Carthaginians reportedly fled in terror from a Greek army in 310 B.C. when a general named Agathocles released trained owls that settled on the shields and helmets of his troops as they advanced.

My attempt to explain the owl controversy once to a group of African

journalists visiting Seattle simply mystified them. They shifted restlessly, and finally one of them interrupted my talk. "I do not understand why you are telling us this, why you are so preoccupied with
owls," he said. "In Africa, owls are bad luck. If a farmer finds one,
he kills it."

The juxtaposition of respect and fear may be what makes owls such
a potent symbol. In the early 1970s British television surveyed 300
people for their attitudes toward animals and found owls ranked twenty-
seventh in popularity. (Dolphins were number one.) In response to
questions, those queried described owls as cruel, strong, not cuddly,
and unapproachable—but also clever, sad, fascinating, and beautiful.

The secret to the owl's hold on the human imagination is its anat-
omy. Far more than other birds, owls look like people.

Owls sit directly upright, their plumage hiding their talons and their
boxiness giving them a shape reminiscent of the human trunk. The
likeness is heightened by the face. Though most owls are only one to
two feet high, their eyes are as large as human eyes—in fact, the
sockets for an owl's eyes take up more space in its skull than its brain.
Moreover, because an owl's eyes can't rotate from side to side like
those of humans, it must always look directly at whatever it is observing.
The effect of that direct stare, sometimes shrouded by a half-wink, can
be both charming and disconcerting.

To make up for the inability to shift its eyes, an owl's neck is
unusually flexible. It is able to twist 270 degrees, compared to 180
degrees for a human. Early observers of owls had seen them swing
their heads backward to look, and then snap forward with a motion
so quick it couldn't be followed by the human eye. Because of this
some thought the owl was swiveling its head in a complete circle, and
folklore held that if a person walked in circles around an owl its head
would keep swiveling until it twisted itself to death.

A small beak is positioned on the owl's face similar to the placement
of a human nose, and tufts of feathers on the forehead of some owl
varieties look like ears, making the owl a kind of caricature of a human
or mammalian head. A saucer-shaped disc of feathers around the eyes,
designed to direct sound into an owl's true ears (the large ears on the
side of the skull are hidden under its plumage) exaggerate the compelling quality of an owl gaze. It is as if the bird had donned spectacles.

Forsman's fascination with owls was increased by his respect for
their ability. Owl eyes are estimated as being fifty to one hundred times

more efficient than human at seeing objects at night. Their ability to home in on prey is improved by their superb hearing: the fact that the right ear opening is set higher than the left and that there is a differential of .00003 of a second in sound reaching one side of their head before the other enables them to determine what angle a sound is coming from. Laboratory experiments have shown owls adept at striking prey by sound alone.

To allow this hearing to function and avoid warning hunted victims, owls are one of the world's most silent fliers. Softened edge feathers and a lightness in relation to wing span keeps wind noise and flapping to a minimum when they dive for dinner, an attribute studied by aircraft designers. The result is a ruthless efficiency as they swoop to seize mice, squirrels, muskrats, and other prey in their talons. An illustration of their effectiveness was once found in the middle of Washington, D.C. A pair of owls roosted in a brick tower of an old Smithsonian building. When scientists climbed up to inspect the nest site, they found 454 skulls of small mammals killed by the birds.

Thus it is not surprising that Forsman's curiosity was piqued when a pair of northern spotted owls repeatedly glided down into the guard station clearing that summer in response to his calls. What made these owls even more intriguing to an ambitious biologist was that, "Essentially, there was nothing known about them." No nests had ever been described, no census had ever been made, and the owls had only been seen in Oregon, not in Washington State or British Columbia. Nothing was known about where they lived or what they ate or how they bred. It is one thing to discover an unknown insect or plant, given the millions of species estimated to exist. Here was something rarer: the opportunity to study a big woodland species. It was like finding a previously unknown kind of deer. Almost all other large raptors had already been studied.

Even better, this was the first owl Forsman had encountered that did not fly away when approached. "They have a complete lack of fear of humans," he said. Instead of being fierce and wary, a spotted owl would come when called and would perch a few yards from an investigator, seemingly as curious about humans as the scientist was about it. "It is one of the easiest wildlife animals we know of to study," Forsman would eventually conclude.

By 1990, scientists ranked the owl among the top one hundred or so wild species of which the most was known. The trust the bird seemed to put in people had an emotional effect on those who studied it, heightening their awareness that the owl's survival or demise depended on human decisions about harvesting the forest.

Environmentalists view the owl as an astounding gift. The problem with protecting an endangered species is that defenders need to prove it is indeed endangered in order to argue for protection, yet data can be scant because of an animal's very rarity. It is a paradox the owl overcame. "Can you think of any other wild species that comes when you call it and lands a few feet away?" asked Andy Stahl of the Sierra Club Legal Defense Fund. "That carries radars? From the viewpoint of collecting a lot of information in a small amount of time, the owl was ideal. We know more about the spotted owl than any other rare species."

The spotted owl came to illustrate two enormously significant trends: the increasing importance people are placing on preserving a diversity of species, and the growing political power of science.

The first trend is marked by the value humans have begun to place on species that have neither obvious utility—such as cattle or deer or dogs—or a particularly striking nobility—such as lions or whales or eagles. Since the 1970s biologists have been well aware of the growing tendency of Americans, especially those who lived in cities, to anthropomorphize animals, to attribute to them human and cuddly aspects they don't really have. Bob Moorhead, a biologist in Olympic National Park, has a theory about this. He believes that as urban society becomes more technical and impersonal, there is a corresponding increase of yearning for what he calls "touchy-feely" things. There has been a steadily increasing appetite for television documentaries and books about the natural world. The animal lovers have been a biologist's biggest ally and worst pest, helping focus research spending on the critters and yet objecting to animal population management or sometimes necessarily cruel research techniques. Yet the passion of these enthusiasts helped set the stage for strange new ideas, such as managing the landscape for obscure species.

With the stage thus set, perhaps it is not surprising there was immediate concern for the owl, particularly among bird watchers. Yet the spotted owl's very obscurity and nondescript nature took human attitudes toward the natural world another step. It made the calls for the owl's preservation a challenge to an older, more human-centered view of the world, where the kinds of animals people cared about were the kind they were familiar with. Here was an animal few people had ever seen, and yet many people were willing to assert it mattered.

This shift in attitude began in the 1970s among scientists at universities such as Oregon State. It was a natural outgrowth of the new science of ecology that had drawn increasing interest among biologists in the 1950s and 1960s, a science that suggested that more familiar and popular species were inextricably linked to a larger web of obscure creatures, great and small. For many scientists, the transition has not been an easy one.

"Things you could shoot and trap had been the focus," Forsman said. "Very little attention had been spent on the majority of wildlife."

Nearly two decades later a big-game biologist named Jack Ward Thomas would become famous in the Pacific Northwest for heading a landmark owl study which concluded that vast acreages of old growth should be set aside for the birds. When Forsman was beginning his research, however, attitudes were very different, Thomas recalled. Shortly after Thomas came to work for the Forest Service in eastern Oregon as a research biologist in 1973, he met with officials at Oregon State University to determine which university studies the Forest Service might support with grants. One of Forsman's professors, Howard Wight, suggested the bright young student's work on spotted owls. Thomas laughed. "I said, 'Hell, Howard, what's the bag limit on *those?*' "

Thomas was reflecting a common attitude, when wildlife departments were still called game departments. Forsman can recall one of his professors at Oregon State University telling the class that the region's old-growth forests were "biological deserts" because they were devoid of big game. In the convenient dogma of the time that fit the standard logging practices of Oregon's biggest industry, the professor taught that clearcuts were necesary in part because the brush that grew up after logging created forage for deer and elk. This assumption had never been challenged because the old-growth ecosystem that was being cut down had never been studied in any detail by scientists. Brush-foraging species were easily seen while many old-growth inhabitants, such as spotted owls, were more invisible. Coincidental to Forsman's owl find, other researchers at Oregon State and the University of Washington—including a Forest Service ecologist named Jerry Franklin—began poking into, finally, the most obvious and overlooked thing in the Northwest: the ancient forest.

"As we got into the old-growth, things started to swing the other way," Forsman said. "Scientists found things were a lot more complicated than the number of deer and elk there were to shoot."

Thus the owl came to represent another trend, as well: the growing political power of science.

This was not entirely new. The ability of science to interpret, manipulate, and thus influence the world had been growing exponentially since the Renaissance. What did prove new in the Northwest was the ability of science to offer a research-based "truth" in a debate over forests that seemed hopelessly divided between those who coveted trees for their economic value and those who worshipped them for their scenic and spiritual quality. Initially in this debate there seemed to be no objective set of facts or cultural agreement even on what a forest was *for*. The ecologists seized the high ground in this debate by suggesting that dollar values were too narrow a measurement and aesthetics were unreliable as a guide. What was important was the ecosystem, they argued, the natural machine, and all the bits and pieces like owls and old growth that made it work. It was the machine, the web, that was fundamental to existence. This could become the agreed-upon truth, scientists argued, on which political decisions should be made. The evolution of this new scientific power was slow, but by 1990 it had penetrated Congress and shifted the perennial preservation debate from dividing the landscape between recreational and industrial refuges to pondering how to manage the entire landscape to preserve complex ecosystems.

The spotted owl proved crucial to this transformation of the debate. A great deal of what scientists do is sort through the seeming chaos of everyday reality and count, name, and classify things, creating an understandable order. The ability to map and count the owl was a crucial first step to understanding it. Because it could be counted, it could be quantified. Because it required large blocks of native habitat, it would eventually be chosen by the U.S. Forest Service as an "indicator species," a kind of canary in the coal mine. If the canary died, miners knew toxic gases were building to dangerous levels. If the owl disappeared, it meant the forest system itself was collapsing: that a prehistoric ecosytem inherited by the pioneers was in danger of being entirely wiped out. The owl came to symbolize first an entire kind of forest, and then a worldview: a way of seeing nature, and man's role in it, different from anything the general public had accepted before.

Back in 1968, Forsman had no way of knowing the spotted owl would take on such significance. He was merely excited that he had successfully called down a rare bird, and he told his friend, Dick Reynolds, about his find. The two began driving the logging roads of Oregon, Reynolds looking for goshawks and Forsman for spotted owls. At this point the search was somewhat random: just where owls could be expected to live was not yet clear.

The search was soon interrupted when Forsman was drafted into the army in August 1970. He trained as a medic and served in Germany. Meanwhile, a pioneer of the shift in scientific interest toward nongame species in the West was OSU professor Howard Wight, who began to get interested in raptors as a result of Reynolds's encouragement. In March 1972, Wight asked Forsman if, after he mustered out, he would like to return to Oregon State to work on a master's degree on the spotted owl. Forsman agreed immediately. Three days after leaving the army he was in the Oregon woods, hooting for the birds.

The ability to call the owls was crucial, and eventually Forsman and other researchers would catalog at least thirteen different spotted owl calls. The obvious first step was to find out where the birds were, and for the next two decades owl searches using these hoots would consume thousands of hours by dozens of biologists.

Through trial and error by Forsman and many others, owl mapping evolved into a standard technique. It was best done, scientists quickly established, in spring and early summer when the owls nested and took prey back to their young. The biologists walked or drove forest trails and roads at night when the owls hunted; every few hundred yards they would hoot for owls, either with their own voice or by using a recording. Experience had taught the scientists that the birds could pick up the calls at distances up to half a mile. Then the humans waited in the dark, listening for a reply. The ability to hoot was fairly easily mastered; the ability to pick out an answer from the background cacophony of a forest at night—crickets, birds, howling coyotes, wind, the creak of swaying trees—was not. It could be lonely, tedious work, but also fascinating: years later, on the Olympic Peninsula near Forks, a Forsman team would regularly spot prowling cougars that are almost never seen in daytime.

An owl that called back at night, however, might never be seen.

Certainly its nest could not be tracked in the dark. Accordingly, if an owl was heard, the researchers would return to the same spot during the day and call again for the now-sleepy raptor, this time trying to lure the owl to the ground. The object was to locate its nest, and thus learn which trees around it were most critical to be protected from harvesting. The ability to trail an owl to its nest was discovered somewhat by accident. Forsman early on began trying to net owls in order to fix radio tags on them, and found the best way to lure them near a suspended net was to tether a live mouse next to it. The owl would swoop down and snatch the mouse. Sometimes the owl was caught in the sprung net, but at other times it would flap free and, carrying the mouse in its talons, make in a straight line for its nest to offer the food to its mate or young. Other owls had never been so habitually domestic, but here was one that conveniently pointed straight home for the price of a mouse.

What Forsman had been doing by accident he began to do on purpose. A mouse would be tethered to a log, would scamper back and forth, and the owl would strike. Its prey clutched, the bird would typically fly fifty to one hundred yards and then pause on a branch before resuming flight. The scientists would note the direction of its flight and "run like hell" in Forsman's words, bounding across logs and thrashing through underbrush in what was often steep, wet terrain.

An owl glide of an eighth of a mile across a canyon might mean a half-mile run by a researcher down into the bottom of the ravine and back up the other side. If the nest was very far, it was common to lose the owl. Then the hooting would begin again and, if the owl was in the mood, a mouse would be snatched and the chase would resume. In this manner, nest after nest would be painstakingly located and mapped. The discoveries were valuable because, unless disturbed, the owl pairs were likely to return to the same nest site year after year. Spotted owls commonly live fifteen years.

The owls were tractable in other ways. Their habit of roosting curiously near a human made it possible to catch them with a looped snare on a pole, often a fly rod, which proved safer than the nets. Of about 1,000 owls captured by 1990, only three died, an encouraging ratio for wildlife work. The owls also proved adaptable to carrying electronic beacons. Radio transmitters were fitted into tiny backpacks and strapped onto owls' backs, one strap around the bird's neck and another around its middle below the wings. An antenna was strung down the length of the body, ending at the tip of the tail. The instrument allowed the wide-ranging hunters to be tracked.

Still, the work was rugged and difficult. It could take a new owl surveyor eighteen months to learn not just the variety of calls but necessary techniques such as radio telemetry to fix an owl's position accurately on a map. The job description could be formidable. Ideally a researcher had to be able to drive a four-wheel-drive rig over rugged roads, climb trees, use a chainsaw to cut away trees that sometimes fall across roads, read a map and aerial photos, triangulate radio signals from tagged owls, snowshoe, cross-country ski, pilot a snowmobile, and above all not get lost in woods that are easily disorienting. The glamour of the work could be elusive. Owl field-workers were sometimes dubbed "pellet counters" to distinguish them from academicians spinning theories back in the ivory towers. The name comes from the deposits the biologists pick over. Owls often swallow small rodents whole and the indigestible bones and hair are excreted in pellets that can give biologists clues to their diet.

Slowly the search pattern for owls widened, from central Oregon south into the California redwoods and north to the Canadian border. The search became especially critical on the Olympic Peninsula, where the donut-pattern of preservation and logging had forced the owl to use huge ranges of up to 10,000 acres to find enough food to survive. "The Peninsula is pretty tough walking," said Stan Sovern, an OSU wildlife graduate who signed on with Forsman to look for owls there. "It's real steep, real brushy, and most of the time it's real wet. It can really try your patience, looking for owls in that stuff."

The most mundane things could be frustrating. The nets that were used initially to catch owls were forever getting snarled in the underbrush. Even handling the captive mice used for bait could be a chore. They stink, for one thing, Forsman said, and they're fragile for another. If they get too hot, for example, they die. "You're always worrying about your mice."

Working hours were also long, and weird to human biorhythms. Crews typically called for owls until two A.M. or even dawn, slept until late morning, and then in daylight went back to where owls were heard to call in hopes of finding nests. The nighttime work was usually on logging roads or trails, but the daytime frequently required bushwhacking cross-country to get to a nest. The biologists quit to eat dinner, then returned to the roads at nightfall for more calling. Rain and high winds would bring a respite because it became difficult to hear owls, but the biologists could feel isolated while waiting for the weather to improve in communities such as Forks. "Right off a lot of people knew who we were," recalled Sovern of the two years he spent in Forks. On a few occasions he drove its residential streets with an antenna stuck out a truck window, trying to draw transects of owl locations in the surrounding hills. "They were kind of standoffish— we really never dealt with people in town at all. Nobody was nasty to us, but they didn't want us around, either."

Forsman got the same impression. In the two years the wildlife team was on the Peninsula, he said, it got only one invitation to speak, on a radio talk show. None of the logging communities asked the biologists to make any presentation on what they were finding. "All we got was flak," he said. Forks residents turned the complaint around, saying the biologists were reclusive and made little effort to brief loggers on their research and its possible implications.

At times, the owls seemed to have the same standoffish attitude. "They're not too concerned with what they lead you through," Sovern said, remembering the tangles he would smash across, plunging forward to follow the owls. In Washington's Wenatchee National Forest, he tracked owls by transmitter from a snowmobile through the winter to learn their habits. "I remember being out there at two A.M. in a snowmobile, in the middle of a blizzard, trying to track a spotted owl. I thought, This is ridiculous. I don't know where this owl is, and I don't care."

On the steep terrain of the Peninsula, many of the roads, he described, "are like they are drawn on the side of the hill with a pencil. There's a big drop-off, sometimes on both sides. In the winter you get a lot of ice. We'd have a four-wheel drive creeping with all four wheels chained up and our hands on the door handles, ready to jump if we went over the edge."

One thing quickly became apparent as Forsman hiked and drove the back roads, hooting into the trees. The only places he seemed to find owls were in stands of virgin old-growth timber. It wasn't clear why, but Forsman and Wight made some early guesses. Perhaps the owl's preferred food, such as flying squirrels, lived in old growth. The bird seemed to prefer nesting in the broken tops of big old trees. Scientists realized the owl rarely built its own stick nests, often appropriating the abandoned nests of other raptors. Old growth has other advantages for any bird of prey. Stands tend to have a variety of trees from young seedlings to standing, dead trees called snags. The top of a dead snag, barren of needles or leaves, makes a much better lookout than a young green tree where foliage blocks the view. Additionally, tree trunks in the old forests were bigger but more widely spaced, and there was more room for a swooping owl to fly.

Timber industry scientists would later find owls in second-growth redwood in northern California and some second-growth forests in eastern Washington. They complained that the owl's adaptability had been underestimated, and that its need for old growth had been exaggerated. Forsman was criticized for concentrating his search in old growth.

Forsman and other scientists responded that such sightings were exceptions due to particular growth characteristics that did not hold over most of the owl's range. In western Washington and western Oregon, the key ancient forest battleground, maps that traced the wanderings of radio-tagged spotted owls showed an almost finicky preference for old growth, the birds overflying huge acreages of smaller trees to roost in the survivors. "We have not gone to old growth because we like old growth—it's because it is where you can find the birds," Forsman said.

The connection was to have enormous political consequences. Years later, scientists would still shake their heads at the role played by the bird. "I'm surprised the question of old growth focused on this cryptic surrogate," Jack Ward Thomas said in retrospect. "If fifteen years ago you had asked if there is going to be a fight over old growth, I'd have predicted yes. If you'd asked me if it would be a fight over an owl, I'd have laughed."

3

THE OPENING IN THE TREES

▲▲▲▲▲▲▲

The Olympic Peninsula is made of circles. There is a circle of mountains, a circle of sea, and by the end of the 1980s circles for owls: places on the map where a 2.1-mile radius had been drawn around each discovered owl nest. Biologists urged that not more than half the old-growth forest within those circles should be harvested. Ten thousand acres per nest! If the loggers had any remaining doubts the government had gone crazy, drawing those owl circles proved it. What the loggers didn't know—what no one would have believed, at the time—was that such circles were just the beginning of owl-protection proposals, not the end.

Highway 101 also rings the peninsula in a circle. No road penetrates through the rugged heart of the Olympic Mountains. Instead, the highway skirts their periphery. People in Forks express dismay that Olympic National Park and its forest are hidden from the tourists who drive around the Peninsula to weigh how many old trees are left. "I guarantee you that anyone saying there aren't enough hasn't walked through that park," said Jerry Leppell, the saw shop owner in Forks. "Let 'em walk through it and then tell me how many more acres they need."

But most people don't walk the park's nearly 1 million acres. Instead they circle it, leaving the main highway to poke up into the Hoh Valley or switchback up to Hurricane Ridge and then come back out again. In their circumvention of the fifth-most-popular park in America, they drive through communities like Forks, and thus see a different landscape and a different need. The town is on the western arc of the highway, and it can be approached from either the south or north. Either path is unflattering. Or maybe just honest, depending upon your point of view.

Forks lives on timber, and high-production logging on the Peninsula has long meant clearcuts. From the south, as Highway 101 leaves the ocean beaches of Kalaloch in the coastal corridor of Olympic National Park and winds inland, the clearcuts seem to multiply in frequency as one approaches the community. The fight over logging owl habitat near the park has pushed some operations down next to the road. On private land that lines the highway, some owners have decided to harvest before the environmentalists set their sights on them. And in the summer of 1990, with the spotted owl battle at fever pitch, big new swathes of second-growth forest on state-owned land were cut right at the turnoff tourists take when they drive into the Park's Hoh Rain Forest. No polite curtain of trees along the road. Just raw earth and stumps.

Those who saw these roadside bites into the forest were understandably confused by the complicated land-ownership mosaic around Forks. There was federal park land where logging was prohibited. Then there was federal national forest land where it was allowed. There was state-owned timberland, and private timberland owned by big corporations such as ITT-Rayonier, and private patches of ten or twenty acres owned by individual families, some of the titles kept in families since homesteading days. Many folks didn't know the difference. Some thought the loggers were cutting down the national park. The motor homes that trundle along 101 each summer would pull off to the side of these brown swathes of slash and debris and their occupants would snap pictures. Geezus, they'd mutter. Does it have to look so bad? Don't these loggers know what a rarity this land and this forest is? Up at the Hoh Visitor's Center rangers trying to give nature talks on the rain forest were interrupted by questions about clearcutting. People were upset. You could hear the tourists shaking their heads and muttering about it in the campgrounds each evening.

The timing of the cut did seem peculiar, even reckless. Some residents of Forks darkly suspected environmental enthusiasts in the state Department of Natural Resources of having planned the cuts deliberately to heighten public opposition to logging and change department practices. That suspicion amused urban tree huggers who believed "DNR environmentalist" was an oxymoron and that those stationed in Forks in particular were "timber beasts," the slang for particularly pro-logging government foresters. (The Forks DNR boys got in trouble one year when they put a float into the town's Old Fashioned Fourth of July parade that featured a spotted owl being chased around the float's periphery by a logger with a chainsaw; Seattle environmentalists got wind of it and raised a stink.) Perhaps the roadside clearcuts were simply honest, but they seemed almost defiant in their prominent ugliness, as if to say, See, this is the reality of the modern forest. Sure, you can drive up the Hoh River Valley into the park and dip your toe into that ecological museum, but this is the reality of our civilization. Here is where your home and furniture and newspaper and toilet paper come from. Go ahead, take your snapshots. They are only the mirror of your own desires.

The clearcuts were even more frequent along 101 to the north and east of Forks, and the contrast with the park even more jarring. In the north the circular highway follows the winding shore of ten-mile-long Lake Crescent, a breathtaking fjordlike jewel cupped in mountains that are included in Olympic National Park. Carved by glaciers during the Ice Age, the lake is up to 600 feet deep. The edge of it shimmers a clear aqua when the sun shines, but the bottom drops off quickly and a few feet from shore, the water is an opaque, chilling blue. Until the highway was improved it was not uncommon for cars to swerve or slip and disappear into its depths, and so precipitous was the drop-off that the lake had a reputation for not giving up its dead. Or, if it did, accomplishing mysterious things. One graceful female body floated to the surface after years in the depths, preserved but ghost white: somehow the cold, coroners said, had changed her fat to soap, preserving all but her face and fingers.

Despite such morbid tales the lake remains lovely. Beyond it, however, Highway 101 climbs up over a divide and drops into the Sol Duc River Valley. The valley was railroad logged in the 1920s, and now a second crop of trees is being logged again. The highway straightens here through what were called the "fiberboard flats" back in the high-roller days of the '60s and '70s when the log trucks ran nearly bumper to bumper.

To the experienced eye, the clearcuts offer an ecological archae-ology. There are the fat, high stumps of the first old growth logged and carted out by railroad. Between them are the lower stumps of the second crop of trees cut by chainsaw and trucked away, sixty to seventy years later. And between those there are the seedlings of a replanted third crop. The hills beyond have the familiar stepping-stone pattern of regrowing tree stands of varying heights. Some of the regrown trees are big enough now, one hundred and more feet high, that many tourists think these relatively puny second-growth specimens are the old growth environmentalists are fighting for. As if to underline the point, the DNR has put a campground in a second-growth grove that used to be a raw clearcut and logging camp.

The highway runs west to Lake Pleasant. The hills above it were shaved by chainsaw again recently, as if to mock the lake's name. There is still a stand of tall second-growth timber behind the home of logging truck drivers Dick and Barbara Mossman, but ITT-Rayonier is expected to log it soon. Dick accepts this philosophically, like a farmer ready to concede the harvest of a field of waving wheat—even though he won't live to see the stand grow that high again and even though the lack of a wind break will probably mean the loss of the handful of conifers in his backyard to storms. To deflect the criticism of outsiders, the DNR and ITT-Rayonier have erected signs in places to explain when the sites were logged and replanted and when, in the twenty-first century, they will be logged again. "Jobs grow with trees," the DNR signs say.

That is about as close as the industry will come to apologizing for the ugly front porch of Forks. The cut patches—many sprouting conifers the size of Christmas trees, the firs and hemlocks exploding upward three and even four feet a year—underline the point that this is a working town, by god. Outsiders don't understand, locals say; they don't grasp how this forest changes and rots and regrows. The inevitable defensiveness draws the town together but also produces a weariness, like worldly adults having to explain a harsh reality to children.

Bert Paul, one of the town's two leading grocers, likes to take visitors up on Willoughby Ridge where a striplike clearcut follows the crest for miles next to a tongue of Olympic National Park. The circular logic of Northwest logging is represented here: the trees had to be cut to pay for construction of the logging road that had to be built to take out the trees. The U.S. Forest Service has more road than any agency in the world, 343,000 miles of it, about seven times the length of the interstate highway system. It is a monstrously ambitious network, impossible to properly maintain. Each winter sections of it sheer off in heavy rains and slide into creeks. Only recently have biologists gently suggested that maybe not all these roads are absolutely necessary for all places for all time, since the trees may only be cut once every hundred years. But the roads also make possible forest fire fighting, hunting, and hiking. There's nothing like a clearcut to expose scenery; in Eastern Oregon the Forest Service sold off trees next to a road in Hells Canyon National Recreation Area and named the timber sale

"Vista View." Argue about roads and you get very quickly to the heart of debates about man's role in the forest: if a tree falls, does it make a sound if no one can drive out to hear it?

Paul doesn't bring visitors up to Willoughby Ridge to talk about logging roads, but rather to compare the fat, old, and tired lean of old growth with regrown tree crops. Paul served on a state commission that preserved for at least fifteen years the old growth to the south that this road was supposed to doom. He has heard all the preservationist arguments. Still, he doesn't understand why otherwise sensible people get excited about the harvest of overripe, decaying trees. As with so many people heard from in this green country, ideas about religion and human purpose creep into his conversation. "I feel God had more purpose in creation than to let this forest fall over and rot," Paul said, gesturing at the big trees that appropriately look gray and wrinkled in the marine fog. "He put these here so people could use them."

On the way down, Paul remarks that he likes the look of the young trees coming up between the stumps. They are a bushy, bright green— puppies of the plant world. He argues they have a beauty of their own, an intimate charm as worthy of consideration as an old forest. Perhaps ten years old, the young conifers planted on a clearcut have grown up and together in a thick, interwoven carpet that rolls away into the mist.

Of the beauty of young trees healing a human scar, there is no question. On a golden autumn morning, its frost melting and then steaming in the sun, a cut-over and replanted patch west of town shimmers with tinseled light. It is the end of the summer season when Northwest spiders reach their biggest, and here they have woven hundreds of webs, glossy with dew, between the young conifers. The rising sun lights them as if they were made of silver neon. The effect is magical, as if life is physically stitching together the interstices of the vanished big forest, endlessly repairing itself in a cyclical rite of rejuvenation that those who live here argue is as sacred as an ancient grove.

Forks's layout is like that of a thousand other American rural communities, fronting on the main highway the way frontier towns once fronted on the railroad. Yellow ribbons flutter from a line of young fir at the western outskirts, symbolic of an industry that feels it is being held hostage by environmental extremists. Other yellow ribbons, most of them faded and tattered from the lengthening battle, hang from pickup aerials as well. A logging locomotive is on display in the city park, and up in the center of town next to the Vagabond restaurant there is a graying slice from the trunk of a spruce, its diameter higher than any head, and a sign noting proudly that the tree sprouted before the arrival of Columbus. Above it is a sign reflecting Forks's claim of the 1970s: LOGGING CAPITAL OF THE WORLD.

At the peak, before the go-go overcutting finally slowed, the volume of wood that rumbled out of this town on the back of trucks was indeed as great as any place in the United States. This tree, placed in 1977, is apparently not the first such trophy put on display. Back in 1939, when a similar tree was cut near the Hoh River, the intention was to display it in Port Angeles. The plan was abandoned when it was discovered the trunk was too fat to fit through a tunnel on the way to that city so they put it in Forks instead. These cross-sectional chunks of the vanishing forest are as commonplace in Northwest logging towns as racks of antlers. They are indicative of the traditional way of seeing trees, of a trophy approach to nature.

The main street of Forks has a single stoplight and the usual strip of commerce: gas stations and convenience stores, motels, restaurants: the coffee shop at the Pay-N-Save that is the social hub, the Vagabond, Hungry Harry's, Sully's, the Smokehouse. There is a gun and tackle shop, a barber, a gift shop, and the papered-over windows of a small department store that folded. The lone movie theater, where Indians used to sit on one side and whites on the other, is closed; there are several video outlets instead. Most of the taverns are gone now but there is still the Hang-up, scene of a legendary scuffle between a pack of motorcyclists and the loggers on the Fourth of July back in 1979. The bikers lost, of course—in earlier days loggers brawled a lot, and a man who fell under the caulk boots of an opponent got what was called "logger's smallpox"—and stories about the scuffle made the wire services. Some folks admit they kind of enjoyed the brief notoriety; others complain the fight gave the town a roughneck reputation it never deserved.

A visitor can get a clue about the dilemma of Forks by noting that the town's biggest office buildings are the headquarters of the Forest Service and DNR. Forks is an island of entrepreneurial zeal in a sea of government timberland, a place of capitalist conservatism based on a wood-driven economy about as socialistic as any you'll find in America. What no one likes to talk about much is that government timber policy made Forks, government overcutting helped cheat it of its future,

and government environmentalism is shutting it down. Forks is suspicious of government as only a dependent can be.

That is about all of Forks most travelers ever see. The everyday town
of post office and utility headquarters and schools starts one street over,
and the residential areas spread out beyond that. The neighborhoods
extend out onto a flat prairie, surrounded by foothills wooded with
young conifers about forty years old that have grown back since the
Big Fire of '51. Forks is quieter and prettier back there off the highway,
and there are no clearcuts in sight. On the yards and in windows are
yellow signs that read, "This family supported by timber." One sees
similar signs in the shop windows: "This business supported by timber."
It is both a statement of fact and a plea. The high school canceled its
vocational class that taught logging to the students there; while parents
struggle to hang onto the forest, they expect their children to have
different choices.

Out toward Paul's grocery store there was a cross somebody put up
until the chamber of commerce complained. For a while it had owls
roosting on the crosspiece and logging equipment scattered at its base.
If the symbolism seemed a bit mixed, the message was not—it was
the logger who was being crucified.

After objections from religious groups, the owls perching on the
cross were taken away, as was the logging equipment. Instead someone
mounded dirt at the cross's base, making it appear as if there was a
grave there. The sign over the grave read, "This family *was* supported
by timber."

In sum, you can't escape Forks's identification with logging: and yet
that identity came slowly. From the Civil War to World War II, Forks
thought of itself primarily as a farming town, just waiting for a harbor
or a railroad or a highway to link it to markets. By the time a good
highway came dairying was fading, however, and hops and peas and
other dreams were plowed-under failures. What was left was the
timber—the trees that toppled around the town in '21, the trees that
delayed the completion of Highway 101 until the Depression, the trees
that almost burned the place to a cinder in '51. The damnable trees
that finally, in the last few decades, brought a burst of prosperity and
finished converting Forks's self-image.

Forks traces its start to 1877, when a Civil War cavalry veteran
named Luther Ford arrived in Washington Territory after a postwar
odyssey in search of a healthy climate that by varied accounts had

taken him to Iowa, Indiana, Florida, and California. Those were the days when logs were still being skidded down Seattle's streets, and Portland, Oregon, was nicknamed Stump Town, the stumps white-washed so that wagons wouldn't collide with them at night. Seattle's pioneer mill owner Arthur Denny offered to sell Ford eighty acres of what would become downtown Seattle for $400, and Ford could have paid for the land by working at Denny's sawmill. But Ford had little interest in Seattle's steep terrain. He wanted to farm. Tales had drifted back to Puget Sound of a rich, rain-soaked flat prairie on the western end of the Olympic Peninsula. There were no trees that needed clearing on this prairie, the stories went. It might even have wild cattle, left by earlier pioneers who had failed to stick there.

Ford was not the first would-be homesteader to hear of this place, burned annually by the Indians to keep it an open grassland for elk and other game. Word had come back from lone trappers by 1860, and a number of settlers migrated from the community of Dungeness, on the northeastern Olympic Peninsula, about the time of the Civil War. They had dreams of a new community, and even tried to form Quillayute County on the western peninsula in 1868. They were too early, the country still too remote. There were not yet enough settlers even to fill the county offices. It was the first of recurring, abortive moves over the next century to form a separate government for the remote, cantankerous West End.

The prairie was so isolated that by 1871, the original settlers had drifted back to Dungeness, disappointed at the lack of opportunities for commerce. The few white settlers left clinging to the area lived near the mouth of the Quillayute River. It emptied into the Pacific Ocean at an Indian village called La Push.

Ford and his wife Esther were intrigued by the reports of the prairie. In a land half-suffocated by dank forest, here was open country, un-claimed and promising. The only problem was getting to it. There were no roads to the reported prairie. The only way to approach was by sea. They boarded a schooner in Seattle and sailed west down the Strait of Juan de Fuca to Neah Bay at the northwestern tip of the Olympic Peninsula. It was December 1877.

The targeted prairie was only about twenty miles south from Neah Bay as the crow flies. But it was twenty overland miles through rugged foothills and some of the densest forest on earth. The crudest trail between Clallam Bay on the strait and the prairie area would not be opened for fourteen more years. Even then, the fallen trees blocked the way like a series of walls, some of the trunks twelve and fifteen feet in diameter. When Martin Konapski began running a three-horse pack string in 1891, he cut steps up the side of these monsters and taught his laden horses to mount them like circus ponies. It was easier than hewing through the logs with an ax.

Accordingly, the Fords decided to skirt the rocky Pacific coast south to La Push by Indian canoe. The mammoth canoes, carved out of a single cedar log, were formidable vessels that reached up to seventy feet long and sometimes had sails made out of woven cedar bark. The fierce Makah Indians of Neah Bay used them both for war and whaling.

No transport could have been a better introduction for the land they were about to enter. The high prow and sleek shape of the canoes gave them grace and power, and their primitive origin from a single tree made the canoes seem fundamental somehow, a gift from the gods.

The cedar, one of several conifers native to the Peninsula, was the most prized of all trees by Northwest Native Americans. They called it the "tree of life" and would later compare its utility to that of the buffalo for Plains Indians. Cedar is decay resistant like redwood, so much so that fallen trees persist on the wet forest floor for centuries. Its sinewy bark can be stripped and woven for clothing or baskets or wound to make twine. Its wood is easily split and worked and has a pungent perfume of its own. Cedar was used to make the plank long-houses, the totem poles, the canoes.

Cedar groves were also places of spirits and worship. Washington Indian tribes would successfully petition the Forest Service in the late 1980s to set aside some tree groves as places for traditional spirit quests. A Lummi Indian named Sam Cagey once took me into a cedar grove far up the Nooksack drainage in Washington's Cascade Mountains, and matter-of-factly talked of the magic the trees performed there. Objects sprang out of the wood, Cagey said. The trees had the power to touch the mind. The fasting Native Americans, who plunged into the nearby icy stream and meditated beneath the soaring cedars, came in touch with other worlds. "You can really receive a power," Cagey said.

More than a century after the Fords' first cedar canoe trip, a reformed logger and recovering alcoholic named David Forlines—part white, part Native American—would help revive the craft of canoe building at La Push. By then it was difficult to find cedar of the necessary girth and age (at least three hundred years) to make a canoe. Forlines combed state land on the western Peninsula and marked thirty-one old-growth cedar trees he thought suitable; when he returned to check on them most had been cut down.

Still, he managed to save some, and enlisted the help of locals to carefully take a few down for canoes. Some of the region's best veteran loggers eagerly pitched in to help. Their job had not numbed their fascination with the big trees.

One does not simply cut down a suitable canoe cedar, Forlines instructed. One speaks to it first and explains one's intentions. You have to promise the cedar the use you intend, and deviation from the promise can make you sick, or cause the canoe to fail and drown its crew. You are making a pact with a living thing, giving it a new purpose and different guise. As the craftsman speaks he circles the tree, waiting for a feeling of acceptance. Even this is not enough: "You use your imagination, you wait until you see the canoe in the wood of the tree." Michelangelo talked about this, how his sculptures were already in the marble and only needed to be revealed. In a canoe tree, however, this vision is not automatic. Forlines recalled that one favored specimen refused to reveal any canoe and continued to look, frustratingly, like a cedar tree. The disappointed Forlines began walking away and then decided to try one last time, wheeling to address the cedar with a plainspoken threat. "You know, I have come to speak to you before the invader comes. He intends to cut you down and chop you into shingles for homes in California." The canoe appeared.

Even after the live tree has agreed to its own sacrifice and transformation, Forlines said, cutters must turn away when the tree falls, so the cedar does not see who toppled it and so will not direct its anger at them later, when it is bearing them at sea. Then the cutters wait to give time for the little people to scramble out of the tree. Forlines said many loggers will support his belief in the little people: they have heard the rustling and the crying of children after a tree comes down.

To make a forty-three-foot canoe out of a five-hundred-year-old log took Forlines nine months of spare-time work on the ocean beach at La Push. The period may have been appropriate. "It's like there is a bonding between a craftsman and his tree," he said of the long hours of hollowing the log. "It is almost like a male giving birth." In 1989, the Peninsula Indians paddled several of the newly made canoes to Seattle to mark the state's centennial.

This kind of symbol of the forest was what the pioneer Fords climbed into for the last leg of the sea journey to their new home.

The western Olympic coast remains today the most undeveloped stretch of coastline in the continental United States. Rocky headlands and half-submerged stone towers called sea stacks breast the long, gray breakers like the prows of ships. The spray that comes off the surf wreaths the wind-twisted spruce and cedar above the beach in constant moisture. In places waterfalls plunge down the cliffs to the ocean below, and offshore, dark-red undersea forests of kelp roll restlessly in the surge of the sea. Dozens of sailing ships have gone down along this coast in the decades since the Fords canoed here.

Accompanying the Fords was Dan Pullen, who had staked a claim at La Push in 1872. Pullen was already something of a legend with local Indians, regarded with both awe and dislike for his prowess as a fighter. When a Makah warrior showed up at his La Push store to question his pugilistic ability, Pullen reportedly felled him with one punch.

As the party paddled southward along the forbidding coastline, the weather began to worsen. The short hours of winter daylight disappeared, rain began falling, and the seas steepened. The party tried to put ashore at Ozette to wait out the weather, but the breakers were already too rough. They struggled on southward, toward La Push. Eventually the canoe seemed caught in the swells and began to be propelled toward the booming breakers, despite the urgent paddling of the tiring Indians. Finally the natives despaired of clawing free of the coast, put down their paddles, and began wailing a death song. Esther Ford was desperately seasick in the swells and no doubt wished she were anyplace else on earth, but her two daughters, Winnie and Myrtle—crouched under warm blankets in the bottom of the canoe and oblivious to the danger—were charmed at the Indian chanting. Mrs. Ford would later recall that some of the songs seemed to be hymns taught the Indians by Christian missionaries.

Pullen was not ready to resign himself to fate. He snapped at the Indians, urging them to pick up their paddles and make a last try at pulling clear of the surf. After some argument (and probably just as important, some rest) they did so. Digging in furiously they drove the canoe back clear of the breakers and fought southward again. Finally the craft knifed through the steep waves that crown the sand bar at the mouth of the Quillayute River and coasted into the little harbor at La Push. It was four A.M., fourteen hours after leaving Makah Bay. The Fords were at the very end of the continent and there was little prospect of going back. Luther Ford had just seven dollars.

There were two prairies east of La Push, one a few miles inland at

Quillayute and a larger one further up the rivers. The Fords pushed up the rivers to the bigger prairie. There was not even a trail to follow.

They came to a 3,000-acre plain of black clay, covered with grass and bracken fern so high it could almost hide a horse and rider. All around were foothills shrouded with dark, ancient forest. Ford claimed 160 acres of prairie a mile east of what is now downtown Forks. The family built a cabin, and began farming. The following year Esther waited nervously with her daughters while Luther Ford journeyed back to buy dairy cattle on Puget Sound, land them on the beach at the Strait of Juan de Fuca, and drive them down the ocean beach to La Push and then up to his homestead. Because there were no roads through the forest, cattle were also driven back along the beach to market. The first such drive, by the Pullen brothers, took seven weeks.

Three bachelors already lived in the area, but Ford brought the first permanent pioneer family. His second daughter Winifred, aged twelve when she landed at La Push, married one of the bachelors, Eli Peterson, at age sixteen. But the first white child born on the prairie was Oliver Ford, son of Luther and Esther. He would live in Forks all his life, toward the end of it facing down a forest fire with a garden hose.

Eventually the settlers in this remote, roadless community proposed naming their community Ford's Prairie. The U.S. Post Office reported back that there was already such a name in Washington Territory and so the pioneers chose Forks instead. Here the Calawah River joined the Bogachiel, and the Bogachiel the Sol Duc, and together they formed the short Quillayute that poured into the Pacific and up which salmon would swarm every fall.

The name "Forks" would prove prophetic, in a way. Here the argument would be most intense about the fork, or split, in the way humans viewed nature and the forest. Here would be a town forced to examine its own reason for being.

4

THE OWL

▲▲▲▲▲▲▲▲

There is a sign on an office door at the National Council for Air and Stream Improvements in Corvallis, Oregon, a wildlife consulting firm hired by the timber industry to find out if spotted owls can survive outside old-growth forest.

SINCERE BELIEF MIXED WITH CRAFTY DECEPTION IS CONSPICUOUS BY ITS PREVALENCE IN THE HISTORY OF BOGUS SCIENCE, the sign reads.

Larry Irwin, a wildlife biologist who heads the company, does not accuse owl enthusiasts of bogus science. Irwin himself served on an owl study group that called for 7.7 million acres of designated habitat for the owls. The Bush administration tried to debunk the Interagency Scientific Committee report headed by Jack Ward Thomas and couldn't, because it was written by some of the best wildlife and owl experts in the world.

Still, Irwin cautions that scientists are human, as vulnerable to peer pressure, groupthink, and outside influences as other people. He realizes his own hire by the timber industry instantly makes his research more suspect.

What Irwin argues is how little we really know about the habitat requirements of a species such as the spotted owl. "Here we have an animal that weighs twenty-two ounces and uses five thousand acres of forest," he said. "Once the mind-set was that old growth is needed for spotted owls, people went to old growth to find spotted owls. . . . It's sort of a social process—if you are going to be in the in-group of scientists, here's what you have to think about things." Irwin was hired by the timber industry to test the hypothesis that owls are limited to old-growth forests. He was hired to, in theory, ensure a final objectivity by challenging from a new point of view.

The complaint that owl policy was outrunning owl science grew as momentum for owl and old-growth preservation built in the Pacific Northwest. A minority of scientists, many linked to the timber industry, complained that old-growth preservation proposals were being driven by environmental ideology, not science. "Beware of scientists bearing solutions," warned sociologist Robert Lee of the University of Washington, "particularly if they are based on myths or land ethics."

This criticism stemmed from a split in approach as old as environmental debate. The timber industry argued that if policy makers could not be certain a particular tract of trees was necessary for spotted owl survival, society should allow logging to proceed. The burden of proof, they contended, should be on the owl and its biologists. Environmentalists maintained the opposite, that if there was not absolute certainty then logging should stop until there was.

The scientists who headed owl research argued that it was the industry biologists who were stretching things, ignoring the bulk of the evidence collected over two decades and seizing on refugee owls pushed out of old growth by relentless logging as proof that the bird could survive in industrial forests. "There is more information available on the spotted owl than on any other species ever considered under the Endangered Species Act," said Charles Meslow, an owl researcher with the U.S. Fish and Wildlife Service. "There is no shortage of data." When Jack Ward Thomas learned that the industry's American Forest Resource Alliance had hired three statisticians to hold a press conference challenging the certainty of owl plans, he confronted one of the researchers. "I asked, 'Have you ever been to the Pacific Northwest?' He said no. I asked, 'Have you ever seen a spotted owl?' He said no. I asked if he was paid. He said he spent five days on his report for six thousand dollars and six hours reading our plan. I said, 'You're a pimp.' "

What such confrontations illustrated is how important the assumptions and motives of individual scientists had become. In an age of uncertainty and moral confusion, we tend to enshrine science for the truth it seems to offer. And in fact, over time science does tend to be ruthlessly objective, with even the most sacred theories fair game for scrutiny and challenge. But the stereotype of the scientist as objective to the point of being emotionless and socially naive is rarely accurate. Scientists' background colors their observations, which in turn drives their research. Nor do they live in a social vacuum. Even in the early

1970s, Eric Forsman and Howard Wight were almost immediately aware of the implications of being able to call, and find, spotted owls. And Forsman decided not to keep quiet about it.

The stage for controversy was well set. In the Pacific Northwest, overall timber harvests had doubled in volume since World War II. The annual cut on the largely untapped old-growth forest of the national forests had grown even more. In 1946 the national forests in Washington and Oregon cut less than a billion board feet of timber. By 1968, when Forsman first saw the owl, the annual volume cut had soared to 5.1 billion board feet. It was a near record, but even that huge cut would be eclipsed in the 1980s: in 1987, when environmentalists sought protection for the owl as an endangered species, a record 5.6 billion board feet were cut on national forests in the two states, most of it old growth. In the more than two decades that elapsed between Forsman's meeting with the bird and government admission that the owl was threatened with extinction, more than a million acres of old growth were cut.

As early as 1969, the U.S. Forest Service published a study warning that old-growth forests in western Washington and Oregon were being rapidly depleted and that timber harvests could fall as much as 30 percent when it was gone. (In fact, as early as March 1938, the federal government's Pacific Northwest Regional Planning Committee forecast that forest harvesting on the Olympic Peninsula would decline drastically by the end of the 1980s. "This Pacific Northwest region marks the end of the trail so far as virgin timber is concerned," the committee reported to President Franklin D. Roosevelt. "So far as merchantable timber and the timber industry are concerned, substantial depletion may come about in a relatively short time with respect to the national lifetime. At the rates of production of the 1920s, this may occur perhaps in five or six decades." The prediction was ignored, but it proved uncannily accurate.)

Moreover, there had been a shift from selective cutting practiced before the war to more economically efficient clearcutting. As thousands of miles of new logging road were punched into wild areas and favorite trails were swallowed by clearcuts, public complaint about forest management was beginning to grow. Now Forsman and Wight appeared to have found a rare bird that nested only in uncut, virgin, old-growth forest.

Oregon State University, where Forsman was still a graduate student in 1973, is located in Corvallis. Accordingly, some of Forsman's first spotted owl survey work was conducted not on federal land, but in the nearest forest he could find: the city's 10,000-acre watershed. Within a week Forsman found three nest sites, doubling the number of known spotted owl nests in Oregon. Logging, however, is a source of revenue for many municipalities with forested watersheds. Patches of the Corvallis watershed were periodically harvested to raise money for the city budget. Shortly after finding his nests, Forsman learned the city planned to cut 100 acres of trees within 100 yards of a spotted owl nest.

In the spirit of the era's student activism, Forsman decided to object. In September of 1972 he wrote Floyd Collins, the city's water supervisor, to advise him of what he found. The exchange of letters and arguments was remarkably prescient in setting the outline of the debate that would boil for the next two decades.

"I cannot overstress the requirements of this species for old growth timber and dense forest understories," Forsman wrote Collins. "In a statewide search for this species, I have yet to find it in anything but old growth timber stands of approximately 300 acres or larger. . . . As proposed, clearcutting or thinning in this area would destroy the nest site and the habitat now being used by these owls."

Collins replied with a brief acknowledgment, pointing out that the nest Forsman immediately feared for was not actually threatened by current logging plans (there was some confusion in the mapping) but noting that another nearby nest site might be. He invited Forsman to discuss the issue further.

Forsman did so in April of 1973. "As I told you before," he wrote to Collins, "I have only been able to find the nest sites of three pairs of owls on the entire 10,000 acres which comprise the watershed. I consider it of utmost importance that we seek to preserve known nest sites of this species, because they are nearly impossible to find. Because they are never found, they are never preserved, and so goes the story of the spotted owl. . . . It seems to me that on a watershed of 10,000 acres it would be possible, for the moment at least, to plan the harvest areas such that critical habitat areas are avoided."

Forsman did not stop there. "I was appalled at the suggestion made by the Watershed Study Committee in the [newspaper] last night that timber harvest be increased on the watershed," he went on. "The paper states that trees on some parts of the watershed have become decayed as a result of 'disuse.' Disuse by whom, certainly not spotted owls? I recognize that most old growth stands contain a high incidence of decayed and often diseased trees, but this is exactly the factor which attracts the spotted owl. Old growth trees provide an abundance of nest cavities for owls, squirrels, bats, woodpeckers, tree-mice, wood-rats, Vaux's swifts, etc., etc. Old decaying deadfalls which litter the forest floor in old growth stands provide habitat for innumerable rodents, insects and reptiles."

This time Collins replied at length, arguing that the old-growth trees Forsman wanted to save were more apt to be damaged by fire or wind, and if so could topple and cause soil damage. The area Forsman wanted saved, he wrote, "represents an area that has reached its maximum potential for additional growth and increased economic value. . . . [I]n viewing the economics alone on a 300-acre parcel, you have placed a value of 2 million dollars per nest on these areas. . . . I'm sure you can appreciate the responsibility that the City of Corvallis has to the citizens of this city to manage the watershed and all of its resources in a manner that provides maximum service to the citizens."

Forsman—in youthful candor he would not use in later years— replied in writing that he was "displeased and very digusted" at Collins's answer. Old growth did not represent the soil hazards Collins claimed, he wrote, and added, "I do not question the dollar value you place on the trees. . . . I am not talking economics, however, I am talking simple biology and the preservation of a unique community of animals."

Here was a value system the city of Corvallis did not yet understand. Preserve animals for what? For whom? Forsman took his case to the city council at its regular meeting and was rebuffed. "They reacted pretty negatively," he recalled. He wrote letters to the editor, drew some sharp rebuttals, and aroused the interest of the Corvallis *Gazette-Times*, which wrote a brief story that put the spotted owl into the news. The local Audubon Society chapter began asking the young biologist to tell local bird-watchers what he was learning. Forsman also began peppering the Forest Service and Bureau of Land Management, both major landholders of old-growth forest in Oregon, with information about the spotted owl.

The initial response was quick. The owl was included on a list of species the government drew up as potentially endangered in 1973, the same year Congress passed the federal Endangered Species Act. In Oregon, the director of the state Department of Game, John McKean, spearheaded organization of the Oregon Endangered Species Task Force that formed in 1973 and began looking at the owl. In

California, the Forest Service's Gordon Gould began surveying for spotted owls in 1973 using Forsman's techniques and found far more than anyone had expected.

The Endangered Species Act of 1973 was the culmination of a series of laws dating back to 1900 aimed at protecting America's threatened wildlife. Earlier, weaker versions written in 1966 and 1969 had proven inadequate to stem development. The new law superseded the older laws. It put the survival of species above economic considerations: including "any member of the animal kingdom," and adding, for the first time, plants. It provided a means to preserve ecosystems on which endangered species are dependent. In the 1980s, about $232 million was spent by the federal government on species protection.

But administration of the act has been uneven. The inspector general of the Interior Department found in September of 1990 that while 550 species had been listed under the act, another 600 known and 3,000 probable endangered or threatened animals and plants had not been listed. In response to the inspector general's report, the U.S. Fish and Wildlife Service replied it didn't have the money to adequately study and make a determination on more than about fifty species a year. Moreover, while the inspector general estimated it would cost $4.6 billion to adequately provide recovery for endangered species already listed, the annual Fish and Wildlife budget for that purpose is only $8.4 million. The practical effect of this has been delay and dissatisfaction on all sides. The spotted owl became a prime example of this.

Opposition to protecting the owl quickly formed, once it became apparent what protection implied. Scientists had hypothesized that at least 400 nests must be protected to ensure that enough pairs of owls survived to genetically continue the species, and that a minimum of 300 acres of protected old growth was needed around each nest site. Even though that many nests had yet to be located, owl researchers led by Forsman and the state of Oregon asked the federal government to set aside the acreage in 1974. The timber industry thought scientists must be joking. Set aside 120,000 acres of prime timber for owls? Even a modest estimate of the value of wood on that land would indicate a potential sacrifice of $10 billion. The Forest Service and the Bureau of Land Management rejected Oregon's proposal, justifying the rejection on the grounds that more study was needed. The refusal set a pattern of delay and study that would continue for seventeen more years. The modest 300-acre reserves would not be adopted until 1977, and even then were hotly opposed by the timber industry.

The industry's nightmare was just beginning, however. By 1981, scientists were calling for 1,000-acre preserves, not 300, based on radio telemetry data of where owls flew. "We came to realize 300 acres wasn't even close," Forsman said. The more the flight pattern and feeding habits of the owl were studied, the more the acreage grew. By 1988, the proposed habitat areas would balloon to as much as 10,000 acres per nest site on the Olympic Peninsula, where owl prey was less abundant. In 1990 even that was deemed inadequate and scientists called for preserving huge blocks of owl habitat: 7.7 million acres in all in Washington, Oregon, and California; 5.8 million acres of it outside existing parks and wilderness areas and 3.1 million acres of it considered commercial timberland. That was a minimal plan that under pessimistic assumptions would preserve about 2,200 pairs of owls by the year 2100, the scientists said: a decline of 40 to 50 percent in the owl's estimated numbers. The dollar value of the old growth biologists wanted protected became stratospheric. One estimate was that owl set-asides would cost the region's economy $27 billion in the next fifty years. Job loss estimates by the year 2000 ranged from 14,000 to 105,000.

Yet just one year later, that acreage was dwarfed again. The U.S. Fish and Wildlife Service had, after a court order, declared the owl a threatened species (a category that under statute was slightly less dire than "endangered") but had failed to designate critical habitat for it as required under the Endangered Species Act. Working under a tight deadline imposed by a further court order, in April of 1991 the agency designated 11.6 million acres outside of parks as "critical habitat" for the owl. While that figure would be adjusted, its scope was unprecedented. "The Endangered Species Act has never been done at this scale before," former congressional aide Don Barry, an expert on the act, said.

The owl issue became a political black hole, sucking more and more agencies, industry representatives, and environmentalists into the owl's once-obscure biology. Washington State followed Oregon and began its own owl research in 1978, formed its own study group in 1979, and set up its own national forest reserves around nests in 1980. When the Reagan administration successfully pressured the U.S. Fish and Wildlife Service not to list the owl as threatened or endangered in 1987—a decision that would later be reversed after U.S. District Court Judge Thomas Zilly found the agency's decision to be "arbitrary and capricious"—Washington's Wildlife Commission would defy the federal government and list the owl as endangered on January 15, 1988, after an exhaustive seven-hour meeting of acrimonious testimony. "It was a gutsy thing to do," recalled Harriet Allen, an owl researcher who became the department's endangered species coordinator. "They said science and biology must prevail, and the political aspects are not relevant."

It was back in 1981 that the U.S. Fish and Wildlife Service first described the owls as "vulnerable" to possible extinction but not yet threatened or endangered. Then, in 1982 the federal government set up an ambitious research program to study the owls in depth. In 1986, the forest industry belatedly started its own research program in self-defense. Some of its leaders complained scientists weren't looking hard enough for owls on logged lands, a suspicion that would eventually lead to Larry Irwin being hired. Forsman, however, said the industry became the victim of its own lack of interest in wildlife biology. "We have tried since the very beginning to get the industry interested in doing surveys," he said. Industry representatives would not finance them. In the timber recession of the early 1980s, timber companies slashed both their scientific research and public relations staffs, cuts they would come to regret a few years later.

Forsman can sympathize with the eventual dilemma timber executives found themselves in. The spotted owl was becoming the tar baby of the Northwest woods, the wildlife Vietnam that never seemed to end. The more owls the biologists found, the more concerned they seemed to become about their survival. And the sparser the owls were in any one place, the more land scientists claimed the birds needed. For example, the surveys showed that the density of the owl population declined as one moved northward from California to the Canadian border, presumably because the northern forests had less prey. Accordingly, recommended preserves for owl survival increased from as little as 1,500 acres in the south to 10,000 near Forks. It was the owl's huge range that caused the problem to begin with. The owls were threatened with extinction precisely because they required so much land to survive. Timber companies didn't know what to do. Should they look for owls on industry land to prove they could survive without old-growth forest? Or avoid any search out of fear any owls found would produce a stampede of biologists trying to lock the tree farm up? Eventually they hired Irwin and other wildlife consultants and began arguing that owls and modified logging might not be incompatible. The dispute frustrated people such as mill owner Larry Mason of Forks. If owls on the Olympic Peninsula needed so much range, he argued, why not concentrate protection where spotted owl prey was more abundant: southern Oregon, for example. Why did owls have to survive everywhere?

"It's pretty crazy, is what it is," Forsman would later say of the industry's dilemma.

Still, the fact scientists went from locating a handful of nest sites to more than 2,400 known owl pairs across three states—with 3,000 to 6,000 pairs suspected as the total population—did not lessen the owl's significance, Forsman said. "What's the problem? That we keep finding more of them? The fact that we're finding more all the time simply tells us more people are involved looking for them." By the mid-1980s, a single monograph describing what had been learned about the spotted owl would credit forty different biologists from four agencies, three universities, and two companies. Dozens of other scientists were also contributing to the research. "At the same time we're finding more of them, their population seems to be declining in areas we've studied for a long time," Forsman said. "Reproductive rates don't balance out with survival."

In Oregon in the first decade of study, owl numbers declined an average of .8 percent a year, biologists concluded. At the same time, the Forest Service estimated, old-growth timber was disappearing at a rate of one to two percent a year.

The problem was that an owl's chances were not easy in the first place, given the cruelties of the natural world. A mature spotted owl might live for fifteen years but nesting is irregular, egg laying occurs on average just every other year, and the mortality rate of owlets is high: 80 percent in one Oregon study, and a disastrous 89 percent in another California survey. With that kind of mortality rate, a pair of spotted owls might have to produce one to two dozen young in their lifetime just to replace themselves. Young spotted owls could fall prey to great horned owls. More aggressive barred owls (more commonly known as "hoot owls" in the East) had appeared on the West Coast in 1970 and were competing for spotted owl range.

In a few instances barred owls have bred with spotted owls, a trend owl biologist Meslow judges not unusual and genetically insignificant to date, but still adding to the confusion of calculating the health of the species. Moreover, there is little genetic difference between the northern spotted owl and the California spotted owl (though more so with the Mexican spotted owl). At present, all three are considered subspecies of a single species. The presence of southern neighbors led some in the timber industry to hope the spotted owl count could be broadened into Mexico and the owl's peril be discounted, but Meslow said the more likely result is that all three subspecies will be found to be threatened and critical habitat will be expanded, not reduced.

The owls are not cuddly in their personal habits. They rarely build nests, preferring instead to either appropriate the abandoned nests of other raptors such as hawks or find a cup-shaped cavity in a broken-topped tree. The cavity nests are cushioned by rotting wood, randomly accumulating needles, and leaf litter, and in older nests by the powdered bones of dismembered prey and old pellets. When the weather warms, the nests draw blood-sucking flies that attack the young owlets. Scientists theorize that one reason spotted owls leave the nest before being fully capable of flight is to avoid the energy drain of these biting insects.

The male and female owls part and lead solitary lives during the winter but by early March join again, often returning to the same nest site. At least two to three weeks before eggs are laid the pair copulate after a brief courtship of calls. They then both continue hunting until about a week before egg laying, when the female begins spending most of the time near the nest. The male, the smaller of the pair, brings food.

Typically two eggs are laid, though one is not uncommon, three were observed, and four are reported in historical records. The eggs usually hatch in April or May. The owlets are born covered with white down, their eyes not opening for the first five to nine days. At ten to twenty days their juvenile pale-brown plumage begins to grow, and by thirty-four to thirty-six days it is complete enough for the young owl to leave the nest, though its flight tends to be short and awkward for a couple more weeks. It is not uncommon for owlets to fall or jump prematurely, however, the majority are either killed by the fall or eaten by predators. Some spend ten days on the ground before gaining the necessary feathers to fly, in the meantime climbing trees with their talons and grasping the trunk with their wings when tired.

Few live long. Of those owlets observed in one study, a third that successfully left the nest were missing by the end of their first summer, probably killed by predators. In times of scant prey, owl parents may ruthlessly feed only the firstborn and drive others from the nest.

But when prey is abundant, spotted owlets are efficient killers themselves. Within three weeks of leaving the nest the owlets are typically able to tear up prey on their own. By late July they are capturing crawling insects, and by September they typically can hunt mice.

However gritty the owls' rugged existence, there is something compelling in their nature that seems to affect most people who come into contact with them. The willingness of a wild creature like the owl to submit to human inspection close up can be hypnotic. I ate lunch with some timber industry executives once beneath a tree housing a mother spotted owl and her fledgling youngster, his down puffed out like a carnival Kewpie doll. The owls seemed at least as curious about us as we were about them, swiveling their heads to follow us as we crashed clumsily through the brush. They were strangely unafraid, never starting or fleeing. The spotted owl comes across a bit as a trusting pet, blinking its soulfully large eyes, as if assuring visitors of its confidence that humans will ultimately do the right thing. We sat in amiable companionship for more than an hour with the birds, our intrusive chatter drifting up into their trees, enjoying an easy proximity impossible to obtain with almost any other wild animal. The effect is powerful: the timbermen said they had no intention of logging this stand.

"You can take the most negative critic in a group, take him into the woods, and he can't help but be affected by this owl," Forsman said. "It just sits and looks at you. Everyone comes away with a different perspective."

Stan Sovern, the owl surveyor who worked with Forsman, compares the owl to a cat. "They have a neat personality," he said. "They'll watch things kind of like a cat does. During the day they'll doze off, like a cat does. Sometimes on a sunny day I'd walk into the woods and find them way up on the top of a tree, basking in the sun, like a cat. And they do things that are surprising. Just when you think you've got them figured out when you're radio tracking, and you know just where they'll go next, they end up miles away. We don't know why."

Even with the high mortality, the owl could hold its own as long as its habitat was intact, scientists concluded. What it could not do is persist in heavily logged areas.

Slowly this data sifted into the consciousness of environmentalists. By the early 1980s briefings on the owl were becoming a common part of environmental meeting agendas. In 1985, the National Audubon Society formed a blue-ribbon advisory panel to review the status of the spotted owl in Washington, Oregon, and California. Still, the idea of challenging the Northwest's biggest industry over a little-known bird struck the most politically savvy of environmentalists as risky. Was the public prepared for such a step? "That was when environmental groups as a whole made the only strategic decision they ever made— they decided *not* to go for listing" the owl as an endangered species in 1985, recalled Andy Stahl of the Sierra Club Legal Defense Fund. Despite the years of study, as late as 1987 national environmental organizations showed little interest in owls or old growth. Any attempt to get the owl listed still struck many as premature. Stahl made a special trip to northern California to dissuade a pair of earnest environmentalists known as the Beckwith brothers not to petition to list the owl. Environmentalists felt unready for a showdown with the timber industry. The general public still had little exposure to the owl issue. The term "ancient forest" had yet to be coined for the big old trees.

In October of 1986, the issue was forced. Defying the calculation of mainstream environmental groups, an obscure Cambridge, Massachusetts, group called GreenWorld petitioned the U.S. Fish and Wildlife Service to put this owl, 3,000 miles away, on the government's list.

Northwest environmentalists had no idea what GreenWorld was. "I think maybe it was a guy and his girlfriend," said Stahl. "The calls I would get from him were always from a telephone booth, with traffic in the background." The initial request had the owl's scientific name wrong and was rejected by the government because it lacked the word "petition." GreenWorld amended its request and sent it in again on November 28.

GreenWorld was small, but it was more than a guy and his girlfriend. According to the organization's director, Max Strahan, the group was formed in 1982 by environmental radicals frustrated with what they saw as a tendency to delay and compromise among mainstream environmental groups. Its first campaign was to seek protection for caribou in northern Idaho, its president being a northern Idaho attorney named Charles Sheroke. While GreenWorld only counts about twenty active members, it has had an impact out of all proportion to its size. By 1990 it was working on protection for ten different animal species.

GreenWorld's frontal-attack approach to environmental issues was evident even in its recorded telephone message, a blunt, "This is GreenWorld. We save endangered species. Who are *you*?" Strahan, who was thirty-two years old when the owl petition was filed, is a longtime radical activist who has protested and led campaigns on such issues as the Seabrook nuclear power plant and low-income housing. He has a physics degree from the University of Massachusetts, and a booming voice with a Boston accent that rises rapidly in volume when discussing the alleged timidity of mainstream environmental groups such as the Sierra Club and Audubon Society. "The reason we got involved in the spotted owl issue was because no one else was," he said. "We knew the spotted owl was in trouble, but National Audubon and the Sierra Club were always cutting all these deals with the Forest Service. The bigger these clubs get, the more conservative they get. They go for quick, simple solutions. They love working with federal agencies, love getting crumbs from them. These guys become the government—there's no difference."

GreenWorld decided that more than a decade of government delay on the owl was enough and it was time to force the issue. By that time the stakes were immense. Some were calling the owl the "billion-dollar bird," a tag that was to prove to be a woeful underestimate. On the Olympic Peninsula near Forks, the now-harried Forest Service drew circles 2.1 miles across around each owl nest and halted logging inside them. A few months later scientists declared even that inade-quate, and by mid-1990 huge swathes of the forest were recommended to be set aside by the Jack Ward Thomas committee as "habitat con-servation areas." The owl became a media star, and mainstream en-vironmental groups such as Audubon, the Wilderness Society, and the Sierra Club were leading the old-growth and owl preservation campaign.

Meanwhile, Strahan concluded that even the new conservation areas, sprawling across 7.7 million acres, were inadequate, because they would allow the owl population to decline 40 to 50 percent. By the fall of 1990, he was campaigning for a more ambitious recovery plan. "We think there should be twice as many owls, not half as many," he said.

In March of 1988, Andy Stahl addressed a group of environmen-talists at the Western Public Interest Law Conference in Eugene, Oregon. He tried to explain what made this bird, still seldom seen by any hiker or logger, so significant to what was becoming an escalating battle over old trees.

There were no laws protecting old-growth ecosystems, Stahl ex-plained. There were, however, laws protecting wildlife. "It's quite biologically sensible to hypothesize that one or more species of wildlife would, in fact, be unique to old-growth forests because such forests for millennia were the dominant forest type in the Pacific Northwest," he said. "In addition, wildlife are measurable and you can count them . . . and thanks to the work of Walt Disney with Bambi . . . wildlife enjoys substantial, substantive, statutory protection."

"Well, the northern spotted owl is the wildlife species of choice to act as a surrogate for old-growth protection," Stahl went on, "and I've often thought that thank goodness the spotted owl evolved in the Northwest, for if it hadn't, we'd have to genetically engineer it." It was an inside joke. Stahl's father, a University of Oregon molecular biologist, was sitting in the audience.

"It's a perfect species for use as a surrogate," he explained. "First of all, it is unique to old-growth forests and there's no credible scientific dispute on that fact. Second of all, it uses a lot of old growth. That's convenient, because we can use it to protect a lot of old growth. And third—and this is more a stroke of good fortune in one sense and, in another sense, an indication that environmental groups tend to wait too long before they act—it appears that the spotted owl faces an imminent risk of extinction. That's very important, for if it didn't, federal agencies could argue that they could continue to log old growth and not hurt the spotted owl. It's important that it not only face a risk of extinction, but that we haven't gone too far because then federal agencies could argue: Why should we bother to protect old growth; it's too late already; the spotted owl is doomed. In other words, we have to be right on the edge and by good fortune, it appears that we are in this decade right on that edge."

Two decades after it first answered Forsman's hoot, the owl had become the center of one of the biggest resource controversies in the nation. Yet the northern spotted owl, as crucial as it was, was still just an indicator of a much broader issue. The debate was rapidly broadening to encompass an even more ambitious and nebulous idea than species protection: protection of the owl's entire ecosystem.

5

THE TOWN

▲▲▲▲▲▲▲▲

"Trees! Such monsters, all crammed together as thick as corn stalks," wrote pioneer Amantha Sill of Oregon's coastal forest in 1861. "God put them there, he must know what for. It is a great cave for animals to live, and Indians to come up on you so sudden. . . . Every day and night, I pray to be taken back to Indiana."

How different the forest must have seemed when it was unbroken. It affected the women in particular, often left alone in cabins set in a dark clearing hacked near the bank of a river. The wall of surrounding conifers whispered in the wind and stretched two hundred or more feet high. The men would leave to hunt or fetch supplies or log for a few dollars and the women would stay behind, often with young children, sometimes miles from any neighbor and any help. Dora Huelsdonk, wife of a prodigiously strong pioneer known as the Iron Man of the Hoh, used to wonder what would happen to her toddlers if she had an accident during her husband's treks to hunt cougar for bounty.

The forest is glorious in the glittering sunlight of high summer, of course. It is glorious in winter too, but in a darker, lonelier way. "You drove here down a tunnel of trees," recalled Lorraine Maris, who came to Forks from the east side of the Olympic Peninsula in 1954 and who used to run the Forks newspaper. She remembers not being able to see the stars, so narrow were the gaps of sky. She recalls electricity going out as long as five days because of the rain of limbs on the line. The shade would cause the black ice that formed on the roads to persist despite winter sun. It was claustrophobic until the big logging started. "Most women hated it here," she said. "The biggest cause of divorce was that forest. You felt like you were buried alive. Until you've been where you don't see the sun, you don't know what it's like."

Those who had lived in the forest inevitably had a different view from those who would later visit. It seemed inexhaustible in size, overpowering in structure, and a danger in its threat of fire or windfall. Robert Lee, the forestry sociologist at the University of Washington, has been researching the origins of these conflicting attitudes between rural and urban residents. Lee, a self-described political conservative who grew up in a backwoods home and worked in a redwood mill in California before going to college, argues that the rural view is the more realistic one, that rural residents understand that all life lives on the death of other life. "Rural residents can live with the ambivalence of loving nature and cutting trees," he said. "It's an acceptance that that's life." They see a cycle. City dwellers, he argued, are more likely to feel guilt toward nature, and thus be more in favor of trying to preserve some of it unchanged. "Urban people are more disconnected with nature, and are very likely to regard trees as a symbol of immortality, of continuity." The split, he said, almost takes on religious overtones.

Part of the explanation of attitudes in Forks comes from its difficult history. In the earliest days Forks's prairie was like an island, connected only tenuously to the outside world. Only slowly were corridors punched through the woods. Supplies those first years were infrequent. In a strange three-way commerce, the Indians brought seal pelts and fish to traders such as the Pullens in exchange for store goods, and then traded some of those store goods to the white farmers for vegetables. Only the smallest vessels could breast the breakers at the mouths of such rivers as the Quillayute and Hoh. In the 1890s a thirty-foot ketch called the *Surfduck* run by a Captain Hank brought supplies over the river bars until it disappeared in a storm.

From the beginning, Forks struggled to overcome the limitations of its own location. After Merrill Whittier homesteaded the present site of downtown Forks he and several settlers started a hops-growing operation, building a large drying shed. But the only transport was at the river mouth at La Push, where storms across the bar could keep vessels from entering or leaving for weeks. The hops rotted waiting for stormy weather to clear.

Accordingly, growth was slow. While Forks had its post office in 1884, the town's street plan would not be laid out until 1912. It would be 1929 before the town would have its first formal garbage dump, 1930 before it searched earnestly for a bank. There was only one obvious wealth to this land, the trees: so many of them. But they were so remote from other cities, that momentarily at least they were for all practical purposes valueless.

Slowly the West End of the Olympic Peninsula opened up. In 1892 the settlers turned out to improve the road from Forks north to Clallam Bay on the Strait of Juan de Fuca. Small communities took root at Beaver and Shuwah and Mora. But progress was frustratingly inconsistent. Shortly after the turn of the century there was a fever of excitement as four different railroads sent survey crews struggling through the dark woods and brush of the West End, seeking a route for tracks to head north from Aberdeen and Hoquiam or west from Port Angeles. Then a recession hit in 1907. Not a single rail was laid.

The first end to isolation came from a timber baron, Mike Earles. An enthusiast for the curative powers of hot springs, he acquired the rights to Sol Duc Hot Springs tucked up in the Olympic Mountains. (Sol Duc is an Indian name meaning "sparkling waters.") To get tourists from Puget Sound to the remote location, Earles ferried road-building equipment west across Lake Crescent and carved a $100,000 road up through the forest to the springs. Then he spent $500,000 constructing a lavish four-story hotel in the wilderness. Opened in 1911, it had European tapestries, golf links, and tennis courts.

The hotel burned to the ground in 1916. Legend has it that the heat started the mechanism of the mechanical organ in the hotel lobby, and it played out Beethoven's "Funeral March" as the grand edifice crumbled. The hotel was not rebuilt, but the trail from Forks east to Lake Crescent was widened into a road to link up with what Earles built, giving settlers access to the eastern Peninsula via the Lake Crescent ferry. It was the first ambitious extension in the West End of what would become Highway 101. In 1922, a winding road carved into the cliffs was completed on the south side of Lake Crescent, and from 1924 to 1931, Highway 101 was pushed south of Forks. But Forks's dreams of prosperity remained frustrated by its isolation.

Logging had started on the western peninsula to the north and south of Forks in a big way after the turn of the century. To the south the Quinault Indian Reservation would be raped of wood, much of the native land turned into a fiber desert of broken slash where nothing could regrow. Grays Harbor County was so relentlessly logged that a history of the period is titled *They Tried to Cut It All*. To the north, in the Hoko and Pysht basins, camps for loggers were built and trees were cut, the conifers dragged and floated out to the Strait of Juan de Fuca and then rafted east to the big mills in Port Angeles and Bellingham. But Forks itself was still isolated from the transformation.

An explanation for this was the lack of roads, not just major highways but gravel and dirt logging roads such as the system that today crisscrosses the national forests. Flat valleys alongside railroad tracks could be logged, but to get up into the steep foothills trucks were needed. There are many explanations for the explosive cutting of old-growth federal timber after World War II, one being that the simple extension of roads made trucking logs feasible.

Earlier, just before U.S. entry into World War I, it had seemed railroads might do the job. In 1917, the best wood for airplane framing was spruce, which for its weight was the strongest wood in the world. The western Olympic Peninsula had some of the biggest spruce trees anywhere.

In response the army organized the Spruce Production Division, a 30,000-man unit in Washington and Oregon designed to punch roads and railroads into the coastal forests and take out the spruce that thrived on heavy rainfall. Loggers were recruited from throughout the army, paid civilian wages, and put into logging camps modeled on the ones Merrill & Ring Company had built on the Pysht. In the spring of 1918, construction began on a railroad along the northern shore of Lake Crescent and up the Sol Duc River Valley, terminating at Lake Pleasant near Forks.

It was an epic feat of construction. Some thirty-six miles of railroad were built in six months through steep, thick country. At one point along Lake Crescent, a 460-foot tunnel was blasted. The world's great flu epidemic hit that fall and truckloads of bodies were taken from the work camps, but the work pace hardly slackened. Working at breakneck speed, the Spruce Division completed the railroad on November 30, 1918—nineteen days after the war ended.

Not a tree was ever harvested for the war effort around Forks. Once again, the community's time had not yet come. The world had a surplus of biplanes, the spruce market plummeted, and the railroad, and the private land around it, went up for sale.

The frustration continued. Bloedel Donovan, a timber company headquartered in Bellingham across Puget Sound, was intrigued by the postwar prospect of the railroad. They began negotiating with Clallam Lumber Company of Grand Rapids, Michigan, to buy its

12,000 acres of holdings around the rail line for a million dollars. The deal was done, the paperwork flowing, when the hurricane of January 21, 1921, hit.

The storm was queerly focused: it hit north of the Columbia River and cut a 100-mile swathe northeastward. Forks, which boasted only a dozen homes, three stores, and two hotels in the town proper, was directly in its path. The worst of the wind spent itself in just three hours, but estimates of its top speed were as high as 120 miles per hour. The forest it struck was one of shallow-rooted conifers, and in that brief period an estimated 8 billion board feet blew over, or about 20 percent of the forest around Forks. Logs from the disaster were still being salvaged in the late 1970s.

"The noise of wind and rain and falling trees and branches was as deafening as a continuous thunderclap," Grace Fletcher, a member of one of the region's pioneering families, would later recount. "Several people, who had been able to see the hills before darkness blotted out all sights of the storm, reported having watched the trees on the hilltops go over like tall grass before a sickle."

Another Fletcher, Lena, was in the Hoh River Valley south of Forks. "We were astonished to see the flying timber," she later wrote. "We now saw a 200-foot hemlock crash straight towards our cabin, landing only a few feet short of it. Looking out we saw the branches of thousands of trees sailing overhead across the sky from one divide to the other."

Despite the havoc, most escaped injury. A Mrs. Klahn braked her Model T Ford to a stop when a tree fell in front of it. Her attempt to back up failed when a tree fell behind her. Prudently, she crawled into a ditch. A tree came down and crushed her car.

At the end of the new rail line at Lake Pleasant, work crews played cards at either end of a rail car, waiting for the storm to pass. A tree came down and cut the car in two, blowing out both ends and the men with it. Miraculously, none were hurt.

Highway 101 north from Forks was just a narrow gravel road at that time, and in minutes it was a snarl of thousands of trees. Forks residents counted three hundred across the roadway in the first mile. It took ten days to cut through the windfalls and reopen the road to Lake Crescent.

The wind again delayed exploitation of the great forest. Bloedel Donovan balked when it learned perhaps a fifth of the forest it wanted to buy had blown over. Although the deal had been made, Clallam Lumber finally agreed to cut $250,000 off the purchase price to avoid a protracted legal battle. Still, Forks had to wait. Negotiations over use of the government railroad broke down, and finally Bloedel built its own railroad from the strait south to Sappho, and then along the Spruce Railroad tracks to Lake Pleasant. In 1924 logging finally began, and by 1928 1,500 men were cutting timber from railroad logging camps. In one day, 320 railroad cars were loaded with logs. By the time the Depression hit, most of the area within easy reach of the railroads was denuded. Up on the Pysht, more than forty square miles had been cut by a single company, Merrill & Ring, by 1944. On the highway between Lake Crescent and Forks today, most of the forest a traveler sees is second growth that has grown up since that period.

Forks grew slowly from this first great harvest. The timber industry was still evolving, from remote forest camps primarily filled with migratory bachelors to family men who would commute by truck on a vast network of forest roads. The loggers of legend came from these camps, where a two-man saw was called a misery whip and the stacked bunks were sometimes so confined that the occupant could climb in from only one end, and thus called his bed a "muzzle loader." The city of Aberdeen south of Forks had celebrated brothels called Harvard, Columbia, and Yale; collectively the red-light district was referred to as College Row. From these frontier beginnings, only slowly did timber communities of families, tied to a fixed radius of forest, come to be the norm. One push for change came from the World War I Spruce Division. Colonel Brice Disque created a "Loyal Legion of Loggers and Lumbermen" to speed the harvest, forcing logging contractors to accept an eight-hour day, forty-hour week, and livable camp conditions. These were the same goals that the Industrial Workers of the World, or Wobblies, had been agitating for—sometimes violently— before the war. Their institution, and decent pay, changed the logging work force from essentially migrant labor to middle-income employees who could afford to support families.

The federal and state governments hastened the transition by beginning to market public timber at a pace that was promised to be sustainable: by the time the last tree of the virgin forest was cut, the first of the regrown was supposed to be big enough for harvest. In 1937 Congress passed the Sustained Yield Act that pushed the U.S. Forest Service into this program and promised rural logging communities stability. Later harvest reductions to protect old growth would be interpreted by these communities, with some justification, as government betrayal.

In Forks the transition did not firmly fix the community's identity as a timber town until after World War II. In the decades before the war, farming and tourism were both continued disappointments, the former because of Forks's distance from markets, the latter because while the town sat between a spectacular coast and mountain range, it had no view of either. In the end it was periodic disaster that rescued Forks from its frustration. The modern era came first from fire, then another windstorm.

The Northwest Pacific coast has some of the wettest winters in the world, but the great forest from northern California to the Olympic Peninsula has remarkably dry summers. In most temperate areas of the world, moisture is distributed fairly evenly throughout the year, but in the Northwest, summer rainfall is as little as a tenth that of winter. Rain can hold off for weeks, even months. These droughts are one explanation for the dominance of conifers; the lack of summer moisture puts broadleaf trees that have foliage only in the warm months at a disadvantage to evergreens, which can photosynthesize nearly year-round.

In a dry wind, the normally wet conifer forest can become a tinderbox, able to be ignited by lightning or careless humans. Indeed, most western forests have evolved and been shaped by fire. It is fire that destroys the shade of overhead canopies and this in turn allows a species such as Douglas fir to outcompete its shade-tolerant cousins. It is fire that favors thick-barked Ponderosa pine over faster-growing but less-hardy competitors. It is fire that melts the resinous coating around the seeds of lodgepole pine, allowing it to regenerate. Scientists estimate as little as 60 percent of the Northwest forest that pioneers encountered had lived long enough to qualify as old growth because stands were ravaged so frequently by fire and wind.

The era of great forest fires is mostly forgotten now, just as is the era of urban blazes that would level entire downtowns in Chicago and San Francisco and Seattle. (San Francisco burned six times in eighteen months at the start of the 1849 gold rush, creating the first big market for Northwest timber. Briefly, timber cost a dollar a board foot, a price it would not reach again for a century and a half.) But early in the twentieth century 200,000 forest fires annually plagued the West. Together they were scorching 30 million acres a year, or an area the size of Pennsylvania. Not all the trees were killed over such vast areas: fire in the West weeded and renourished many ecosystems, consuming brush but leaving the thick-barked trees unharmed. Still, the hottest blazes could be disastrous. The Yacolt Burn in southwestern Washington burned 700,000 acres and left thirty-five dead in 1902. The Tillamook Fire in northwestern Oregon in 1933 burned as much timber in ten days as the United States would consume all year.

The summer of 1951 was particularly dry, the blue skies slowly drying out the valley of the Calawah River. Sparks from a yarding engine ignited a small blaze in late August, but it was extinguished— or so the crew assumed. In reality, embers smoldered in the duff of the forest floor, waiting for an opportunity to break out.

In the early morning of September 20, 1951, flames licked up past the surface and fed greedily on oxygen. A wind out of the east was blowing, and the blaze flared quickly. In eight hours, it raced seventeen miles down the valley.

In Forks, the sky turned an ominous black and red. It was so dark from smoke at midday that the town's streetlights came on. At two-twenty P.M. sirens sounded, advising residents to evacuate. By official count, 269 did so, fleeing north and south on Highway 101 with their headlights on and their cars piled high with clothes, bedding, furniture, and mattresses. Some arrived in Port Angeles with the paint of their autos blistered from the heat.

"The sky has been so dark with smoke that no one can tell when daytime ended and night began," wrote Earl Clark, city editor of the *Port Angeles Daily News*. "Fine ashes rained down the sky in a ceaseless flow, filling eyes, hair, ears and mouth, and coating everything with a fine powder. There were only three kinds of sounds—the roar and crackle of the flames eating into the town, the scream of sirens as fire trucks raced through the empty streets, and the urgent shouts of men's voices. In the north end of town, flames exploded houses like matches."

Doors were left swinging open in the rush to flee, furniture was abandoned in yards, and clothes were still hanging on wash lines. One man staggered out of his house with a new washing machine on his back; another rushed back inside to snatch and save his wife's negligee. A deer plunged out of the forest, almost crashed into a firefighter, and disappeared. Dogs howled mournfully. A herd of goats huddled together. A battery of bottled gas containers went up with a roar. "It felt like a flame thrower hitting me," a Port Angeles fireman told Clark.

Some didn't flee. Oliver Ford, the first white child born on the prairie, now seventy-one, stood all day on his porch with a garden hose. The flames came within 200 yards of his house.

At the climax, 450 firefighters were battling to save Forks and head off the flames. A fire line had been carved by bulldozer around the town in 1938, and perhaps that helped. The fire burned in a half circle around the tiny town, then halted. The hot wind out of the east shifted, cooler air blowing in from the ocean. On September 23 a light rain fell, and the danger was over. The fire had run for twenty-five miles, destroyed twenty-eight houses, four garages, a mill, a ranch house, and three barns. It had consumed fifty-five square miles of timber. No one was killed.

The fire had not finished Forks, but rather given it new impetus. The black snags in the dead valley could be salvaged for lumber, and for the next few years local loggers did just that, cutting the dead trees and returning home each night covered in ash. Joe Dahlgren, who would head the community's biggest surviving logging company by the late 1980s, moved to Forks in 1952 with his wife Ingrid to drive a log truck hauling salvage logs from the fire.

One more disaster was to set the stage for Forks's brief boom as the world's logging capital: Hurricane Freda.

On October 3, 1962, aircraft began tracking the developing tropical storm near the Philippine Islands as it began drifting across the Pacific Ocean, going north and east. About 1,750 miles southeast of Tokyo the circular hurricane itself lost cohesion, but its powerful winds continued to be driven with the prevailing westerlies. On October 12, Columbus Day, the storm struck the Pacific Northwest with savage fury. At Naselle in southwest Washington, a sustained wind speed of 150 miles per hour was recorded.

It was the biggest Northwest storm in history. It took forty-six lives, blew down 15 billion board feet of timber (equal to about one year's harvest in Washington and Oregon), and damaged 53,000 homes.

This time the Forks area experienced little damage. Instead, the impact was indirect. Big timber companies such as Weyerhaeuser suddenly had an enormous quantity of wood needing salvage and no American market that could absorb that much.

Someone thought of Japan, beginning to rebuild at breakneck pace. U.S. executives began aggressively marketing Pacific Northwest timber and Japan responded to what were often bargain prices. As a result of this beginning, log exports shot from 210 million board feet in 1960 to 4.2 billion board feet—a twentyfold increase—by 1988. Ninety percent of the wood came from the great conifer forest of Alaska, Washington, Oregon, and California. Nearly two-thirds came from Washington State alone.

Here was wood demand that could finally defeat the time and distance problems of remote Forks, a demand that would increase some wood prices fivefold in the 1980s. An hour's extra haul on the highway was barely a cost factor if a log was going all the way to Japan. In the decade of the 1970s Forks's population doubled and it took on a boomtown atmosphere, with rollicking taverns and go-go enterprise. A man who wanted work didn't need to know the difference between a choker cable and a splitting maul. All he had to do was stand in the parking lots of gas stations in the hours before dawn and wait to be picked up by a labor-hungry crew bus. Even the state government hurried to get in on the bonanza. The biggest nonfederal block of virgin timber left in Washington was in the state-owned Clearwater River drainage south of Forks, left untouched until the 1970s because of its distance from markets. A former Forks logger and schoolteacher named Bert Cole had been elected Commissioner of Public Lands, and he decided the time was ripe to punch roads into the Clearwater and clean out its old growth. Federal, state, and private harvests exceeded a billion board feet a year on the Peninsula, or five times what it would fall to by 1990.

The euphoria quieted in the timber recession of 1979–1983, but even then another disaster intervened to keep the loggers of the Logging Capital of the World employed. The 1980 eruption of Mount St. Helens scorched 150,000 acres, 68,000 of them part of a Weyerhaeuser tree farm, and leveled millions of trees the timber industry wanted salvaged. For the next three years, many woods workers like the Dahlgren family temporarily migrated to southwest Washington to take part in the harvest.

The robust economy that began in the 1970s gave Forks a cocky self-confidence and as the iconoclastic town came into its own, it was not shy about going its own way. Environmentalism was viewed with suspicion and contempt. In 1976, a contingent from the town had unsuccessfully lobbied Congress to prevent addition of more ocean shoreline to Olympic National Park. In 1981 when Peninsula rivers were proposed for possible addition to the nation's Wild and Scenic River system more than 600 residents of Forks packed the high school gym to protest and successfully kill the idea. Forks was like a gnarled stump sucked at by the currents at the mouth of a river, used to holding out against the larger tides.

By the mid-1980s timber prices were soaring again and there was a new flush of prosperity in Forks. The town was rich with green gold.

Yet change was in the wind. Union power in the big timber companies was eroding. In the era's speculative, buy-out fever, timberland was beginning to rapidly change hands, and the new owners, saddled with debt, seemed to have even less interest in sustainable forestry than the old. State and Forest Service officials trooped to community meetings in Forks to warn that the bonanza from their lands could not last. In the urban centers of Washington and Oregon, environmentalists were beginning to challenge the logging head on.

When Luther Ford rode over the La Push bar with his family in 1878, most of the Peninsula's 2 million acres of old growth still stood. By 1990 less than 20 percent of it was left, most in Olympic National Park and adjoining wilderness areas. The Wilderness Society estimated that only 3 percent of low-elevation old growth survived in Olympic National Forest, and virtually none on private lands. What was left was fragmented into isolated patches.

The foothills around Forks were a rolling panorama of brown and bright green. A new kind of forest had been invented, one that was the product of decades of research. The monstrous gloom of old growth had been replaced with plantations of clone-like conifers, the same age, the same height, the same species. Clearcuts were burned clean for this progeny, planted so densely that competing vegetation would be squeezed out, and sprayed, thinned, and fertilized for maximum growth. To those who raised doubts about this transformation of the forest, the foresters and economists had charts and studies defending the utility of their practice. By the 1980s estimates varied on when the last of the original forest would be converted to this improved variety—some said thirty years, some fifty—but there was no question conversion would occur. Most foresters considered it an improvement.

Yet even as Forks finally triumphed over its isolation, even as it finally capitalized on its final forest, a new generation of scientists was emerging from studying the ancient groves. They were about to challenge all the assumptions that communities such as Forks had been built on: and in doing so, turn forestry on its head.

6

THE GURU

▲▲▲▲▲▲▲▲

Standing waist high in pink fireweed on the crown of Gold Mountain, Jerry Franklin looks down a slope of Washington's Cascade range to see an example of his ideas put into action. A score of U.S. Forest Service employees from the Darrington Ranger District northeast of Seattle have accompanied the scientist to look at one of their first attempts to produce what Franklin calls a deliberate "dirty clearcut." It is one of many bits of verbal imagery he has coined to get his ideas across. This most recent logging pattern on Gold Mountain puts into practice Franklin's theories about "New Forestry," his name for an attempt to integrate ecology with wood production.

The views are spectacular and troubling this late summer day. To the east, between Prairie and White Chuck peaks, a series of clearcuts stripe a ridge that runs in front of the Glacier Peak Wilderness Area. The slope is like an unrolled scroll documenting controversial government logging practices. On several of the clearcuts the steep slope, thin soil, and dry sun have defeated repeated replantings. Some of the vertical slashes through the forest have been nicknamed "ski runs" for their chute-like pattern. Another oddly shaped clearcut, designed in an apparently vain effort at encouraging reseeding from surrounding mature trees, is called the Playboy Bunny: its round patch has two shaven "ears" that cut uphill. From this distance, it is as if someone cut patterns on the mountainsides with a lawn mower. The Mount Baker-Snoqualmie National Forest doesn't look very managed from this vantage point. It looks abused.

Below the crest of Gold Mountain, the Forest Service is trying something new. Its latest clearcut is deliberately messy. While most of the trees have been logged, about 10 percent of the dead snags and green conifers of what was an old-growth forest stand have been left standing. The intention is to provide a refuge for surviving wildlife. Quite a bit of wood has been left on the ground as well, as if the loggers quit before they were quite finished yarding their harvest. Phyllis Reed, the district wildlife biologist who helped lay out this sale with its surviving trees, explains how the trees and rotting logs will provide shelter to animals.

Like this attempt to modify clearcutting, Reed is a symbol of how fast the Forest Service is changing. When her boss, forty-nine-year-old District Ranger Fred Harnisch, joined the agency in 1963, it was almost exclusively male. The Forest Service was divided between timber-oriented "foresters" who spent much of their time planning timber sales, and engineers who spent most of their time designing logging roads. Most were from the rural West and they reflected the assumptions of their region. "The people in the organization knew we should be changing, but the direction was to get the cut out," Harnisch recalled. "One guy [outside the agency] told me that we worked hard, but the one problem was that we didn't listen to people. We didn't have time. Our nose was to the grindstone."

Now the district staff is 45 percent female and has biologists and archaeologists and hydrologists who look at the forest as a place to do more than grow wood. The new mix is typical of the entire agency since Congress passed the National Forest Management Act in 1976. The change has been slow—it took fourteen years for the Mount Baker-Snoqualmie National Forest that includes the Darrington District to finish a radically revamped plan that Congress called for in that 1976 act—but it has also been significant.

As a young wire service reporter in Washington, D.C., I covered the often tedious and technical hearings that produced the 1976 Act and wondered at the time if earnest lobbyists had not overblown its significance. The law was prompted by a court ruling halting clearcutting on federal land in West Virginia, but went beyond that issue to force the Forest Service to consider other forest values. "The days have ended when forest can be viewed only as trees, and the trees only as timber," Senator Hubert Humphrey told his colleagues. Yet in the years after the law passed, Humphrey's declaration seemed hollow. Little immediately changed in Forest Service practices.

The reasons for the legislative tedium are more apparent now. Some Forest Service officials call the law the most important for their agency in this century. Since it was passed the Forest Service has gone from 284 to 688 wildlife biologists, 75 to 236 fisheries biologists, 47 to 206

archaeologists, 7 to 84 ecologists. The new disciplines attract enthusiasts from across the United States, many of them more liberal,
worldly, and wildlife oriented than their predecessors. On the Darrington District one comes from Brooklyn, another from Manhattan.
Phyllis Reed served in the Peace Corps. They bring new perspectives,
and it shows up on the ground.

Loggers can also adapt to change. Jim Bryson, the Forest Service
employee who helped persuade a contractor to make this peculiar cut,
advises his colleagues to use some psychology when approaching loggers with these newfangled ideas. "If you tell them to do it, they'll
cuss and yell," he said. "But if you make it a challenge, they'll do it.
It's surprising what loggers can do if they want to."

Franklin's theory is that leaving these trees and logs comes closer
to mimicking what nature accomplishes with fire or windstorms. Forest
fires tend to skip and hop, destroying part of the forest but sparing
enough to recolonize the damaged areas. The trees and logs that are
left become homes for insects, reptiles, birds, and mammals. Franklin
calls it a "biological legacy." He jokes about the scientists' new love
for rotting logs. "I worked around logs for fifteen or twenty years," he
said, "climbing over them, swearing at them, kicking them, viewing
them as a fire hazard, without ever thinking they had an ecological
function."

The idea of leaving such material was conceived when Franklin and
a team of researchers visited the scorched slopes of Mount St. Helens
after the volcano exploded with the force of multiple atomic bombs
in 1980. The blast laid trees over like a giant comb, burning off the
needles and covering the mountainsides with logs like matted brown
hair. Ash covered the duff of the forest floor. Humans and large animals
caught in the blast were suffocated and roasted. But scientists were
surprised at how many small creatures and plants survived the searing
heat and began immediately to repair the ecological fabric. Fireweed
poked through the ash. Ants scuttled across the gray powder. Gophers
burrowed to the surface, beginning to mix the old soil with the new
deposits. Insects and seed began to blow across the moonscape. It
dawned on the scientists that leaving woody debris behind speeds the
recolonization of the forest after a disturbance, be it volcano or clearcut. Musing later on the twists and turns of his life that made him
one of the Pacific Northwest's most famous and controversial scientists,
Franklin remarked on the propitious timing of the eruption that jolted

ecologists' thinking: if the blast had not leveled those 150,000 acres of trees, the campaign to preserve millions of additional acres of forest may not have developed quite the same way.

Franklin is at his best when he is explaining his ideas to working foresters. On this day on Gold Mountain, he expounds from an old logging landing above a clearcut, pink and white from fireweed setting seed. The logged hillside overlooks the logging town of Darrington, a community of immigrant Tarheels from the North Carolina Appalachians that is dependent on timber and boasts one of the best bluegrass music festivals in the Northwest. Franklin fits easily in such a milieu, relaxed and folksy for this sermon on a mount. His talk is one of hundreds that Franklin has given in recent years, ranging from testimony in front of Congress to classroom lectures. His effectiveness has earned Franklin the tag of the "guru of old growth" in the media.

He has drawn the less-flattering sobriquet of "Chairman Mao" from jealous academic rivals dismayed at the success of this heretic at challenging the tenets of traditional, commodity-oriented forestry. Chad Oliver, a colleague of Franklin's at the University of Washington, implied to a roomful of timber industry executives once that Franklin's ideas are so untested they are equivalent to the debunked claims made for cold fusion. "Let's not go out and do something without having thought it through," said Oliver with a trace of bitterness at Franklin's attack on traditional tree farming. "I don't want it done in (television) sound bites."

Franklin is hardly a sound-bite scientist, however. Three decades of painstaking research and technical writing gave him a solid academic reputation long before the spotted owl crisis drew attention to his ideas. He coauthored a massive tome on the biology of the Northwest forests and has authored dozens of technical papers on ecology and the impact of harvest techniques. His critics want him to produce a similar bible on New Forestry, a detailed prescription of hypothesis and proof that can be tested and assaulted, a project he intends to tackle in the mid-1990s. Meanwhile, Franklin complains he is attacked one moment for allegedly going too far and too fast with New Forestry, the next for not having already written a cookbook specifying every management detail. "I get bloodied all the time that we do not yet have sufficient research to quantify all the effects of New Forestry, both positive and negative," he said. Yet, during this Gold Mountain trip, the harvest of Northwest trees was averaging four to five square miles every week.

It is not that Franklin is unused to challenge: two forest supervisors and the Northwest's regional forest supervisor tried to get him fired in the 1970s over his studies asserting the value of old growth and the dangers of unbridled logging. In his office at the University of Washington is a photograph of him shaking hands with Dale Robertson, national chief of the Forest Service. Robertson's note at the bottom gives some idea of Franklin's mixed reputation with his bureaucratic superiors. It reads, "I too agree that it's great for a 'loose cannon' to get recognition for a job well done."

Franklin fits his role as logging heretic well. His parents seem to have signaled his future direction by giving him the middle name of Forest. He is six-foot-one and has the rangy lope of a man who has spent a lifetime traversing rugged terrain. He can fit with ease into a marbled congressional hearing room in Washington, D.C., but up on Gold Mountain he gives a hint of his talent for dramatizing an issue with his red suspenders and a floppy Stetson a bit like an Indiana Jones hat. He is gentle in look and manner and voice, with graying hair and round, wire-rimmed glasses that in this context inevitably give him a bit of an owlish look. One suspects that Franklin's boyish enthusiasms and the delight often mirrored on his face have led opponents to underestimate him.

For most of his adult life he has led a cadre of friends on once-a-year rugged hikes across untrailed terrain in the Cascade and Olympic Mountains. While it took the Press Expedition six months to break trail across the Olympics, Franklin's group rambled the same distance on alpine ridgetops in a week. At age fifty-three, time is slowing down the ambition of such treks, but it hasn't dampened his love for the woods.

"He's a delight to hike with," said his wife, Phyllis. "He's like a child. He whistles, he yodels, he names birds, he talks to the animals, he points out every new little flower. He expresses awe at every change of color around the seasons."

When Jerry Forest Franklin married for a second time in 1987, he took his new wife to a grove of old-growth trees at Government Camp in Washington's southern Cascade Mountains. It is a long journey from the couple's new home on Squak Mountain, more than two hundred and fifty miles, but Franklin felt it was important to do this early in their marriage. He wanted to explain himself to his new bride. "He wanted the trees to meet me," she recalled.

This was the place where, at age eight, while camping with the Boy

Scouts in Gifford Pinchot National Forest, Franklin had a kind of epiphany. It is not customary anymore to concede to the natural world the power to touch us in ways beyond the obvious five senses, to attribute any meaning to all but the most prosaically concrete. Yet the majestic grove spoke to Franklin in some powerful way.

"He felt he received a mission," Phyllis said that Franklin explained to her. "His mission was to speak for the trees." The scientist sat with her in the grove, explaining this mysterious thing that had driven him since childhood as the trees reared like pillars overhead. He cried a bit, she recalled. It was not the sort of feeling a scientist would display in public, of course. But it was a necessary introduction to their marriage, one that would explain the long hours Franklin would spend in coming years at meetings and hearings and speeches. "This feeling is very, very strong," she said.

This instinctual appreciation would, at times unconsciously, guide Franklin's subsequent research. "I came to old-growth forests with an intuitive feeling that these forest have value," he would later recall.

Does this intuition, this passion, invalidate scientific research? No one who understands the enthusiasms scientists bring to all sorts of questions, large and small, is likely to think so. "Scientists are just like other human beings in terms of motivation," Franklin said. "There is a myth of objective science."

For decades the bias and motivation tended to run in the other direction. Pacific Northwest forestry schools got most of their donations from the timber industry, and it was natural their research would focus, often narrowly, on the most efficient ways to cut down and regrow trees. When the federal government made money available in 1969 to study basic forest ecology, the scale began to tip the other way.

Science is ultimately objective. Unlike other fields of human thought such as religion and philosophy, science is based on hypotheses that can be tested. Its portrait of reality is constantly changing. New ideas run a gauntlet of skepticism and challenge and revision, and Franklin has no doubt that most of what we understand about the forest today will seem quaint and myopic in half a century. He talked about that on Gold Mountain, how one *sees* the forest based on present knowledge and how any scientist is probably overlooking profound and basic facts that someday in the future will seem painfully obvious. "They'll look back at us and say, 'Gee whiz, how could they have missed that?' " he said.

But the ways scientists see are inevitably affected by their culture and background and era, he added. Americans generally are "oriented toward products and efficiency," Franklin said, which explains why historically, most of the value put on forests has focused on the commodities they could produce. Scientists, he thinks, tend to split on more abstract lines, between the technocrats and the naturalists, between those who like the simplified order of tree farms and those more comfortable with, or appreciative of, the seemingly disordered complexity of natural systems. Franklin almost instinctively liked the chaotic rationality of the original forest. The reasons why probably date from his boyhood.

Franklin, who has kept the easy twang common to the rural Northwest, grew up as the son of a pulp mill worker in Camas, Washington, on the Columbia River across from Oregon. "His father introduced him to the beauty of trees," Phyllis explained. With the end of gas rationing in 1945, Franklin's family began to camp in the nearby Gifford Pinchot National Forest and at Mount Rainier. By age nine, he knew he was going to become a forester.

Franklin's skills as a communicator developed only as an adult. In high school he was introverted and an indifferent student, and found adolescent solace in long, solitary walks in the woods near his home. Once in college, the relative academic freedom appealed to him, however, and he quickly excelled, settling finally on pursuit of a degree in forestry at Oregon State, the Northwest's leading forestry school. There, Professor Bill Farrell got him a student trainee job at the Forest Service's Experimental Station nearby. Franklin had found his niche.

Dick Miller, a soils scientist who was then a student at the University of Washington, remembers meeting Franklin at a conference in 1959. "He was all enthusiastic about ecology," Miller recalled. "We thought the action was going to be in soil science, and we gave him a hard time" for concentrating on this new, nebulous idea of ecosystems and biodiversity. But it was Franklin, whose skill was going to be the ability to synthesize the research efforts of numerous scientists, who would prove to have recognized the significance of a systems approach to biology.

A pivotal event in Franklin's career was a United Nations–inspired research effort called the International Biological Project in 1969. Financed by taxpayer dollars through the National Science Foundation, the project made money available to study the workings of some of the earth's major ecosystems. Franklin was put in charge of a group of scientists who went to the H. C. Andrews Experimental Forest near

Eugene, Oregon, to study Pacific Northwest old-growth conifer forests.

It was the dominant coastal ecosystem of a large part of North America, but curiously, no one had ever studied the ecology of old growth in any detail. This final forest was so pervasive, so obvious, that it was largely overlooked. By the conventional thinking of the time, virtually everything humans did to it was an improvement. A preliminary Forest Service study of old growth had been abandoned eight years earlier with the conclusion that old growth was adding little, if any, net wood fiber. Therefore the best thing to do would be to harvest it as quickly as possible and replace it with young, fast-growing trees.

"I got a heavy-duty education at Oregon State in the traditional view, that there was value only in wood and that these forests needed to be converted," Franklin recalled. "The idea was that these were really negative ecosystems."

Instinctively, the scientist remained unconvinced. Simply as pieces of biological engineering, the Pacific Northwest's conifers are extraordinary organisms. A mature Douglas fir can contain 70 million tiny needles, which together present an acre of surface area to the atmosphere. The trees are like mighty combs, brushing the air to collect moisture and sunlight and to cleanse the atmosphere of the grit of pollutants. Their height of 200 to 300 feet is near the limit of a plant's ability to pull water against the force of gravity from its roots to its tops. "I thought there's got to be value in there," Franklin said. "They can't be negative ecosystems—it's got to be the way we're looking at them."

The team of assembled scientists started digging into the soil, measuring the streams, and climbing into the canopy. They looked at the impact of shade and fallen logs and dead standing snags. Cycles appeared. Adult salmon spawned in clean streams, died, and their carcasses fertilized the trees. Underwater insects hatched, flew to the nourished trees, flourished themselves, and died. Their bodies in turn fell into the water at the time the baby salmon emerged from their eggs, providing food. Everything fed everything. Yanking out the trees was like pulling an ace from a house of cards.

"Early on, there was a lot of, 'gee-whiz' astonishment," recalled Ted Dyrness, a close colleague of Franklin's who coauthored the pair's ecology text. "Everywhere we turned we thought, 'Gee whiz! We're going to have to rethink the whole way we manage timber! It is not just analogous to raising corn!' "

Old growth, thought to be a biological desert for its lack of big game, turned out to be teeming with little-noticed life. Here were 150 species of mammals and perhaps 1,500 of invertebrates. More than 100 species of birds, fish, reptiles, and mammals seemed dependent on old growth: martens, fishers, pileated woodpeckers, spotted owls, salamanders, to name a few. There were some tree voles that spent their entire lives in the forest canopy, dining on fir or hemlock needles, never seen from the ground.

The links in the system were elegant. In the Olympic rain forest, a graduate student named Nalini Nadkarni used climbing gear to get into the tree tops. She found that the mats of suspended mosses and lichens were not parasitic squatters on the branches they colonized. They metabolized fertilizing nitrogen from the air and fed the tree that supported them.

Forest ecologists such as Chris Maser discovered that some tree voles descend from their branches to eat truffles buried in forest humus. These truffles are fungus colonies that develop from mycorrhizal fungi, which in turn live on root hairs and help the roots of trees extract nutrients from the soil. The voles eat the truffles, scamper to new sites, and excrete droppings that contain undigested mycorrhizal spores. "It may be the elimination of old growth and the removal of small animals will affect the dispersal of mycorrhizal fungi," explained Marty Raphael, a Forest Service wildlife biologist. "If you don't have fungi, the trees won't grow."

Even the very thing that drove traditional foresters crazy, dead and rotting wood, was found to have purpose. Woodpeckers, for example, usually can't find their insect prey such as carpenter ants or bark beetles in young healthy trees. The wood is too hard and resistant to host insects, it won't succumb to pecking beaks, and it will gum the birds with sap. Jeff Peterson, a forester at Oregon State, has estimated that simply leaving dead snags in a tree stand will increase bird numbers by 30 percent. Dead wood is equally important on the ground. Peterson said 70 percent of Northwest amphibians and 85 percent of the region's reptiles needed downed logs to survive. They live in the wet, rotting hollows.

The wider spacing of trees in old-growth stands, where wind and decay has weeded out other trunks, provides flying room for predators such as owls and sunlight for a second layer of younger trees, turning a grove into a kind of multilayered apartment building. Old growth is warmer and more snowfree in winter, providing animals with better shelter and feed. It is cooler in spring and summer, conserving snow and soaking up rain, preventing flooding and erosion. As a result, old-growth streams also tend to make better fish habitat. Biologist Jim Sedell of Oregon State University has concluded that a stream in old-growth forest raises seven times the fish of a counterpart in a harvested area.

Franklin's importance was in quickly realizing the overall significance of the bits and pieces of research and synthesizing it. As the elegance of the system became apparent, he became ever-more insistent on speaking out. He can seem tireless, working until eleven P.M. and rising at five A.M. Once he bolted upright at three A.M., muttering something about elk. "He must dream this stuff," his wife said.

Franklin did not begin to assemble his findings into a program of reform until the mid-1980s when he took a leave from a dissolving first marriage and increasing tension with Oregon State administrators about his anti-clearcut research. He went on sabbatical to Harvard Forest, an annex of Harvard university located about eighty miles west of Cambridge at Petersham, Massachusetts. Franklin arrived out of energy and out of ideas. There he met Richard Forman, a Harvard professor who began to push Franklin further into the new field of landscape ecology.

Forman's explanations reverberated in Franklin. Shortly before, in 1983, tens of thousands of trees blew down at the edges of clearcuts in Mount Hood National Forest in Oregon. Pondering this, Franklin wondered if the Forest Service's attempt to soften the impact of logging was in fact making it worse.

Scientists had known for years that clearcutting on a massive scale could have catastrophic consequences, causing flooding and loss of wildlife. The Forest Service's solution to this has been to make its clearcuts small and pepper them through the forest in shotgun fashion. This scattering requires a tremendous road system, however, and a lot of small clearcuts have more edge—the point where the clearing meets the surviving forest—than a single big one of the same acreage. All that edge exposed a lot of trees to wind, Franklin realized, increasing the chance of blowdown. Additionally, wind and sun could penetrate about seven hundred feet into the surviving old growth, creating a different kind of microclimate than the deep forest Northwest life had evolved to. The Forest Service policy of small clearcuts, he realized, was creating less old-growth habitat, not more.

Franklin was seized by excitement. He immediately contacted the Forest Service chief on his new finding, urging a change in cutting patterns. Later, Forest Service landscape ecologist Miles Hemstrom would experiment on a computer with modifying clearcut patterns on a 12,000-acre block on Willamette National Forest in Oregon. By clustering clearcuts, he learned, the amount of edge could be reduced from 135 miles to 95 miles.

Franklin returned to the Northwest, leaving Oregon State University for Seattle's University of Washington. Then, at a conference in 1988, he listened as different scientists presented the research findings, and jotted notes. Franklin was scheduled to speak but uncertain what he would say. Suddenly it seemed to click. The whole approach was backward: clearcutting, its pattern, the massive road network, the burning of leftover slash. It ran counter to how the forest evolved. He broached the idea of "new forestry" just as the political battle over the spotted owl and clearcutting was beginning to penetrate the public consciousness.

When Franklin began his career with the U.S. Forest Service in the late 1950s, the agency was abandoning past experiments in selective cutting of Northwest old growth and swinging firmly behind rapid clearcutting. The swift harvest could help provide affordable postwar housing. Coincidentally, it made necesary a swelling of the Forest Service bureaucracy to handle the timber sales. As clearcutting accelerated, however, the result was an increasingly bitter clash with environmentalists. That ultimately led to a division of the national forests between wilderness areas and what amounted to industrialized tree farms.

Franklin has elicited praise and ire from both sides for trying to stake out a middle ground. He wants not just part of the virgin timber preserved, but the entire forest managed on firm ecological grounds: to modify harvesting enough so that the natural ecosystem can persist. A forest is not eternal, he stresses. The "ancient forest" that hikers revere is in fact in constant transition, its steady successions of species interrupted by fire and wind. Its average life cycle, before natural catastrophe intervenes, is about seven to eight centuries. Logging could be seen as one more interruption. But Franklin argues that logging that takes every tree, burns the remaining wood waste, and replaces a complex forest with a simple man-made one is an unnatural disruption.

Franklin envisions a forest with mixed ages of trees, refuges left for wildlife, and the soil nurtured with rotting wood. He talks of pattern and balance and diversity.

Some in the timber industry have reacted to this with fear. In Hoquiam, a timber city south of Forks on the Olympic Peninsula, someone posted a sign that read, LOOKING FOR THE NEW FORESTRY. Next to it was a dummy with its head down a toilet.

The federal government has become increasingly receptive, however. Forest Service Chief Robertson "hates the term New Forestry— a lot of people do—because it carries the implication that the old was bad," Franklin noted. But Robertson's agency has gingerly decided to experiment with the same ideas under the tag, "New Perspectives," including an ambitious program to test it in the Shasta-Costa unit of Siskiyou National Forest in Oregon.

Franklin doesn't really care what you call it. He sees the possibility of having his ideas drastically modify the management of millions of forest acres. His phone rings constantly, both at the University of Washington in Seattle and at his home on Squak Mountain east of the city. The house is a fitting eyrie. It has a panoramic view of the front range of the Cascades and several portraits of the spotted owl. He has seized the moment the owl has given him. "I've been working on this all my life," he said.

Franklin had begun the day he went to Gold Mountain speaking to rangers at the Darrington grange hall, explaining that he was trying to achieve a synthesis: to look at the entire forest landscape and ensure enough diversity to maintain the Northwest's original ecology. Wilderness areas are not enough, he told the Forest Service workers. Most of the acreage in them is high-altitude alpine meadows, rocks, and snow. Trees in the West tend to shrink in size as elevation is gained. The remnants of lower elevation old-growth forest of truly big trees are too small and fragmented to provide an adequate ecosystem for species such as the spotted owl. "What we do on our commodity lands [the lands devoted to timber harvesting] really makes the difference on whether we have sustainable forests and biodiversity," he says.

Franklin took the foresters to a grove of 200-year-old Douglas fir trees outside Darrington. The stand is old enough to have developed some old-growth characteristics: A wider spacing of trees, downed rotting logs, a canopy of leaves and needles at several heights instead of one. More than that there is an instinctive rightness about a forest of that age that even the most untutored visitor senses, a lack of human manipulation and artificiality. "There is a gestalt," Franklin told his listeners. "You can *feel* an old-growth forest."

Decision makers seldom respond to feelings, however, so Franklin offers some statistics. One researcher counted sixty-one species of invertebrates such as insects in an old-growth stand; in an adjacent managed forest where all the trees were planted at the same time, only sixteen invertebrates were counted. Many of the additions in old growth are carnivorous insects that eat their vegetarian cousins, particularly the aphids that thrive in tree plantations. These predators disappear in humanity's simpler forests, with the resulting possibility, ecologists suspect, of insect infestations getting out of control.

Some of the foresters listening this day seem a bit frustrated by the imprecision of Franklin's prescriptions. It has been customary for them to think of one species at a time, to plan one clearcut at a time, and to worry about the next one-mile extension of the nation's 343,000-mile logging road network. Franklin's vision is revolutionary but so all-encompassing as to seem vague. He wants them to look not at one animal but whole ecosystems, not at one clearcut but entire landscapes. He talks about trying things that will take decades, even centuries, to prove right or wrong. It is exciting, daunting, confusing.

Franklin has specifics: replant trees further apart to delay the growing together and closure of the evergreen canopy that chokes off light and life underneath; leave logs and other coarse woody debris behind; leave green trees in a clearcut; provide different ages and species of trees; leave standing dead snags. He said that rather than slowly pocking a stream drainage basin with clearcuts like an excruciating environmental water torture of the landscape, foresters should consider logging it intensively for a brief period but then pull out, closing the roads, to let the land recover.

"Our basic paradigm in forestry was, 'Let's simplify the forest,' " Franklin said. He wants complexity to make a comeback.

Still, the specifics can get sticky. Does leaving some trees standing mean more acres will be cut to make up for the lost wood? If not, how *does* the nation make up the difference? Will the wood debris left behind dry out and fuel forest fires? If canopy closure is delayed, won't brush and weed trees such as alder infest regrowing conifer tree stands? If roads are closed, how will fire crews get back to battle forest fires?

If Franklin's "dirty clearcuts" allow old-growth species to persist in harvested areas, could New Forestry harvesting techniques be used as just another excuse to log more old growth?

This latter question is particularly significant to the environmental community, to whom for a brief period Franklin was a guru. Initially, he seemed able to lend scientific credibility to the desire not to cut old-growth forest. "Environmentalists decided way back in the 1960s that science would probably be their ally instead of their enemy—that science would be useful to them," Franklin noted.

Eventually, however, the enthusiasm of environmentalists for New Forestry cooled. Franklin did not think the ecological solution was simply to create new forest preserves as a de facto extension of the wilderness system. Politically, Congress would never set aside enough land to maintain the biological diversity of the ecosystem, he reasoned. Franklin was more interested in modifying logging and managing all land for wildlife. "These owls are living in stands of mixed structure," he said. "We can recreate those stands." He predicted a regrown stand of trees could attract owls in as little as seventy to one hundred years after planting. This was not something environmentalists seeking old-growth protection wanted to hear. They became wary. Could this new reform be turned on its head, and used as justification for continued logging of old growth? "These concepts didn't serve either group's interests," Franklin noted.

Jack Ward Thomas, the wildlife biologist who found himself embroiled in the owl controversy, said this confusion is natural. "These are quantum jumps in the recognition of complexity," he said. "We were trained to look like this." He cups his hands around his face, peering down at the ground. "Jerry Franklin wants people to look at entire forests. A lot of things that come along in concept are necessarily nebulous in the beginning. New Forestry is nebulous, but you are seeing it defined more and more precisely all the time. Ecosystems were a nebulous concept thirty years ago. Someone [ecologist Frank Egler] once said that ecosystems may not only be more complex than we think, they may be more complex than we *can* think. New Forestry is simply the recognition that standard forest practices to maximize wood production [are] not universally applicable to achieve the desires of the public."

"It's old-fashioned foresters versus the ecologists," said Bill Atkinson, a former researcher with Crown Zellerbach timber who now heads the Department of Forest Engineering at Oregon State University.

Atkinson unabashedly puts himself in the camp of the former. "Jerry has pretty much sold this as an operational silvicultural system, but it hasn't been tried by anybody," he said.

Atkinson's attacks on Franklin have gotten pointed. During a summer 1990 media tour of the H. C. Andrews Experimental Forest in Oregon, where Franklin developed many of his ideas, the break came out into the open. Atkinson complained to the media that the guru's gospel was proving so effective that forestry traditionalists were getting afraid to speak out against it. As reported by journalist Paul Roberts, Atkinson compared it to China's Cultural Revolution, where Mao Zedong proclaimed flowerbeds an ideological distraction. "The next morning everyone is outside, pulling up the flowerbeds. Of course we don't have Chairman Mao. We've got Jerry."

Franklin, who laughs quickly and gets angry quickly, was open-mouthed at the personal assault in what is usually—at least in public view—constrained scientific debate. (In private, scientists can be strongly competitive, in both jealous and friendly ways. Franklin tells a story of walking into a scientific committee chaired by his longtime friend Thomas and Thomas quipping, "Ah, here's the Pope now!" Franklin had a comeback for his colleague. "Yes, and I've come here to get the word from God!")

As Atkinson walked back to the tour bus, Franklin strode up to Atkinson's side and asked, "What are we doing out here, Bill?"

"You should've controlled what's being done in the name of New Forestry, Jerry," Atkinson replied. "You let it get out of control."

"Bill, the same thing could be said for plantation forestry, that *it's* gotten out of control," Franklin replied.

"Well, it has," Atkinson admitted.

"Well, why don't you stop it?" Franklin asked.

There was no answer.

"Bill, we've got to start working together on this or the industry's going to be wiped out."

In an interview, Atkinson expanded on his fears about New Forestry. All the things learned about growing high-value Douglas fir, in an environment ripe with biological competitors, Franklin seems to be throwing out, he complained. "The result will be brush patches instead of forests."

Yet when pressed, Atkinson admitted modern tree plantations, while efficient producers of wood, are ecologically simplified and relatively sterile of wildlife. "No doubt what we think are wonderful plantations for growing wood never created much wildlife habitat," he agreed. He suggested improving tree farms by shrinking clearcuts, leaving more strips of uncut trees, increasing the number of snags, and slowing the burning of waste wood. Told that sounds like New Forestry, he said, "I think there's a common ground here." But it is clear that while foresters trained in wood production may have sympathy for wildlife— may even understand that *feel*, that gestalt, that Franklin expresses— they do not rank it as high in importance.

Atkinson is correct that there are practical reasons for the kind of clearcutting that horrifies the public.

The sheer volume of wood in Pacific Northwest old-growth forests is an obstacle to harvesting it. Unlike tropical forests, trees in temperate climates decay slowly, thus making the ground a crisscrossed obstacle course of fallen logs. Trees also grow tall and have narrow branch structures, allowing the forest to pack a lot of stems into a small area. As a result the total biomass, or total weight of living matter in these temperate forests, is typically four times that of the densest tropical forest. Some redwood forest groves in California have been measured with twenty times the biomass of similar sites in the tropics. Those who dislike preservation of these forests argue that if wood consumption does not decline, setting aside Northwest old growth could come at a high environmental cost, globally: it could take ten to thirty acres of taiga forest in northern Canada, Alaska, or Siberia to produce the wood of one acre in Washington State.

This astonishing volume makes harvesting the forests lucrative, but the trees and downed logs are so dense it is difficult to log selectively by cutting only some of the trees. Those cut can damage the survivors when they fall, and can damage them again when dragged across the ground to be loaded onto trucks. It is expensive to work around standing trees, and those left may topple or shed branches that could injure loggers. Even if they survive logging, critics contend, the trees left behind may blow down in high winds.

Additionally, old-growth forests leave so much woody debris and half-decayed logs on the ground that it can be difficult to simply walk through a harvested patch, or find bare ground to plant seedlings. In the 1960s and 1970s old growth was typically clearcut, the cut burned to consume branches and needles, seedlings planted, and then the cut sprayed with herbicide to kill the broadleaf alder and similar brush that also thrived in the sunlit cuts.

Over time, every practice had a defending argument. Burning the wood waste, foresters argued, consumed fuel that might otherwise contribute to forest fires. Logging roads opened the forest to recreationists and fire fighters. The clearcuts ensured that no snags would poke upward to endanger airplanes and helicopters that swooped low to apply herbicides. The brush that sprouted while the conifers struggled to get started provided browse for big-game species such as deer and elk.

Yet even as foresters seemed to justify clearcut logging of the nation's last old-growth forests, a chorus of objections began to rise. Slash burning created vast plumes of smoke that polluted Northwest cities. The animal browse was choked out after twenty years or so as the young Douglas fir grew together, creating a darkened forest floor devoid of almost any vegetation or wildlife for three decades or more. The herbicides were applied too heavily. The forest was being mined: so much wood was either harvested or burned that some scientists such as Chris Maser warned the soil fertility was threatened.

Erosion and flooding increased from clearcut areas. There typically is an eight- to ten-year period when the roots of the harvested forest are rotting away while the roots of replanted trees have not yet developed to fill the gap. The result is to make landslides more likely. Lee Benda, a geologist at the University of Washington, estimates that clearcuts are 2.8 times more likely to have landslides than the natural forest. Roads, he calculated, are thirty times as likely to slide. A similar study, by fisheries scientist Chris Frissell at Oregon State University, showed that landslides in southwest Oregon had increased sixfold since World War II as the loss of original forest harvested had shot upward from 24 percent to more than 80 percent.

On the Hoh River near Forks, cutting on steep slopes by the Department of Natural Resources resulted in disastrous mudslides in the winters of 1989 and 1990 that ran into river tributaries and destroyed salmon-rearing habitat prized by the Hoh Indian tribe. "That area won't fully recover for 150 years," forecast Bob Naiman, a hydrologist at the University of Washington.

Visually, clearcutting became its own worst enemy. Timber companies and the Forest Service began to leave strips of trees along highways to shield from view the devastation behind it, like the false front of a Potemkin village. To combat this illusion, environmentalists enlisted the aid of Project Lighthawk, a volunteer group of pilots who flew public officials and the media over some of the most heavily logged land in the Northwest to drive home the extent of the cutting and erosion. George Atiyeh, nephew of a former Oregon governor and a logger himself until 1981, flew me once over the heavily cut ridges north of Mount Rainier National Park. "I firmly believe if we could get everyone in Washington and Oregon into the air to see this logging, it would stop tomorrow," Atiyeh said.

Such criticism and the sheer shortage of a commodity Northwesterners once took for granted—big, old trees—set the stage for any scientist who could offer a credible alternative. If most were reluctant to offer sweeping prescriptions for such a volatile issue, a few are not. One in particular was questioning the assumptions of modern forestry for most of his adult life. "What I want to do is reform forestry," said Franklin.

The timber industry was ill-equipped to deal with such a challenge. Industrial forestry "has been in a constant process of denial," Franklin said. A National Science Foundation survey had shown the timber industry's typical devotion of revenues to basic research was only about one quarter the rate of American industry as a whole. Few in the big timber companies were paying attention to what the scientists were learning, how environmentalists were interpreting it, and how public acceptance of traditional clearcutting was beginning to erode.

"Industry has had no interest in what's going on," Franklin said. "They considered it irrelevant until it impacted their operations."

By the end of the 1980s, basic research on the spotted owl and old-growth ecosystems—stuff on dirt and mosses and tweety birds and how snow melts, the kind of taxpayer-financed research that seemed so obscure at times it could have been held up for ridicule with a Senator William Proxmire Golden Fleece Award—had set the stage for a public revolt against traditional clearcutting. In 1988, environmentalists would use the government's own science to humiliate the U.S. Fish and Wildlife Service in court over its decision not to give the spotted owl protection under the Endangered Species Act. A few months later, the Forest Service was shown in court to have ignored much of the best research in concocting what was found to be an inadequate and poorly justified plan to protect spotted owls. Words such as biodiversity, gene pools, and mycorrhizal fungi had become part of the routine vocabulary at environmental gatherings.

The scientists had thrown a firebomb into another "ecosystem," however—a human economic, social, and cultural rural society based on cutting down big old trees. In the end the new ecologists were not just challenging a method of forestry, they were threatening a way of life.

Franklin said he views loggers not as villains but victims, people given no warning of the consequences of change. "What is worst is the feeling of being totally powerless about your future," the scientist said. "Those people were reassured for decades it would all be okay. Now they're finding it is not okay."

"We didn't get the information until it's too late," log truck driver Barbara Mossman observed of how science and ecology snuck up on her industry. "Somebody ate the dinner while we were out to lunch."

7
THE INDUSTRY

▲▲▲▲▲▲▲

The kind of forestry Jerry Franklin wants to change is best seen from the air, preferably in winter. Snow turns the modern managed forest into a checkerboard of black and white and gray. The clearcuts are white, and the mature, uncut evergreens black. The regrowing forest is a spectrum of gray, depending on how big the young trees are against the snow. The bigger the trees, the deeper the hue.

This early winter day is a bad one for flying over the Cascade Mountains. The big leaf maples and aspens are still golden down in the valleys, but on this afternoon they are already being dusted with powdery snow. I see this from above, perched in the forward plastic bubble of a helicopter chartered by the Plum Creek Timber Company. The transparent envelope that wraps under our feet provides a magic carpet kind of view, but there is little sense of security as the machine ducks around the dark gray dirigibles of snow clouds and bucks in the gusty wind. The mountains look cold, lonely, and hostile.

Company biologist Lorin Hicks urges the pilot ahead, however. Poor weather doesn't deter him much. Hicks once crashed in a light plane while trying to track elk, crawled out of the wreckage, and carried the shocked pilot out to a road through several miles of snow. Then the biologist climbed into another plane the next day, so necessary has flight become to the modern biologist trying to traverse and understand rugged country.

Animals are strange, Hicks remarks. A spotted owl on Plum Creek land moves only a couple of miles over a year of radio tracking, drifting downslope in winter and back up in spring. An elk, however, can track from the upper reaches of the Missouri River in Montana to St. Louis, its migration seemingly as aimed as a missile but its purpose only

116

guessed at. The more biologists learn about animals, the more they realize how little they understand.

We are pushing the weather this November because Hicks is anxious to show what his corporation is doing to modify its logging. More than any other large timber company in Washington State, Plum Creek was lambasted in the media in the late 1980s for its rapid liquidation of old growth. The criticism spilled into *The New York Times* and *Wall Street Journal*, and one Seattle congressman called Plum Creek the "Darth Vader" of clearcut logging. Its clearcuts in Montana have been pummeled by environmental groups in the Rockies. Plum Creek's clearcuts are no worse than those conducted by any other big timber company over the past century, with two crucial differences: it did not start logging in earnest until most of the region's other privately owned old growth was gone, and some of the land it inherited from its parent, Burlington Northern Railroad, overlooked Interstate 90 east of Seattle where most of Washington State passed by, sooner or later. By the end of the 1980s, Plum Creek had become a subject for cocktail party condemnation in Seattle.

Accordingly, no timber company was doing more in Washington State to salvage its reputation. Early in 1990, Jerry Franklin invited a Plum Creek executive to defend industry cutting practices at one of Franklin's University of Washington classes. In return, the scientist was invited to explain his New Forestry ideas to the company's board of directors. David Leland, Plum Creek's president, was impressed by what he heard. As a result, on 20 percent of its harvest in 1990, Plum Creek experimented with New Forestry ideas at a probable cost of several million dollars. One dirty clearcut at Frost Meadows, south of the Cascades town of Roslyn, is called "The Franklin Cut."

Plum Creek is also unusual because of Hicks. He is one of only four wildlife biologists employed by timber companies in the western United States, and as such is an oddity who tries to straddle two worlds, comparing himself to a long-tailed cat in a room full of rocking chairs. "I've got everything from gophers to grizzlies on a million and a half acres" of timberland stretching from western Washington to western Montana, he explained. He is trying to advise the company how to protect wildlife at the same time it is playing catch-up with other large timber firms by cutting old growth at a feverish pace and replanting its land with younger trees.

Plum Creek is a prime example of the organizational tumult that affected big timber companies in the takeover fever of the 1980s. In the past twelve years, said Hicks, "I've worked for five different companies and never changed employers." In 1980, Congress deregulated railroads through the Staggers Act, allowing them to spin off their subsidiaries. Plum Creek, borrowing the name of a small logging company in Montana, went through several metamorphoses before becoming fully independent of Burlington Northern in 1989.

The breakup had at least two beneficial effects, from a business point of view. The new company can devote itself completely to timber management. And, it is more immune to hostile takeover. The railroad had enormous wood, oil, and gas reserves, low revenues, and no debts, making it a prime acquisition for a raider who would break it up and sell its parts off at a profit. Burlington Northern beat any such raider to the punch. Under the deal the newly independent timber company paid its parent $350 million, deliberately saddling itself with debt to make it unpalatable to gobble up.

To pay that debt, Plum Creek has to cut a lot of trees. It was stung by the criticism of its clearcutting, however, and by suggestions from some environmentalists that the propriety of giving a private company free rein to clearcut on what had originally been railroad grant lands from the federal government should be reexamined. "From the standpoint of the public, we needed to develop some alternatives," said Hicks. The alternatives he shows are fairly remarkable.

As Interstate 90 runs through the Cascade Mountains, the east and west lanes of the freeway diverge at one point, leaving between them an island of trees owned by Plum Creek. The company logged it, but instead of a total clearcut it left a sixty-six-foot-wide buffer of trees on the island's edge, next to the freeway. Then, behind this buffer, it did not cut any trees a foot in diameter or smaller. As a result, from the air the tract looks only lightly touched by chainsaws, yet Plum Creek calculates it removed 80 percent of the merchantable trees and, because larger trees are worth more than smaller ones, 90 percent of its timber value.

South of the freeway is a highway of another kind, a winding belt of dark, uncut trees to provide elk a protective corridor as they migrate in the spring and fall.

Nearby, at Frost Meadows, the helicopter bounces over a ridge and then drops down into a white clearing, kicking up a cloud of snow like a manic flour sifter. We clamber out into the mini-blizzard and find shelter in the 400-foot-wide belt of trees left along Manastash Creek. Such greenbelts are becoming more common in the industrial forests of the Northwest: scientists have concluded they can help contain erosion, conserve water, and shade streams in the summer, making them more habitable for cold-loving salmon and trout. The stillness in the forest after the helicopter blades shut down is soothing. The only sound is the murmur of the ice-rimmed stream and the pad of our footsteps, muffled by snow.

On one side of the creek, the company managed to legally log near a spotted owl nest by taking only some of the trees in corridors along short logging spur roads. Here, the 15 percent of the trees cut yielded an estimated 50 percent of the site's merchantable value.

Crossing a log across the creek to the other side, we follow a logging road up to the ninety-acre Franklin Cut. The timber harvesting is much more obvious on this patch, the ground crisscrossed with logging roads and strewn with slash. But 15 percent of the trees, including some of the biggest, have been left uncut. The site is dotted with western larch, a beautiful conifer that turns orange in autumn and sheds its needles. Because it loses foliage and is well rooted, it has a reputation for being windfirm and less likely to blow over in this "dirty" clearcut. Larch has the densest wood of any Northwest conifer and its thick bark makes it extremely fire resistant. The natural seeding of the larch is expected to supplement the fir the company will replant artificially. At the edge of the cut, a goshawk nest has been left unmolested.

The company has made other concessions, pledging to do only selective cutting, not clearcutting, in back of the town of Roslyn, setting for the television comedy "Northern Exposure." In the early 1980s a citizen's environmental group called RIDGE first called attention to the company's decision to rapidly accelerate its harvest of old growth. A former coal mining town, Roslyn was built in a turn-of-the-century clearcut but now is surrounded by mature second growth, some of it subject to pine beetle infestation. The company wanted to remove much of the 13,000 acres of that second growth, but a new generation of urban refugees attracted by the area's sleepy charm protested loudly.

The compromise has only partly mollified RIDGE, which points out Plum Creek is still cutting far faster than can be permanently sustained and is not modifying clearcutting on the other 80 percent of its harvest. One reason for the dissatisfaction is that by the late 1980s

Plum Creek had tripled its annual harvest in the Roslyn area, to about 5,000 acres per year. Some creek drainages were so heavily cut they almost looked nuked.

In response, the company announced it was slowing down plans to liquidate its old growth; had entered into negotiations with the state and Indian tribes to protect water quality in the Yakima River basin; and agreed to a proposal hammered out with environmental groups that would have required the forest industry as a whole to leave behind 10 percent of its trees in clearcut areas to protect streams and provide habitat for wildlife. (The compromise was later rejected by both sides.) Still, environmentalists were suspicious and timber companies astounded at Plum Creek's turnaround. "Reaction ranges from New Forestry is bad forestry to simply, 'Why are you guys trying this?' " said the company spokeswoman, Sharon Kanareff. "We decided we wanted to get ahead of the curve."

That curve was described by Washington Lands Commissioner Brian Boyle in a speech given to an annual assembly of the state's timber executives shortly after Plum Creek explained its experiment in New Forestry. There is a new urban majority in the state, Boyle told the group, that is "less sympathetic [to the timber industry] than the Washingtonians of twenty years ago. By and large they feel trees are for scenery and wood comes from lumberyards. They are fundamentally changing the political equation in the state." I can see some of what Boyle is talking about as Plum Creek's helicopter flies back to Seattle and its suburbs that lap at the foothills. We skim several forested plateaus that have already been earmarked for massive housing developments. In the 1980s, Oregon and Washington together lost an average of 75,000 forested acres per year to development.

Big Timber is reacting accordingly. In a sense, Plum Creek compressed the history of the Pacific Northwest's timber industry into a few years: rapid clearcut logging, a clash with the public in a rapidly urbanizing region, a recognition of likely political restraint, and steps toward reform. Plum Creek began and ended a freewheeling era in less than a decade.

Plum Creek's responsiveness to the new ideas boiling in the forest is the exception, not the rule, in its industry. The biggest timber corporations lurked like an elephant hoping to blend with the wallpaper. They were conspicuous by their eerie silence. The very fact that the spotted owl did *not* seem able to survive on their tree farms was the primary reason logging on public lands had to be severely curtailed. By the same logic, the owl's absence on private lands seemed to be the potential salvation of the corporate giants. It suggested they would be allowed to log the second and third rotations of their timber crop without political molestation. In theory, at least, ancient forests were a moot issue to companies that had already cut them down.

In fact, alarm over the disappearance of ancient forests was a pry bar environmentalists could use to open all kinds of debate about private forestry practices. If there are ghosts of the vanquished old growth, they haunt most numerously on corporate lands. Most of the grandest old-growth forest—the biggest trees on the flattest, most fertile soil—was given to private landowners, frequently railroads, in the nineteenth century. In the main, this eventually passed into the hands of timber companies or the corporate giants that hold timberlands, such as John Hancock Insurance or International Telephone and Telegraph. Except for some old-growth remnants held by exceptions such as Plum Creek, the annihilation of ancient forest on this prime land is virtually complete. In Washington's southwest corner, an area as big as the Olympic Peninsula, there are only a few museum patches of the virgin cedar left in bogs so swampy it wasn't worth going after them. Only the wonderfully lit, startling black and white photographs of the late nineteenth century show what an empire of colossal giants there once was in the lowlands, trees so big that a squad of loggers frequently had their picture taken sitting in an undercut as if it were a small cave. They wear an expression of doughty pride.

It is not that the big companies do not have ties to that vanished forest. The pattern of its first harvest pretty much dictates the pattern of its second, explaining the frequent concentration of logging in a single creek basin where all the trees reach maturity again at the same time. But the ancient forest that is gone is a matter of only historical interest to the big corporations, as interesting and irrelevant as the mastodon. They are well on their way to creating their own future: plantations of genetically improved "super trees," big-tired feller-buncher machines that snip trees mechanically and thus partially replace hand cutting with chainsaws, modern mills that require a minimum of labor to saw second-growth sticks into product, and a market driven by global supply and demand.

A large part of the Pacific Northwest's timber industry is left out of this future. Small, independent mill owners have since World War II relied on public land such as the national forests to supply old-growth logs that can be sawed into specialty products. The trees they covet are as much as five centuries old; the trees being engineered by corporate futurists are only a tenth the age, half the height, and perhaps one-quarter the width. They are so small they won't even fit the saws and conveyor belts of old-time mills.

What this means is that politically there is no such thing as "the timber industry" in the Pacific Northwest. Its components—large corporations, small mills, independent loggers, log exporters, pulp and paper makers—are competitors for a shrinking resource of trees, with different needs, goals, and political agendas.

For example, for big companies with their own tree plantations, locking up publicly owned timber on national forests to protect the spotted owl is not a dire threat; it in fact removes the competitive irritant of rival smaller mills and boosts the value of Big Timber holdings. After a 1991 court decision by U.S. District Court Judge William Dwyer suspended most national forest timber sales in western Washington and Oregon, wholesale lumber prices jumped as much as 11 percent in a single week.

The industry is equally at odds over the issue of log exports. By the late 1980s as much as 40 percent of Washington's timber harvest was going overseas, much of it never milled in the United States. Sixty percent of what Plum Creek cut around Roslyn was exported without any domestic milling.

Small mill owners were outraged at this loss of logs from the pool of what they could buy, and in 1990, after nearly two decades of debate, Congress extended an export ban it had already applied to logs from federal forests to state lands as well. All the state-owned trees cut in Oregon and 75 percent of those cut in Washington are supposed to be milled domestically.

Perennial acrimony over this was apparent when the timber entrepreneurs of the Olympic Peninsula gathered in the spring of 1990 at the lavishly restored Empress Hotel across the Strait of Juan de Fuca, in the British Columbia capital of Victoria. It was a strange setting for the Peninsula's annual gathering: a genteel "little bit of England" transplanted to the western edge of the New World where the timbermen could, if they were in the mood, partake of the daily high tea. It was not a cheerful conference; most of the briefings at the seminars consisted of political bad news. It also demonstrated how difficult it was for a group divided by habitual business competition to pull together in defense of the wood industry as a whole. Much of the conversation at one banquet table was an argument between a mill owner desperate for logs and an exporter from Hoquiam whose livelihood depended on sending those same logs overseas. Holding logs here to keep your mill open puts my longshoremen out of work, the exporter insisted.

It was no wonder that the owl crusade had been allowed by big business to gather so much political momentum. Some saw the spotted owl as a necessary agent of natural selection needed to weed out an oversupply of timber mills that for too long had been propped up by public timber sale policies on the federal forests. During a tour of the replanting slopes around Mount St. Helens, a Weyerhaeuser official argued that the Pacific Northwest had an historical oversupply of sawmills because of the relatively low capital cost of setting one up and the plentiful, cheap suppy of publicly owned logs. The mills as a whole almost never operated at full capacity; there were simply too many of them and most were old with primitive technology and high labor costs. Some kind of weeding was inevitable, he said; it simply made economic sense. On the surface, the owl sometimes seemed as convenient to Big Timber as to the environmental community.

Real life was a bit more complicated, however. While scientific arguments centered around the survival of the old-growth ecosystem, political debate focused on the profusion of clearcuts, the eroding and flooding they were alleged to cause, and the fact that 40 percent of the trees cut in Washington State were neither milled nor used by Americans, but instead were sold overseas. It is ten to twenty dollars cheaper per thousand board feet to ship wood from Washington and Oregon to Tokyo instead of New York, because of the cost advantage of sea transport over rail.

A dual battle developed: one to prevent the cutting of the remaining ancient forest on public land; another to slow and modify the kind of clearcutting done on private land. Inevitably, the two struggles became muddled in the public's mind. The timber industry complained that environmentalists were being deliberately impractical when they protested logging both in the steep mountains of the national forests and the rolling foothills of private industry; if they were going to curb harvest on the one they should expect it to shift to the other, timber executives said with exasperation.

Environmentalists didn't see it that way. They argued that overcutting in one area aggravated the erosion, wildlife depletion, and destruction of beauty in the other. They complained industry was being arrogantly shortsighted, when, in the late 1980s, it had cut a near-record volume of timber, was biting into an increasingly short and fragmented supply of old growth, was shipping record numbers of logs overseas—and then expressed surprise at the public outcry.

The timber industry is perhaps like no other in the world. It must plan up to a century into the future and is bound by the conditions and decisions and mistakes of up to a hundred years in the past. "People want to hang on us today's values for yesterday's decisions," complained David Mumper, timberlands resources manager for Weyerhaeuser.

To a consumer, lumber and paper remain an astounding bargain, the legacy of the nation's original vast forest. The contribution of that forest to the nation's wealth is probably not fully recognized, but it not only housed America's rapidly expanding population, it fueled much of its early industry, built its fleets, and was the base for its railroads. Wood has been a strategic resource since ancient times, particularly for shipbuilding and as fuel for such basics as metalworking, cement manufacture, and glassmaking. The ancient Greeks fought wars over forests, and the Mediterranean basin has been substantially deforested from its original condition. The English deforested both their own island and Ireland in quest of wood, and oak timbers for warships were as vital two centuries ago as oil or aluminum is to the military today. The victories of *Old Ironsides* in the War of 1812 were not just a tribute to American seamanship, but to the continent's vast forest that included iron-hard coastal oaks from the South used in the frigate's construction.

The timber industry points out that the United States still retains about 70 percent of the forest land it had when Columbus landed, even if old growth is gone from virtually all of it outside the Pacific Northwest and Alaska. Wood typically represents only fifteen to twenty percent of the purchase price of a new home. The ample supply can in part be attributed to private replanting, which accounted for three-fourths of the 2.3 billion seedlings put into the ground in the United States in 1989.

This planting by private industry is in some ways remarkable. The direct payoff between planting a seedling and selling a two-by-four is agonizingly slow. A forester who plants a tree at the beginning of his career just might, if it is a genetically improved tree in a low elevation stand on good soil that is thinned and fertilized, see it harvested before he retires. Most of what he does will not bring a return to his company until after he is gone, and sometimes after he is in the grave. No wonder foresters strive to cram a tree's normal five-century life span into that of a human career! Cut a tree and you see the result crash down; plant one and you rely in part on your imagination.

Many Weyerhaeuser employees have vivid memories of the catastrophic blast of Mount St. Helens that swept over their tree farm, leaving behind miles of toppled trees under a blanket of ash. On the eruption's tenth anniversary they delighted in taking public officials and the media to see the mushrooming trees they had replanted, a few already up to thirty feet high. The hand-planted tree farm is a marked contrast to the still-barren and scrubby National Monument next door, which at the urging of scientists such as Franklin is being allowed to recover naturally as a vast laboratory. The monument is recovering more slowly and arguably more completely, invaded by a ragtag profusion of species taking hold in the rot of decaying logs and the mix of ash and dirt. The Weyerhaeuser portion is a simpler, more efficient, monocultural tree farm. The side-by-side recolonization of the two areas by animals in the century ahead will likely be as instructive as the volcano itself.

In October of 1966, Charles Bingham and a group of other Weyerhaeuser executives told the company's board of directors at its headquarters in Tacoma that it was time to create a truly managed forest, a tree farm that was indeed farmed: the ground scraped to expose soil; planted with genetically screened seedlings; sprayed, thinned, and fertilized. They would take Douglas fir that had an average life span of more than five hundred years and squeeze its commercial growth into fifty. The annual rings that marked wood growth would swell to two or three or four times their normal width. The newly developed computers had run the numbers, projected the growth, calculated the return, and promised that it made economic sense.

By the time Bingham brought this program to the company's board, he had come a long way. One of six sons who grew up on a stump ranch near Coos Bay, Oregon, as a youth he had helped his father log, haul garbage, gravel roads, and run a roadside cafe to survive. Bingham was smart and ambitious enough to land a scholarship at Harvard and Harvard law, one of the early attempts by the university to broaden its recruiting pool beyond East Coast prep schools. Instead of heading to Manhattan, however, Bingham had defied convention by becoming a corporate lawyer with this timber firm in the Pacific

Northwest. Within four years he had been promoted from the law office into management. Now he was proposing one of the biggest, most expensive gambles the company had ever made, throwing a lot of money into the dirt it would not get back for half a century.

The Weyerhaeuser company already had a reputation as a forestry pioneer. Even in 1900, when German immigrant Frederick Weyerhaeuser purchased 900,000 acres in the remote Pacific Northwest from Northern Pacific Railway for what now seems the incredible bargain price of six dollars an acre (the timber alone would ultimately be valued at several thousand times that), some thought the Minnesota lumber man had finally overreached.

"At the time the land was acquired it was a high-risk capital investment," Bingham explained. "Markets were uncertain and wildfire was rampant." As late as 1932, 53 million acres of timberland burned in the United States, compared to today's annual average of about 2 million acres. Skeptics in 1900 feared Weyerhaeuser's purchase wouldn't stand long enough for him to harvest it. Despite periodic disasters, however, the buy proved brilliant. Weyerhaeuser Co. went on to become one of the biggest timber companies in the world: presently it has about 5.7 million acres of its own land in the Pacific Northwest and South and licenses to harvest much more abroad, including 13.3 million acres in Canada.

Almost from its inception, Weyerhaeuser had proved itself willing to gamble money on the future. In 1925, at a time industry practice was to cut virgin timber and run, Weyerhaeuser had started an experimental reforestation program to demonstrate the value of regrowing trees. The company took this a step further in 1936, at the depths of the Great Depression when many timber companies were abandoning their land for unpaid taxes. Weyerhaeuser determined it would pay the taxes and retain its land, and a year later launched an advertising campaign that argued "timber is a crop." In 1941 the company established the nation's first "tree farm" in southwestern Washington, the Clemons Tree Farm, making there the first experiments at seeding, planting, thinning, and brush control. It was as odd a concept then as spotted owl protection was to seem in the 1970s. J. P. "Phil" Weyerhaeuser, the chief executive officer at the time, thought the name *tree farm* was "something of a gimmick."

The 1966 decision was the next step in this evolution, made possible by a growing worldwide scarcity of trees, rising world demand, and resulting higher prices. Although the Clemons Tree Farm had been a useful laboratory, most Weyerhaeuser land still received only aerial reseeding, if that. No timber company in the ancient forest empire had a nursery, or a seed orchard, or a comprehensive program of hand planting, thinning, and fertilizing. Even at that late date, the forest still seemed vast. Most of the old growth in the West End around Forks had yet to be harvested. "The value the public put on regenerated forest was extremely low as late as the 1960s," said Dave Mumper of Weyerhaeuser.

Bingham's group had a bold proposal. "The computer technology came along so we could simulate the biology of a forest," he recalled. "The computer allowed you to simulate the forest through time." What the board of directors was shown was a simulation for the next 200 years. It predicted that forest growth could be dramatically increased—doubled, even quadrupled—through tree farming.

The board accepted the proposal for a couple of reasons. One was the changing public expectation, beginning about the time of the Great Depression, of the responsibility of private forest companies. "First, we had the realization that the forests created by nature were finite," Bingham said. No one knew better than the timber industry that they had reached the Pacific Ocean and the possibilities for cutting and running—at least in the United States—were over with the end of the frontier. Second, there was growing government concern about the failure to replant harvested forests. Proposals for forest preservation dated back to William Penn in Pennsylvania, but no comprehensive reforestation program had ever been established. In the 1930s, Interior Secretary Harold Ickes had begun to talk of having the federal government take over management of private forest lands to ensure their renewal. "He said you have to put those acres in public ownership—you can't expect private folks to invest," Bingham said. Weyerhaeuser's investments were in part to prove people such as Ickes wrong.

Additionally, agricultural research was belatedly being applied to forestry. What seeding and planting had been done was fairly helter-skelter. Seed cones collected from one part of the Northwest were used to seed another with little regard for genetic and climatic adaptability. A new generation of scientists had identified "super trees"—trees that were the straightest, tallest, fastest growing—and proposed they be used to develop seed orchards. Foresters were also learning to match seed sources to sites, recognizing that individual trees were genetically adapted to different elevations, soils, slopes, and so on.

Critics would later charge that the most optimistic predictions of super tree growth have failed to be realized; and in fact that trees are so genetically varied in their adaptability to site that it may never be realized. One scientist at Oregon State calculated that genetic improvements could theoretically speed tree growth a staggering twenty-two times, but what could be predicted on paper or achieved in a laboratory was difficult to duplicate on the ground. Still, tree farming showed improvement in growth over abandoning areas to recover naturally, where it typically was colonized by "weed trees" such as alder. By the mid-1980s, Weyerhaeuser alone estimated it had planted two billion trees since 1900.

While the forest industry owns just 14.6 percent of the nation's forest land it accounts for 30 percent of the wood harvested, and the annual growth per acre on industry land is about 63 percent higher than on national forest land. Part of this difference was that private lands tended to be lower elevation with better soils, but part was that private industry simply managed its lands more aggressively.

So at least was the promise, since sold to the public through newspaper and magazine advertisements, timber tours, and speeches. That 1966 meeting, however, marked perhaps the peak of postwar American confidence in modifying nature and engineering the future. In the next quarter century, U.S. confidence in technology and human management was shaken. Doubts became common about the prowess of science and the wisdom of engineering ecosystems that were only barely understood.

By the end of the 1980s, Bingham was giving speeches to industry groups pointing out that the public expected private forests as well as public forests to be managed for more than just wood; that water quality, wildlife, soil conservation, and so on would also be regarded as important. "It is a natural resource with a huge amount of public interest," Bingham said. "The nontimber values of the forest need to get more attention than the industry has been able to give." Even two centuries of managed forests projections weren't enough anymore. "I think we need a longer-term view."

Still, the paralysis that the public uproar over forest harvesting caused worried him. "The public needs to make up its mind—do we want these forests managed well and usefully, or don't we? We're not making underarm deodorant. We're making products that are very basic on the scale of human needs," Bingham argued.

The timber industry is already making concessions in response to public pressure. In Washington State, it is leaving uncut about $60 million of trees per year that would otherwise be harvested, in order to satisfy environmental concerns raised in a consultation process with environmentalists and Indian tribes. However, an attempt to go even further with a new ten-year agreement failed to win consensus from either industry or environmentalists in early 1991.

Now Weyerhaeuser executives fear the clamor over old growth will spill over into ecological prescriptions for all forest land and put the value of wood secondary to owls or fish. "The difference between meeting minimum state reforestation laws and optimum investment in the land is a fifty percent difference in forest growth," said Bingham. "Land owners need political predictability before making that optimum investment. We can create a climate in this state where private owners are so uncertain about the future, they'll drop intensive management—but if they do, it will almost cut in half yields over the next fifty years."

"Although the people of the Puget Sound basin are very dependent on timber, they don't think they are," warned Weyerhaeuser's Mumper. "We run the risk of making stupid decisions about this industry."

When Dave Mumper was in forestry school, a professor made an analogy about how the economics and science of growing and harvesting trees becomes at some point a subjective judgment. He cited a nineteenth-century German forester named Martin Faustmann, "who compared the decision of when to cut a tree to the decision of when to open a rare wine."

In recent years the industry decision had been to open its wine, or rather crank up its chainsaws, in about forty to sixty years after planting. If the only object is to obtain a maximum amount of wood, this is not a prime time. Conifers such as Douglas fir grow slowly the first decade or so, typically accelerating their annual addition of wood fiber through at least the first century. Growth begins to slow after that and the chance of fire or wind destroying an investment inevitably increases over time. After a few centuries rot can set in to a tree's core, eventually equaling or exceeding the growth at its circumference. At some point, the tree will die. But the point at which a tree should be cut to produce the most amount of added fiber per year is after eighty or one hundred years, not fifty.

The decision to harvest at about fifty years is dictated not by biology, but by money, and the inexorable logic of compounding interest. Trees at that age are only a pygmy reminder of the forests that came before. Mills have had to be retooled to handle the short-diameter dimensions of this engineered second growth. But any investment in planting a forest has to be compared with the return of putting that same money in a different investment, such as a bank account.

The timber industry typically calculates that a dollar invested in trees, if invested elsewhere, could have earned about five to six percent real interest (after allowing for inflation) per year. As a hypothetical example provided by Weyerhaeuser, that means $200 spent preparing and planting a forest acre today would have grown to $2,293 if invested at five percent real interest compounded for fifty years.

To continue with the hypothetical example, however, suppose Weyerhaeuser now tries to choose between two alternatives: growing trees for fifty years and harvesting two percent of its land each year; or growing trees for one hundred years and harvesting one percent of its land each year. The one-hundred-year rotation will provide a more scenic landscape. At any one time, fewer acres will be clearcut, fewer trees will be small, and the most mature trees will be bigger. The trees will add so much growth in their second fifty years that the amount and value of wood obtained from one percent of the land after a century will be more than from two percent at fifty years. There will also probably be a wider variety of wildlife in the longer-rotation forest.

But these benefits come at a staggering cost from an investor's point of view, because of the tyranny of compounding interest and deferred returns. Over a full century, that same modest $200-an-acre investment would have grown to $26,300. No amount of extra wood can make up for a financial cost a dozen times as high caused by waiting an extra fifty years before harvest. Incentives to grow trees longer declined even further in 1986, when changes to the federal tax code made it even less economically feasible to hold on to timber any longer than necessary.

The problem is that in our present economic system, trees as living things, sitting on land, have no economic value. And companies make virtually no money from wildlife or recreation, though there have been tentative experiments to charge user fees to hunters, as has been done in Europe.

This is another reason why the ancient forest debate has focused on public land, not private. National forests do not answer to stockholders and can, in theory at least, afford to hang on to timber for long rotations. Private companies cannot.

Interestingly, the insulation of private land from the vagaries of politics and the ability to make long-term plans has arguably made them a stabler, more dependable source of wood than their public counterpart in the years since World War II. In Washington State, for example, the annual cut on state land has doubled and the annual cut on federal land has nearly tripled since 1949. On private land, the annual cut has gone up only about 40 percent, and then only in peak harvest periods.

But while the industry has provided a more stable level of cut each year, it has not been able to provide stable employment. Technology is whittling its work force. Near the Olympic Peninsula city of Shelton the Simpson timber company a decade ago built Mill Five, an example of the timber industry's conversion to small trees and fewer laborers. Mill Five is a sawmill with an appetite opposite that of mills requiring large old-growth trees for specialized products. The Shelton mill slices two-by-fours out of second-growth groves so densely packed and so skinny they look like a cluster of flagpoles.

The trees, growing on nearly flat ground, are not harvested by cutters like Russ Poppe, they are snipped at their base by big-tired feller-bunchers with giant scissors that grip, cut, and lay the trees like skewer sticks. A single man and a machine can do in a day what a crew of cutters can do in a week, with less energy and more safety.

The mill shows a similar economy of labor. Laser beams cast pencils of red light on logs that computers are measuring for maximum profit, while a single human supervises furious production from a soundproof booth. The mill turns out 600,000 board feet a week with eighteen people per shift, an efficiency rate better than two and a half times the Northwest mill average.

As a result of such mechanization, timber employment in Oregon and Washington fell from about 160,000 to 130,000 between 1979 and 1989, even though wood harvest in both years was roughly the same. The decline had nothing to do with owls or old growth; it was the result of modernization. The industry was producing almost 50 percent more finished product per mill job than it had a decade before. The trend is expected to continue even if no accommodation is made to the spotted owl. The Bonneville Power Administration projected the timber industry in the two states will lose another 34,000 jobs to mechanization by the year 2010.

An era is passing. Long recognizing the inevitable disappearance of the big trees, Weyerhaeuser owns more land in the southern United States than in the Northwest where it is headquartered. Georgia-Pacific, which moved its headquarters from Oregon to Atlanta in 1982, became the world's biggest timberland owner in early 1990 with 9 million acres. The same year, it closed its last Oregon mill.

Bingham said that while the timber industry is frequently accused of being callous or shortsighted, it is in reality an industry of futurists, having to guess at markets, prices, world demand, and population trends decades into the future.

Timber executives are not convinced the rest of society is taking any kind of integrated view. Americans seem to want the product, at the cheapest possible price, while objecting loudly to its harvest. There is no mechanism in the Pacific Northwest to plan the future of forest land on a comprehensive basis. Each landowner, public and private, does his own thing. The region's residents buy wooden homes on cleared forests and protest bitterly when their picture windows look out on clearcuts.

Mumper recalled a meeting he attended in which it was much clearer what the different sides did not want, than what they did. "Jerry Franklin was the only one who said we have to establish goals for land management," Mumper said. "In that respect, I agree with him. Society is always mucking around with the details, but society never lays out what it is ultimately trying to accomplish."

8

THE TRUCKERS

▲▲▲▲▲▲▲

The logging truck is the first thing a visitor sees when pulling into Dick and Barbara Mossman's driveway. Their white shingled home with its red trim is near Forks at Pleasant Lake, that place where the startlingly shaven hills are fuzzed with brown stump stubble and the green whiskers of replanted trees. The Mossmans' truck is hard to miss. The couple built a big new garage for it with enough headroom to be nearly two stories high, and it almost overshadows the home it is attached to. The height is necessary. When a logging truck isn't hauling logs, the rear set of wheels ride piggyback behind the big brown cab, making the steel tongue of the rear carriage jut up over the cab roof like a stubby lance.

While scientists debate the reordering of the landscape and the timber industry runs computer projections of tree growth and revenue two centuries into the future, it is log truck drivers like the Mossmans who struggle to adapt to change. Several times since the Forest Service first proposed setting aside large blocks of old-growth timber for the spotted owl, furious and frustrated loggers have rallied with these trucks to call attention to their plight, once briefly blocking Interstate 5 south of Seattle. Environmental strategists are not unhappy when loggers do so, since the sight of so many log haulers in one place reminds people better than anything else of the sheer scale of harvest in the woods. But for the frustrated loggers, the steely strength of the trucks serve as a rallying point, a declaration of power to a society that seems to have ignored or cold-shouldered them.

Away from demonstrations, of course, the relationships between people and machines can get more complex. The Mossmans' International was purchased new for $75,300 in 1979, or about as much as a mid-priced house in the Northwest cost at the time. When its cradles are fully loaded, the logging truck and its 350-horsepower, complexly geared diesel engine pull a combined weight of forty tons: this, in the kind of mean country that more frequently points up than sideways. The truck was to be the ticket to a newly independent life for the Mossmans, who wanted out from under the corporate thumb of Weyerhaeuser. They would become independents, paid by the load. Their International represented almost everything they had worked for, and they still refer to it as "she," a feminine personification to express their attachment. But the truck has also been cruel in her demands. "We lost the farm and saved the truck," is the way Dick sums up their struggle to pay for the thing. Because of that they also call her the Brown Bitch. In retrospect, they remember they picked the truck up on Friday the Thirteenth.

The logging truck is still the source of their livelihood. It had more than half a million miles on it by the end of the 1980s, and was probably good for about a half million more. A truck that old, however, is as greedy as a pig in its demands for upkeep: in 1989 it ate $7,200 in tires and more than $10,000 in maintenance and repair, not to mention $14,000 in fuel and $2,300 in road taxes. But now the truck itself is finally paid for. After they first purchased it, when the timber recession hit, the payments drained the Mossmans like Dracula at a blood bank.

In those days, the late 1970s, Barbara had a little dream of a sixteen-acre farm outside the southwest Washington town of Castle Rock. It was her favorite place in the world. Then timber demand and timber prices went into free fall, first as interest rates soared as high as 20 percent, then as the recession bit and brought what home building was left to a halt. They had bought their truck at the end of the spectacular '70s, when stumpage prices and logging volume had soared. They took possession just in time for the bottom to fall out of the industry.

It was ghastly timing and they almost lost the truck. To make their payments first they sold their tractor. Then ten acres. Then the balance of the farm with their house. The one thing they did not give up was the truck, the promise of self-employment. Still, Barbara's heart sank when they pulled out of the driveway of that farm for the last time in the cab of the Brown Bitch, knowing that a good chapter of her life was closing and she would never come back.

The couple hauled freight for a while to survive, the other truckers at freeway rest stops marveling at the extra gearing inside the Mossmans' rig designed to get a log truck around the hairpins and out of the mud holes. This interlude was sort of like a vacation, Barbara recalled: driving around the United States and chattering on the citizen's band radio. But hauling freight wasn't the same as being in the woods. It wasn't what they'd been born to, or knew about, or wanted to do, and it wasn't what the truck was designed for.

What saved them, finally, was the eruption of Mount St. Helens on May 2, 1980. The volcano was still belching periodic after-bursts of ash when salvage of hundreds of thousands of knocked-over trees began in 1981 and ran through 1983. It was a godsend for unemployed woods workers, filling the road down the devastated Toutle Valley with log trucks. At the peak of salvage some 600 trucks were rumbling out of the blast area, carrying 3.5 million board feet of timber each day. Weyerhaeuser, the company that owned most of the timber, was in a panic to get the knocked-over trees out before they began to decay and lose value. Dewey Rasmussen, the agile tree climber who would later have his back broken by falling cedar, got one of his first logging jobs chipping ash off the bark so the chainsaws could bite through them without dulling.

Barbara and Dick came back home to join the parade. There was so much work available that she started driving while Dick ran a shovel, a pivoting steel arm that picks up logs with giant pincers and loads them onto trucks. Log camps and vacation homes near the volcano had been destroyed by the blast, so the couple lived in a fifteen-foot camping trailer with no running water. At night they would line up with other loggers at the state park at Silver Lake, feeding dimes into the coin-operated shower there. Three minutes per dime. You hurried not just because of that, but because the mosquitoes ate you alive.

Barbara fit easily into the traditional, male-dominated world of logging. She didn't mind the rough language of the men up on the ash-gray slopes. "Hey, I'm in *your* world," she assured them when they'd begin awkwardly apologizing for a spate of raw words. Barbara liked the honesty of the language, different from the more calculated speech of other professions. "We're a free and open people," she explained. "What's in our hearts comes out of our mouths."

Loggers tend to be judged not by sex or race or belief so much as performance. Barbara dealt with this in a determined way. She would get up in the dark to be first at the logging landing, thus squeezing in an extra load during the long days on the gray moonscape. They kidded her about that, these men she conned into throwing the heavy binder chains over the log load for her. They called her Greedy Gertie. She didn't mind. Not only was she earning more money by working longer, but it was her statement to the men around her. I can do what you're doing. And more.

Woods workers rib each other with regularity and the man or woman who can't take some good-natured hazing with humor will have an unhappy time. The new choker setter on a logging show may come up at lunchtime to find his lunch box welded shut or glued to a log. His reaction will determine his acceptance. The men jousted with Barbara as well. Once, at the end of a long, wearying day, her back and limbs aching, she moaned that she needed a new body. "If you get a new one, I'll take the old," a male driver cracked.

Barbara gave as good as she got. She asked another driver who razzed her once if he'd like to come hunting with her.

"Hunting?" He was puzzled.

"Yeah, let's go hunting."

"Hunting what?" he said suspiciously.

"Hunting for assholes. I need a decoy."

She had a feel for the truck. Barbara was a tomboy, Dad's only girl. "I would rather be out in the rain than in the house," she said. Both she and Dick were born and raised in Pacific County in southwest Washington. They grew up only ten miles apart but, with Dick seven years older, neither knew the other until they met in a bowling alley after their first marriages failed. Down in Pacific County the future tended to be straightforward: you either logged, or fished, or oystered. Dick's father worked in the woods fifty years before being disabled. His uncle was killed logging. Dick himself got married at seventeen after his girlfriend became pregnant. When he found himself nine days out of high school the father of a son, he went into the woods to support his new family.

Barbara believes she had more options. She had been active in school sports, was feature editor on the high school paper, and acted in school plays. She briefly attended college. "I could have done anything," she figures now. But she married a woods worker and was drawn into the camaraderie of that hard world. She always liked the big trucks. She remembers one of the first times she saw a logging truck up close, as a child. "Something about those trucks was just like a magnet," she said. Over the years she coaxed men to gradually teach her how to drive them. The beasts are fussy, hard shifting at times, and it takes skill to pull eighty thousand pounds around a switchback on a one-lane dirt road that falls off into thin air. Barbara remembers spending a year trying to find a certain gear on a balky transmission—not needing it, necessarily, but nevertheless becoming more frustrated by the month that she couldn't find it. It wasn't until she gave up, just flat stopped worrying about it, that the shifter slid naturally into the notch one day. "If you just want to herd the truck down the road, you can learn it in two days," Barbara said. "If you want to be a Driver—well, that takes a long time."

When the volcano blew and there were suddenly more jobs than loggers, it was natural that Dick, who had the experience, would switch to work at the landings and Barbara would drive. She loved riding the truck up those volcanically shaven ridges—the biggest clearcut in recorded Northwest history, they later called the eruption—and then looking out over the ravaged landscape to the crater where a new lava dome steamed. There was an epic scale to this job.

Still, there were some hairy times, such as the day when Barbara was going downhill with a full load of logs and a leak caused the brakes to bleed empty of air. The truck lurched forward, its emergency spring brakes locking it up just before it skidded over the edge of the narrow logging road. Then it hung there, Barbara's truck plugging the whole salvage show. Dick came down to see what was wrong and found his wife still frozen in the cab, staring out the windshield down the steep slope, hands clenched on the steering wheel, her foot gluing the brake pedal to the floor. "Might as well come out, there's no air in the line and that pedal ain't doing a thing," he told her. She didn't care. "I'm not taking my foot off this brake," she replied.

It went like that over the years, good times and bad, feast to famine with the swings of the timber market and the vagaries of nature. At one point they were down to a loaf of bread and a jar of peanut butter. Barbara swallowed her pride and called her family, and they loaded a box with food.

"We are in a profession we love with all our hearts," Barbara explained. "How many people can say they are doing what they want to do? It's such a yearning that you'll put up everything you have, everything you own, to do what we are doing."

By 1990 they were doing pretty well: the truck paid, a new house purchased, kids out on their own. The house was overgrown and in disrepair when they got it, but the Mossmans worked hard, clearing the yard of brush and repairing and repainting it inside and out. Yet the uncertainty never ends. That year the owl and the preservationists and the people upset about shipping unprocessed logs to Asia kicked the bottom out of the wood market. At the end of 1990, the Mossmans estimated that if they sold their truck it would bring only half what it might have twelve months before. Once more they determined to ride it out, but Barbara's mood was reflected by a gloomy mock newspaper story she typed, set four years into the future. The fictional scenario reported that backpackers are disappearing in Olympic National Park, the suspected victims of enraged loggers. In her dark imaginings, the unemployed woods workers set the park on fire.

In their kitchen, Dick tried to explain the emotional vise gripping the heart of people in Forks. "We're bombarded daily" with bad news, he said. "Have you ever nearly gotten in a bad accident and you feel that flush that comes over your whole body, that emotional reaction? We get a flush like that every time we pick up the newspaper. To have someone on the East Coast dictate our future is really troubling to us. We feel the people in this area have the best experience to handle the forest."

The Mossmans are the couple who said they don't contest the right of ITT-Rayonier to log the stand of second-growth trees behind their new house, even though the resulting absence of a windbreak might result in the conifers in their own backyard being blown over. They see the forest as a place of change: either of harvest and rebirth or decay and waste. They don't think the forest is "ancient" at all, and don't understand the way the urban visitors look on it as a symbol of continuity, even immortality. The forest around Forks is a rumpled record of fire and wind and decay, they argue. It is always growing and always succumbing. The Mossmans reason it makes sense to harvest a tree at its peak, the way you would pick a ripe apple. Dick remembers watching a magnificent stand of old growth being sawn down on the Hoko River, north of Forks. "It troubled you when it hit the ground," he admits, "until you realized the center is rotten. It is a bigger sin to waste the resource than to use it and put something back there, new trees, that will benefit all of us."

This view of the forest as something in transition, rather than static, in one way echoes the Mossmans' experience. Nothing in their life has been very permanent: not their careers or their homes or their fortunes. The job sites are always changing, as is the weather and the seasons and the traffic. A salaried city person in a climate-controlled office, on a steady career track in which life is expected to make predictable parabolas—this urbanite who can find paper at a stationer's and lumber at a hardware store in both good times and bad—might naturally transfer this stability to nature itself. To him or her, the forest seems fixed and eternal. To harvest it is to knock down something enduring, like leveling a mountain.

To a woods worker—who sees the timber market boom and crash, who works furiously in the summer but might be laid off in winter, who has no pension plan or company-provided health benefits or IRA account—to that person the forest may be symbolic not just of opportunity but of uncertainty. And the more the ever-changing forest is left alone, uncut, the more uncertain life becomes. The forest offers security to a rural community such as Forks only through its harvest. The good times are an opportunity to get ahead of the game, to buy that truck or bulldozer or logging tower, to make what one can before the lean years that will inevitably come around again. In such a situation a clearcut is not an interruption, but a place of fleeting opportunity.

To the urbanite, an uncut forest is a refuge. It is a statement that some things existed before scarcely bridled development and are eternal.

Robert Lee, the sociologist at the University of Washington who is sympathetic to the plight of logging communities, has argued that loggers can be just as upset at a clearcut as a hiker. Many loggers *are* hikers, or hunters, or fishermen, or mushroom pickers. They lead physically difficult, unsettled lives in order to stay in the woods instead of moving to a city. The difference, Lee said, is that loggers have what he thinks is a more realistic view of nature, a willingness to use it as well as enjoy it. "They accept the rules of life," he said. "They know somebody has to cut it, so let's do the best job possible."

In a speech on this theme, Lee said that, "Unlike advocates for old-growth preservation and reform in forest management practices, rural woods workers tend to romanticize people and view nature pragmatically. . . . People are humanized and nature is a morally neutral object that is readily converted into a commodity."

Environmentalists, he said, do the opposite, romanticizing nature and dehumanizing those who work in the woods. He called this an "institutionalized victimization of loggers."

Forest preservation, Lee said, has for some environmentalists "taken the place of traditional religion by enabling them to deny the terrifying historical and ecological realities of contemporary human existence. . . . It is the symbolic importance of these forests as enduring symbols of undisturbed nature, not their biological functions, that has such broad public appeal. . . . Humans have always sought to confront the terror of death by developing a sense of immortality—symbolic participation in something larger and more enduring. Four ways of expressing a sense of immortality are most common: biological continuity of a family, theological formulations guiding religious beliefs in transcendence and life after death, creative works such as writing and the arts, and participation in the natural order of the world." Environmentalists, he suggested, take comfort in the latter.

Matthew Carroll is an assistant professor of natural resource sociology at Washington State University who has worked closely with Lee. For his doctoral thesis he got a job as a choker setter in the northern California woods to see the logger's life-style firsthand, and later followed this up with extensive interviews to explore the nature of logging communities.

"Traditional logging culture was kind of hand to mouth," he said. "There wasn't a lot of looking to the future. It was a here-and-now existence. They had the knowledge they would get laid off in the wintertime, the knowledge the logging business goes up and down." They operated, in effect, with a different sense of time: more immediate in focus, less trusting of the future, less interested in the eternal.

The economic uncertainties, the dependence on nature and markets that were largely uncontrollable, produce a folk different from the urban majority, the sociologist theorizes. "There is a warmth to these communities," Carroll said. "There is a mutual helping. Once you are established as okay by your peers, there is an acceptance you will not find in the urban environment." Eccentricities are tolerated as long as the resident proves himself to be a producer. "In large part, they are honest, hardworking people. People like that built the economy of our country. It's the work ethic."

The uncertainty extends to danger. One woman wrote a musical play about logging in which she said that loggers are half dead. By this, Carroll explained, she meant that, "They live with death every day. It's almost as if they accept death. Fallers in particular just expect to spend time in the hospital." Chronic injuries such as "white finger," a deterioration of the hands caused by the vibration of chainsaws, come to be accepted as inevitable. The forest takes on the role of challenger, not friend.

Carroll theorizes that there are at least three principal philosophies found in the woods. The Forest Service and similar government agencies tend to be utilitarian, he said, measuring the forest by how it can provide the most good for the most people. Gifford Pinchot, the first chief of the Forest Service, spelled this out in 1905, writing that, "Where conflicting interests must be reconciled, the question will always be decided from the standpoint of the greatest good of the greatest number in the long run." If the majority wants wood products, the Forest Service responds to that. If the majority wants preservation instead, the Forest Service will eventually shift in response.

Environmentalists, Carroll said, tend to be transcendentalist in approach. They find a spiritual, almost religious experience in nature and tend to stress the values of scenery, wildlife, and ecology: the fabric of natural life that offers contrasts and lessons to human civilization.

The third philosophy, Carroll suggests, is a market philosophy. The forest's value is set by the price society puts on its tangible products. This is the philosophy of the big timber companies, he said, and it tends to be the philosophy of most timber communities such as Forks.

While the ordinary woods worker tends to share the market philosophy of the big timber companies, he doesn't have much more love for Big Timber than he does for the Sierra Club. He can be whipsawed between the most insensitive extremes of transcendentalism and market philosophies. "It is not an easy thing they are facing out there," Carroll said. "They are caught between two elites, the big forest industry and the environmentalists." Historically, timber companies have had a history of layoffs, buyouts, union troubles, and overcutting.

Nevertheless, loggers feel more closely allied to an ITT-Rayonier or Plum Creek or Weyerhaeuser than to urban environmentalists. They see in industry more shared values. "Loggers focus on the fact that society needs products," Lee said. "They are enamored of the free market."

Dick Mossman puts this more colorfully. If much more forest preservation is tolerated, he observes, "It's going to get to the point where a guy is going to be wiping his ass with feathers."

Nothing infuriates logging communities more than the suggestion by urban environmentalists that they are obsolete, that they are about to pass the way of whalers and buffalo hunters. Lee sympathizes with that anger. "The whale oil we found substitutes for," he said. "The buffaloes are no longer utilized. To compare loggers to that is to say we can somehow get wood somewhere else. I don't see that happening."

The sociologist is even more disturbed at the emotional cost of such analogies. People learn who they are in part by how others treat them, he said. "We're denying the reality of these people," he warned. Moreover, loggers as a group tend to be independent, resourceful, and adaptable if so encouraged: the very kind of group American society should be trying to nurture, not destroy, Lee argues.

"We are the kind of people the American dream was built on," said Barbara. "We've always taken care of ourselves out here. We never asked the outside communities for anything. Now they want to tell us how to manage our woods. It's like being molested."

Like so many jobs around Forks, log truck pay is based on tangible production: how much load for how many miles. There is different pay for five different classes of road: ordinary blacktop, gravel, logging, poor logging roads, and logging roads so bad that trucks have to be pulled out of the landing by a caterpillar tractor. The Mossmans had a job on one of the latter at the time I talked with them. It was up on a ridge so high and steep it looked like a person would get a nosebleed just driving there. A cat hauled them the last mile by steel cable. "If that cable breaks," noted Barbara, "you're dead."

On a typical run to Port Angeles—about an hour from the Forks area once a log truck hits paved highway—the Mossmans earned under this complicated formula 5.28 cents a pound for a net load of 52,000 pounds of wood. That equals about $275. Depending on the remoteness of the logging site, they could expect to make two or three round trips a day. It sounds reasonably lucrative until expenses are added in.

"A logging truck, contrary to what people think, is not good money," Dick said. The Washington State Utilities and Transportation Commission has frozen rates since the early 1980s. Even those rates are not always observed: when the Mossmans came to Forks in 1986, they drove for a logging firm that never paid full rates as required by law, and ordered their drivers to shut up about it. If you wanted the work, you took the reduction. If you wanted to complain, there was a line of hungry truckers ready to take your place.

Moreover, the work isn't steady. It can be shut down by markets or weather or mechanical breakdowns at the job site. In one recent winter the Mossmans were out of work for five months. When they finally returned, the rear drive of their truck went out the first day. Eleven days after that, their transmission blew up.

In the years 1987–1989, their net taxable income did not exceed $15,000 a year.

It may well have been more secure and more lucrative for Dick to stick to his original job driving trucks for Weyerhaeuser. He started in the early 1960s after a motorcycle accident injured his body too severely for him to continue working as a logger. Dick was respected at Weyerhaeuser. Once given a job test-driving a new kind of logging truck that could haul more net weight, he suggested improvements, and when his boss in the field ignored him the word came down from corporate headquarters near Tacoma: what Mossman wants, he gets. Make the truck work. Still, that kind of favor created friction with immediate supervisors that proved difficult to later smooth over. He found it hard to fit in with a big corporation.

Once he came home growling, moody, restless. "Do I look like a whore?" he asked Barbara.

No, she replied. What are you talking about?

"So why does Weyerhaeuser always keep trying to stick it to me?" he roared in frustration. A turning point had been reached. The couple decided to get a truck and try self-employment.

Log truck driving can not only offer a sense of independence, but it can also be a social, conversational job with the use of a citizen's band radio. Most logging roads are built for economy, with steep grades, hairpin turns, and precipitous edges. They are mostly one lane, with frequent turnouts to allow the big trucks to pass each other. In the trip up the mountain a radio is used to keep the drivers abreast of who is coming down with logs and who is driving up. Most of the talk is businesslike, but there can be some pleasant chatter as well.

I got a better sense of this when Ingrid Dahlgren, the fifty-eight-year-old matron of Forks's biggest independent logging contractor company, took me up to a harvest site. She and her husband Joe and two sons run a firm that owns no forest land and bids on no trees but instead specializes in cutting and yarding wood others have purchased. She piloted a pickup up a logging road with caution, swerving to the side and waiting whenever we met a truck coming down. The CB kept everyone advised of traffic up and down the mountain.

Like the Mossmans, the Dahlgrens worked on Mount St. Helens salvage in the lean years of the early 1980s to keep going. They first came to Forks in 1952 to truck out salvage logs from the big Forks fire. Ingrid was the daughter of an immigrant Swedish couple who sold farm implements in Everson, Washington. Forks seemed remote, dark, and rainy when her husband took her there. The forest was thicker and more pressing. "Housing was much worse," she remembered. "Forks was wilder. At first the loggers frightened me. There was more drinking than there is now. It was different."

The beauty of the land touched her, however, and perhaps philosophies are more mixed in individuals than Carroll's hypothesis would suggest: a person may see the woods as both a place of market and transcendent values. In struggling to get established in the remote West End, her childhood habit of church attendance fell away. "That's okay," she remarked, gesturing at the young trees that carpet the Sol Duc Valley. "You can see God in nature."

When trucking slowed in the early 1960s Joe switched to logging old-growth cedar out on the boggy flats south of Forks. In 1970 his oldest boy graduated from high school and immediately started working side by side with his father. His younger brother followed him. The sons work tirelessly, Ingrid said, going to work on Saturday to notch the stumps that yarding anchor cables will be wrapped around so that the work will go faster on Monday. By 1990 sixty to seventy-five people worked for the company, but as the owl restrictions went into effect the work force began to shrink. Like farmers, logging contractors often lead relatively modest middle class life-styles but pump their profits back into enormous equipment investments. The Dahlgrens had paid $1.3 million for a steel tower designed to log steep Forest Service land. The tower came with a skyline cable system that lifted logs clear of the ground when yarding and minimized soil damage. It was an investment dictated by the agency's new emphasis on being careful when harvesting, the kind of improvement an environmentalist might approve of. Now the Forest Service, responding to the owl listing, had decided not to sell as many trees as it once promised, and the tower was idle. It was as if the Dahlgrens had been fools for trying to respond to the new rules.

For their fortieth wedding anniversary the Dahlgrens had been thinking of taking a rare vacation, kids and grandkids in tow, to Disneyland. When the woods shut down, they canceled. "It's been like this for two years," said Ingrid. "Not knowing what's going to happen."

In the summer of 1990 the Dahlgrens got so tired of all the newspaper and magazine articles and television documentaries criticizing old-growth logging that they began offering free tours to the tourists who came through Forks. They showed the visitors places that had been logged and regrown. People were shocked at the speed at which the trees grow back, she said. "They basically felt they were being lied to by the environmentalists."

Our ride up the mountain completed, we park a bit below the logging landing on this Olympic National Forest clearcut and walk the last short distance, the dirt road covered by a sheen of mud. Flakes of early snow sleet through the air. The clearcut smells like Christmas. The branches knocked and cut from the freshly cut trees mat the ground with evergreen boughs and their perfume scents the air. The needles will soon brown and the transformation of the forest will look even bleaker, but right now the loggers look like toy figures in a plush green rug. The choker setters seem to be swallowed as they jump down into the mess of shattered limbs to fit the steel cables around the logs. It is as if they are jumping into a green pond.

In accord with Jerry Franklin's ideas of New Forestry, clumps of trees have been left on this site for wildlife. Ingrid doesn't like it. She's afraid one of the surviving trees or snags, now exposed to the wind, is going to fall over someday and crush one of their employees. It might be her husband killed by these wildlife trees, she remarked, or one of her sons.

The gunning of the yarder engine and the distances between the workers make verbal communication almost impossible; the toots of a whistle activated by hand-held signalers indicate where the choker cable is to stop when it whizzes down the main lead line toward the waiting choker setters. A giant shovel pinches the logs with steel claws and stacks them like match wood. The wordless motion is like a silent movie.

"We're the foundation of the pyramid," Ingrid said as we watch the work. "This is the beginning of making something."

It is the day before Thanksgiving 1990, and the Mossmans sound gloomy. Snow and mechanical breakdowns have slowed logging on a site they were hauling from and work is rapidly evaporating elsewhere. "The new log export ban has hurt us more than the owl," Barbara said.

The Mossmans don't like to be idle and are inventive by nature. For recreation they like to bow hunt and pistol shoot, and Barbara shot one elk recently with a black-powder muzzle loader. She used its hide for a variety of projects. Stretched on hoops of wood, a section became a canvas for the wildlife paintings she does. Stitched and beaded, another patch became a checkbook cover, a hole in the bead-work marking where the rifle ball went through the elk's side. She used more hides to make buckskin leggings and jackets for the black-powder rendezvous gatherings the couple sometimes attends, where history enthusiasts recreate the Mountain Man era. She enjoys car-tooning. One of her drawings shows a group of spotted owls sitting around a table, complaining they have been manipulated by environ-mentalists.

The Mossmans have no plans to leave the Forks area. They've survived eleven years with the Brown Bitch, and imagine that, one way or another, they'll continue to hang on. "We've had more than our share of adversity," Barbara noted. "We're still here."

Sometimes she writes letters and guest editorials to the newspapers. When we talked she was working on another one, pointing out that more spotted owls—this seemingly ubiquitous threatened species—have been discovered east of the Cascade Mountains, suggesting the ecosystem may not be at as much at risk as the biologists claim. "The facts are still catching up," she said.

Maybe the loggers can still win, she said. Maybe they can still get their story across, or maybe prices will go up enough for wood and paper to make the rest of the United States take notice. Still, it beats you down, working so hard at an occupation that suddenly seems despised.

"It's hard for people like us to understand the treatment we are getting," Barbara reflected. "It's like a religion, what we do. We feel like we're doing something that is vital and important. We feel a kinship to this land. We were the first environmentalists."

9

THE ENVIRONMENTALIST

▲▲▲▲▲▲▲

In late September of 1988, about two hundred Northwest environmentalists gave up the bright sunshine of an Indian summer morning and crowded into the windowless auditorium of the Mountaineers Club, not far from Seattle's Space Needle. The occasion was an annual conference on wilderness, and the sacrifice of a choice Saturday had become customary: this gathering frequently drew some of the most prominent environmental activists in the nation to speak. Michael McCloskey, a former Sierra Club president turned ecological think-tanker, gave a speech on the world's remaining inventory of wilderness. McCloskey is a member of the environmental establishment, a well-paid representative of the increasingly sophisticated mainstream groups that had given ecological concerns a standard seat at the political bargaining table. But despite McCloskey's stature, Mitch Friedman, a slight, bearded, restless Earth First! activist, found his mind wandering. Friedman's inattention was illustrative of a rift between the best-known environmental organizations and their more radical critics who see the big clubs getting fat, bureaucratic, moribund, and timid. Many at the meeting saw compromise with the existing economic order as not a gain but a softening of losses, a mere postponement of planetary catastrophe. Society didn't need to be bargained with. It needed to be changed.

Friedman was interested in dramatic action, not the painstaking stockpiling of votes and dollars and polls and political chits that go into a legislative lobbying campaign. As his thoughts drifted, an idea for a prank crept into his mind: a way, once again, to draw attention to the heavy harvest of the Pacific Northwest's dwindling old-growth forests.

Friedman's scheme was to park a loaded logging truck up on the sidewalk in front of the headquarters of the Mount Baker-Snoqualmie National Forest in downtown Seattle and then walk away with the keys. Perhaps he'd take some vital engine part, too. The idea was that forest officials couldn't get through their front door to work until they figured out a way to move the massive truck. It made an amusing picture in his mind: a cluster of befuddled federal employees standing around the truck full of butchered logs, a monstrous plucked chicken come home to roost.

It was the kind of stunt that author Edward Abbey might have imagined for his novel *The Monkey Wrench Gang*, an inspirational bible to the most radical tree huggers. Abbey's fictional characters had waged a kind of guerrilla war on developers in the West. Copying their tactics, Earth First! enthusiasts such as Friedman had blockaded logging roads, climbed trees that were about to be cut down, and unfurled a gigantic "crack" across the face of the upper Elwha dam that had drowned a valley in what was now Olympic National Park. Friedman had helped dump sawdust in the offices of the Gifford Pinchot National Forest in Washington's southern Cascade Mountains and blockaded a popular campground in Yellowstone National Park. Someone—no one professed to know who, given the seriousness with which authorities viewed the act—had driven steel spikes into trees to wreck any saws that hit them. They had poured abrasives into the engines of parked logging equipment. Once, in Oregon, demonstrators had dug a ditch across a logging road, filled it with quick-drying concrete, and stepped in up to their ankles. Before they could be jailed they had to be broken out with sledgehammers.

While such tactics were widely condemned in the mainstream media, they also drew reporters' interest—first to the demonstration, and then sometimes to the environmental issues behind them. Earth First! was helping to push the old-growth forest issue in front of a distracted media and public.

There were at least two obstacles to Friedman's latest plan. First, he didn't have a logging truck, or logs to put on it. Second, even if he could get one, it seemed a lot of trouble for a one-time stunt of dubious effectiveness, let alone legality. While Friedman was on the radical edge of environmentalism, he was becoming increasingly concerned that such pranks had come to overshadow the cause they professed to represent.

Suddenly he had a better idea. Why not take the logging truck on a tour around the United States with a gigantic old-growth log on its bed? Wouldn't that show people in other states the stunning scale of the trees that were disappearing in the Pacific Northwest? He still remembered being shocked as a boy during a vacation trip to Colorado that "national forest" did not mean a protected tree reserve, but heavy harvest. Many people east of the Rockies shared that confusion, he was sure.

As the conference took a break for coffee, Friedman excitedly broached his idea to others. Some thought it was a silly idea. The loggers were rallying with logging trucks, for crying out loud. Now environmentalists were going to drive them too? Wasn't the symbolism a little murky? For just this reason, the Wilderness Society eventually decided not to lend financial support to the idea. But others were intrigued. There was a growing sense that the old-growth battle could not be won in the Pacific Northwest. Timber was the biggest industry in Oregon and the second biggest in Washington, after Boeing. Andy Kerr of the Oregon Natural Resources Council would later infuriate Northwest politicians by saying that, "Expecting the Oregon congressional delegation to behave rationally about the end of forest cutting in 1990 is like expecting the Mississippi delegation to behave rationally about segregation in 1960." (Kerr, who took impish delight in waving red capes before the forest industry's frustrated bull, would later note the analogy was one of his most successful one-liners: "*Time* magazine liked it so much they quoted it twice.")

Other environmentalists agreed the issue had to be nationalized. People in other states had to be reminded that since most of the surviving big trees were on national forests, they—not just people in California, Oregon, Washington, and Alaska—owned them too.

If some were confused at the idea of environmentalists at the helm of a logging truck, others liked the notion of seizing the symbolism of the other side and turning it against them. A former logger-turned-truck-driver-turned-environmentalist named Ric Bailey, who was working to promote Hell's Canyon on the Oregon-Idaho border as a national park, was immediately attracted to Friedman's plan. "I want to drive that truck," he said.

Renting a truck was no particular obstacle, though Bailey advised it made more sense to rent a higher-geared flatbed designed for freeway driving than a logging truck itself. Finding a suitable log was more of a challenge. The organizers of what was to be called "The Ancient Forest Rescue Expedition" told log yards that they represented a group of Indians and artists seeking a log for a totem pole or similar artwork.

They found their giant, finally, on the Olympic Peninsula. The following spring, Friedman and Bailey drove a truck to Olympic Wood Products in Port Angeles, a Japanese-owned firm that bought the biggest and best American logs for export to Japan. They picked out a 730-year-old chunk of Douglas fir cut from Olympic National Forest. It was twenty feet long and seven and a half feet in diameter, and cost $3,040.

To emphasize its age the Expedition members stapled dates onto its tree rings. The log's thickness fascinated people. During the log's cross-country tour, one man who clambered up on the truck to grasp the wood wouldn't let go. Only when the truck started pulling away to re-enter the freeway did he reluctantly jump off. In two places, St. Louis and Long Island, men saw the log, quit their jobs, and moved to Oregon to work on the tree issue, eventually meeting and forming a "Save America's Forest Coalition." At a New Jersey Turnpike rest stop, strangers walked up and wrote checks of $50 and $100 in support.

The Expedition was launched with a rally at Seattle's Pike Place Market, an historic downtown farm produce and crafts center. As Friedman spoke to a gathered crowd on the need to curb the logging that was going on, others were working on the carburetor of an ancient Earth First! donated van, a 1969 Dodge, that was to be the chase vehicle behind the logging truck. Finally the van's wheezing engine started. The organizers had decided at the beginning not to make presentations in either Oregon or Montana out of fear the truck tires would be slashed by hostile loggers.

The Ancient Forest Rescue Expedition's first presentation was at Bismarck: a three-day drive. When the logging truck was about two hours from the city, organizers heard on the radio that President George Bush was in town for a tree planting ceremony. The timing seemed propitious. Friedman called ahead to his rally's organizer, a wildlife biologist with the North Dakota Department of Game. Why not call a press conference? he suggested. Then, anxious to arrive before the President slipped away, Friedman transferred from the increasingly balky van to the truck like an admiral transferring his flag, ordering full speed ahead. It was well he did. Behind them, the laboring van blew a tire. The tire was changed, but then the vehicle's transmission went out.

Meanwhile, Friedman entered one side of Bismarck as the President was planting a tree (which later died) on the other. No reporters were waiting. The wildlife biologist was furious that the Ancient Forest

Rescue Expedition was trying to link its campaign to Bush's visit. He was afraid Friedman would say something that would embarrass him and his colleagues. Friedman was crestfallen at this reaction. The Expedition had barely started and here they had already angered potential allies in the first city they stopped at outside the Pacific Northwest. Friedman smoothed bristled feelings as best he could, then worked hurriedly to prepare his talk. The slide projector he was loaned was nearly as ancient as the trees he wanted to save. One of his slides from the carousel got hung up in the machine just five minutes before the scheduled start of the talk. As he tilted the machine up over his head to see what was wrong, all the other slides fell out, cascading across the floor. Meanwhile, word came in from the van, stalled somewhere out on the plains in the darkness. It would cost more to fix the transmission than the vehicle was worth. It was abandoned at a junkyard.

That didn't matter, Friedman decided, going out to make his talk. Only fourteen people had shown up to listen to him. That didn't matter either, he thought. Those who did show up were intrigued. That evening was the first step in establishing a nationwide network of enthusiasts willing to work politically on the old-growth forest issue. Some of the city's foresters came by to look at the big tree after Bush left. So did reporters. Nor did the press miss the irony of the President planting a little tree while a federal agency cut down mammoth counterparts elsewhere: the next day's newspaper had a front page picture of Friedman's log making just that point.

"That day established from the start that no matter what happens," Friedman said, "the show will go on." A few days later, the Expedition purchased a $700 used Pontiac in Chicago to replace the wretched van.

Soon, a rhythm was established. A typical evening's presentation would include a brief talk, a slide show or video on the issue, some folk songs, and a rap session for the audience to trade thoughts on what should be done. Friedman explained the forest issue, while Bailey gave the point of view of a former logger turned environmentalist. The Expedition didn't have money for fuel or food, so people passed the hat or purchased ancient forest T-shirts. The Expedition members were invited into homes for dinner and given living room rugs as a place to spread their sleeping bags. Eventually they would visit forty-four states, in most of them astounding people at just how big trees can get. It was like hauling a dinosaur around.

Children were entranced. In Indiana the truck picked up Representative Jim Jontz—a forest enthusiast who would later infuriate the Northwest timber industry by sponsoring an ancient forest protection bill—and then wound down narrow residential streets to a school playground. Some six hundred cheering youngsters ran out to meet them, Bailey recalled.

Truckers liked to call the Rescue Expedition truck cab on the CB radio when they saw the big log zoom by. "Whatch y'all doin' with that toothpick?" they'd ask. Friedman or Bailey would explain that the nation's last, greatest, virgin forests were being cut. "That's a damn shame," the truckers would respond to the news of overcutting. "Don't blame you a'tall." The expedition members heard that a lot. "Don't blame you a'tall."

Not everyone was impressed. Friedman remembers driving down Broadway in New York City with this titanic log and the banner along its length that read, "Ancient Forest Rescue Expedition." Outside Madison Square Garden a throng of young adults in outrageous punk dress—spiked hair, safety pin earrings, leather and tattoos—were lined up for a concert. Here seemed an ideal captive audience that perhaps could be motivated to direct its energy to environmental causes. Bailey blasted the horn. Friedman leaned out the cab window to shout, "It's the Big One!"—their nickname for the fat log.

"People didn't even turn their heads," he recalled, grinning at the memory. "New York was the only place in the country where we weren't even a sideshow."

One of the best reactions they got was in the industrialized timber country of Alabama, where natural forests and cotton fields have long since given way to regimented plantations of fast-growing pine, the trees frequently placed in sterile rows. The mill workers, used to handling wood only a few decades old when cut, were respectful of the big old tree. "Protect that stuff," they told Friedman. "It's all been cut down here and there's not even a damn squirrel in these woods."

In 1985, Mitch Friedman emerged from a zoology class at the University of Washington, where he was completing a postponed wildlife degree, and saw a sign in the hallway advertising the first Earth First! meeting in Washington State. "What's Earth First!?" Friedman asked a friend. Come to the meeting and find out, he was told.

Friedman was not native to the big forests of the Pacific Northwest. He grew up in Chicago's Lake suburbs, the son of an attorney, a precocious Jewish kid with an early interest in wildlife nurtured by subscriptions to a Cousteau Society magazine and National Wildlife when he was eight or nine. He can't really remember where his identification with wild animals and natural ecosystems came from. While his family visited the outdoors, they were more likely to make a ski trip to Colorado than go camping. Instinctively, however, he seemed to identify with the animals. He cried as a child when his mother came home showing off a raccoon coat.

Mitch was also quick to question conventional authority. "At the age of eight, I was the first atheist I ever knew," he said. If he sensed any God, it was in the world's natural order.

His parents encouraged Friedman's exposure to the outdoors. He went on YMCA canoe trips to the Boundary Waters Wilderness area in northern Minnesota at the age of eight or nine. "That's still my vision of wilderness," he said. He was also fascinated by the West. During a high school vacation he drove out to Wyoming and landed a job as a ranch hand, living in a bunk house that had once been shared by eight or ten cowboys. He helped move cows on two- or three-day horseback cattle drives.

After high school he went to Montana State University to study wildlife. In the summer, he got a seven-dollar-a-day job helping a graduate student track white-tailed deer in the Yellowstone area. He was uncomfortable with the curriculum's orthodoxy, however. "It took me about a year to realize I didn't want to manage wildlife, I wanted to protect it," he said. He dropped out of school, drove a fork lift in Chicago briefly, and then enrolled in an oceanography and sailing course at Woods Hole, Massachusetts. He sailed in the Caribbean until his money ran out. Restless again for change, he thought of the Pacific Northwest as a haven of wild country. He decided to go to the University of Washington for a philosophy degree. Once in Seattle, he switched back to science, earning a bachelor's in a self-designed concentration of zoology and ecology.

Meanwhile, Earth First! had been founded in April of 1980 by five American environmentalists at the conclusion of a week-long desert hike in Mexico. They were led by Dave Foreman, who had been a lobbyist in Washington, D.C., for the Wilderness Society. Foreman was disillusioned by the compromises the mainstream environmental organizations had just been forced to make on the future of roadless national forest lands. He and some friends—Howie Wolke, Mike Roselle, Bart Koehler, and Ron Kezar—were all fans of Abbey's *The*

Monkey Wrench Gang. They decided the environmental movement—
which had evolved from the street protests of the first 1970 Earth Day
to a lobbying bureaucracy of its own in Washington, D.C.—needed
a radical voice. The timing was perfect. Earth First! presented the
perfect contrast to the environmental backlash of the incoming Reagan
administration. For a logo the five organizers picked a clenched green
fist. For a slogan they selected, "No compromise in defense of Mother
Earth."

Any U.S. citizens' movement, in choosing its strategy and tactics,
must grapple with the conflicting allure of revolutionary zeal and the
more lasting but less satisfactory power that comes from political compromise. In philosophy it must find a balance between being ahead
of the crowd and still appealing to America's political center of gravity,
the moderate middle class. The 1980s campaign to save the nation's
final, most spectacular old-growth forests was no different, inevitably
mutating from one strategy to the other. At a time when the national
headquarters of mainstream environmental organizations had little
interest in trees or owls or ecosystems per se—and Northwest environmental leaders saw little hope of combating the economic power
of the timber industry—groups such as Earth First! took on logging
at the front lines.

The no-compromise zealots found the mainstream media a double-
edged sword, which first publicized the group and its issues but later
dwelled, almost exclusively and usually negatively, on its most controversial tactics such as tree spiking and civil disobedience. Still, it
got reporters into the woods.

Earth First! was a grassroots movement that successfully tapped a
keg of fermenting frustration. It and scores of small community-based
coalitions pushed national organizations to get involved before the old
trees were gone. Eventually Friedman would conclude that the message and idealism of Earth First! had become blurred by the debate
over its methods, but he thinks that in the mid-1980s the group played
a critical role. "It was a major turning point," he said. "Back in those
days national groups didn't want to touch the issue—they didn't think
they could win." Sympathetic public reaction to the radical protesters
helped change their mind. "Not only did Earth First! rejuvenate the
environmental movement, it has gone back to the grassroots," Friedman judged. The organization was deliberately disorganized, given
the illegality of some of its protests. No donor lists, no slick magazines,
no upscale headquarters. In Washington State what little communi-

cation there was between different chapters came at quarterly campouts; often one group would take some flamboyant action and the rest would be ignorant of it unless the press reported arrests. The national newsletter was anarchic, sprinkled with outrageous opinion. Earth First! promised not membership, but involvement.

Friedman became part of the larger evolution. The mid-1980s saw him perched in threatened trees, bundled in a sleeping bag to ward off the cold. By the end of the decade he was lobbying in Washington, D.C., looking a bit uncomfortable on television in a suit and tie but nevertheless an articulate advocate for halting the harvest of old growth. By the end of 1990 he had been to Washington, D.C., four times: twice with his log truck to the Capitol grounds, twice for congressional-office lobbying. Speaking and persuasion came naturally, he said, but he added that life was less fun now. The best lobbying advice he had gotten was from David Brower, the ecological archdruid who led the Sierra Club in some of its early battles and later split to found the less compromising Friends of the Earth. "When you know you're right, you have to feign humility," Brower said. The white-haired, red-faced veteran also liked to tell groups that Earth First! made Friends of the Earth look reasonable and that, "What we need now is a group to make Earth First! look reasonable."

Friedman's donning of a suit did not end his iconoclastic habits, however. At the beginning of the '90s he was living in Bellingham, Washington, on about $4,000 a year, sharing an apartment for $100 rent and accepting hand-me-down clothes from his brother in Chicago. "I'm not a purist," he said. "I don't throw things out to teach myself a lesson. But I learned the satisfaction of doing with less." He has remained at heart a reformer of society, not a tinkerer and tweaker of its natural, capitalist momentum. Friedman acknowledges there is a gap between his own convictions and life-style and that of most of the people he needs to persuade. He declines to be preachy about consumptive life-styles. "Who knows what drives people who spend their lives at the mall?" he mused. "But I don't think a lot about that. I don't know what I would do about that."

At the time he originally read about the Earth First! organizational gathering in the student union building, Friedman had already read Abbey, Aldo Leopold, and similar spokesmen for the wilderness creed. But it was this meeting that was to give more focus to his philosophical sympathies to wildlife. The Washington State group was organized by an Oregon Earth First! member named George Draffan who had moved to Seattle a few months before. Draffan had joined the organization after hearing founder Foreman speak in 1981. Appalled by clearcutting in Oregon, Draffan recalled, "It was so obvious something had to be done." Ironically, Draffan worked for the public information office of the Forest Service in Seattle for three years while promoting Earth First! on the side; he kept expecting to be fired but either the agency never made the connection or decided it was not grounds for dismissal. Draffan defends the civil disobedience tactics of Earth First! "It depends whether you believe there's a crisis or not," he said. "If you believe there is a crisis, then you need to use crisis tactics to wake people up."

In retrospect, Friedman is less sure of that. "Now the name has been tainted beyond use," he said of Earth First!. Initially, "there was a period of desperation," he recalled. "The Forest Service was doing some incredibly deceptive things. At that time I thought this was one of those crisis points, I thought this is going to help. Now it's hard to tell. This is a complex world, and media perceptions are everything. Earth First! was never portrayed as Robin Hood, it was portrayed as terrorist. Society doesn't want a crisis dealt with through crisis tactics."

Yet it was just those tactics that made Earth First! so compelling, Friedman explained: "What was fun was acting on your beliefs. It was very liberating. It was empowering. That's the most important experience you can get, something society usually doesn't offer. The objective of organizing is to empower people. Participating in Earth First! was an adrenalin rush as a substitute for the feeling of incapacitation. You came away thinking an individual can do their best."

When Friedman walked into the room for that introductory meeting he felt like he had met his philosophical soul brothers. Here were fans of Deep Ecology, an argument that *Homo sapiens* have no heightened claim on the resources of the earth and should be given no share above that of other species. Here was concern that Judeo-Christian civilization as a whole had taken a disastrous wrong turn in its domination of nature and worship of technology. "I met all my best friends that night," Friedman said. "Earth First! is really driven by relationships."

Earth First! inspired protests against the logging of old-growth forest that had begun in southern Oregon about 1983. Activism started with a blockade of a major logging road the U.S. Forest Service wanted to push into the Bald Mountain area of the Siskiyou National Forest, a wild, rumpled area of incredible ecological diversity. The protesters sat down in front of bulldozers or, when it proved too easy to cart them off to local jails, had themselves buried up to their necks in front of the blades.

Friedman's initiation into heady demonstrations came in 1986. The Forest Service had decided to log what environmentalists had identified as the oldest standing grove of Douglas fir in Oregon, with trees more than a thousand years in age. Protesters called it Millennium Grove. They decided that to prevent the trees from being sawn down, they would sit in them.

Climbing an old-growth Douglas fir is not simple, given the fact that the first branch can be fifty to one hundred feet above the climber's head. The Earth First! contingent knew little about the spurs and looped lanyards that loggers use and most lacked the skill to try them. Instead, they improvised. One method was to fire an arrow with a light line attached across the lowest branch. A climbing rope was then pulled over the branch, and the protesters scrambled up. Another method was to pound climbing pitons into the tree. Either method took a fair amount of strength. Moreover, the trees would sway and sometimes creak in the wind. The experience is not for those who suffer vertigo.

The protesters hauled small platforms up after themselves to nest on. Given that there were more trees than demonstrators, some flung ropes with grappling hooks from their platforms to adjacent trees so that if any went over their roost would be yanked with it. Some would go even further. A woman named Valerie Wade, fearful that loggers were going to drop a neighboring tree anyway, tied a noose from it around her neck and dared them to saw. They didn't.

What Friedman remembers chiefly about being up in the trees was the cold. It was early spring, and he spent several days up the tree in a sleeping bag before coming down. Some protesters spent up to twenty-one days. Finally a truce seemed to have been arranged after a lawsuit against the logging company had been filed. The protesters climbed down after being assured no cutting would take place without two weeks' notice. Meanwhile, a judge was scheduled to rule on the legal challenge to the harvest on a Tuesday after the Easter weekend. Instead, the logging company sent a small army of loggers into the grove that Monday. In a single day, they cut every tree down. The judge, reasoning that the legal issue had become moot, dismissed the case.

Things accelerated quickly for Friedman. He was arrested ten times in the next three years. Most jail stays were overnight at worst, but one judge locked him in the Grants Pass, Oregon, jail for twelve days.

For protection he made friends with the inmate he judged was the toughest there, a safe picker. He found his crude surroundings to be educational. "It's enjoyable in some ways," he said of his brief time behind bars. "I think everybody should go to jail." That remains a minority view, however. Draffan estimates only about one hundred people in Washington State's Earth First! contingent were frontline demonstrators, and many of those—including Draffan himself—were not willing to be arrested. Even those who did usually had to back off eventually under the weight of the establishment; many accumulated enough probation violations that they faced stiff prison sentences if arrested again.

In 1987, Friedman saw his first spotted owl. Washington's Wenatchee National Forest had announced plans to log an area called Swauk Meadow. The Sunday night before logging was to begin a group of Earth First! activists camped in the grove. That evening a spotted owl swooped in and roosted near these humans who were determined to save its trees. Atheist or no, Friedman took this as a sign he was on the right track.

"We woke up Monday morning to chainsaws," he said. He and a companion quickly dashed down a logging road to call Seattle television stations, then moved back to blockade the cutting. As cameras rolled, the protesters were arrested. "That was the first demonstration to specifically protect spotted owls," Friedman said.

Friedman saw another sign of natural approval after another demonstration in Yellowstone National Park. He participated in a group trying to close the popular Fishing Bridge campground because of increasing conflicts between campers and bears. The Earth First! contingent reasoned the bears were there first, and should have priority.

Some of the campers were furious at the blockade. An officer in a local recreational vehicle club decided to bulldoze the bearded demonstrators out of the way with his motor home. Gunning the engine, he rumbled forward. Friedman's group stood their ground. The motor home driver was clearly visible through the windshield: seething, his face red, his hands in a stiff-armed grip of fury on the steering wheel, his mood beyond reason. The vehicle lurched forward, bumping into the protesters' chests. They stepped back a pace. The motor home edged forward again, butting them. Again they stepped back. "Down, down, turn around, sit, sit!" somebody shouted. Friedman turned his back on the motor home and sat on the hot pavement. His comrades did likewise. The motor home bumper grazed up to the back of his neck. Just as he remembers the cold of Millennium Grove, he remembers the heat of Fishing Bridge: the rumbling of the engine, the hot smell of its exhaust, the black pavement frying in the summer sun. For ten or fifteen minutes the infuriated camper refused to switch off his engine. The protesters refused to move. The standoff stretched into a seeming eternity, the heat waves radiating off the pavement. Finally the engine went off. Rangers and police had come. Instead of being run over, the protesters were arrested.

On their way to jail at the north end of the park in a park bus, they passed a grizzly sow and two cubs by the side of the road. Such a sight has become a rarity since the park garbage dumps have closed and tourists have stopped offering food to bears. "The driver said it was the only time since he'd worked the park that he's seen that, the grizzly bears right near the road like that," Friedman said. He took it as another sign.

By 1988, Friedman's protest group had coined a motto: "If you're not irreverent, you're irrelevant."

But as empowering as protest can seem to be, it can also be wearying and distracting. The Earth First! protests, starting in what to environmentalists were the dark days of the early Reagan administration, had made their point. "Maybe the old-growth issue had gotten to where it's mainstream," Draffan remarked in 1990. The heart of the struggle began to shift to the state capitals, Washington, D.C., and the nation at large.

Friedman's approach changed at the same time. By 1988 he had moved from Seattle to Bellingham, Washington, near the Canadian border, and had formed a group called the Greater Ecosystem Alliance. The organization was Friedman's reaction to the kind of ecological research being done by scientists such as Forsman and Franklin. Increasingly it appeared that existing parks and wilderness areas were not well designed to adequately protect important ecosystems such as old-growth forests. Most preserves took in high-elevation alpine terrain but did not include many of the valleys wildlife migrated to in the wintertime. Nor did they protect watersheds to preserve stream quality, or govern timber harvesting and grazing to keep an ecosystem balanced. The new group's first effort was a book called *Forever Wild* that called for a staggeringly huge 8.2 million-acre wilderness in the North Cascade Mountains.

By the end of 1990 Friedman's new group had a back-of-the-building office in downtown Bellingham, but *Forever Wild* was being rewritten.

Simply designating more wilderness was not the point, Friedman had concluded. Existing parks and wilderness areas, he estimated, represented at best perhaps half the original natural ecosystems in the United States. "That's not radical anymore," he said of wilderness designation. What American society needed to do, he was concluding, was not just set aside more preserves but manage all land in an ecosystem—including cities, farms, and commercial forest land—to preserve ecological values. Essentially, Friedman said, people had to discover the correct rate of "sustainable extraction" and modify civilization to fit. To a degree he agreed with Jerry Franklin, Friedman said: "Let's manage the areas better that we've already messed up." Environmentalists had to persuade Congress, he said, that "Congress can't mandate the survival of species by law." The nation was going at its goals backward. It was waiting for species to reach a crisis point and then trying to protect them individually, instead of modifying human development to coexist with the natural world.

"It really comes down to ecosystem sustainability," Friedman said. "We're piecing together a complex puzzle. We know enough that we need to act. Industry argues that if we don't have certainty about every scientific issue we should continue to log. We argue that if we don't have certainty, we need to stop logging until we do. Eric Forsman was talking about protecting spotted owls in 1973," and full protection had yet to be implemented seventeen years later. "What we're doing so far is only slowing the exponential rate of abuse."

What about communities such as Forks? Friedman's own frugal, outdoor-oriented life-style is closer to that of rural loggers than of urban Seattle environmentalists. But he argues that a heedless harvest can't be permitted to continue just to preserve the cultural artifact of Northwest logging communities.

"We've fouled it up," he said gloomily of the human record on earth. "We've throttled evolution. There isn't enough genetic material, there isn't enough habitat, and at the same time we're changing the climate. Something's got to give. It's like we're tapping the brakes when we're headed ninety miles per hour towards a brick wall."

10

NOBODY TO BLAME

▲▲▲▲▲▲▲

Considering that it is a meeting to foment a polite revolution, the gathering in the basement of the Chimacum Community Center on the eastern end of the Olympic Peninsula is disappointingly small. Only eight Forest Service employees have shown up this October evening of 1990 to discuss reform of their agency with Jeff DeBonis, a former agency employee who describes himself as a "timber beast" turned tree hugger. Only two of the Olympic National Forest employees are year-round, full-time. Even the setting seems a bit prosaic for the formation of a cabal. The room is lit a bright, sterile white by fluorescent fixtures, and a couple of freezers hum in the background. Still, it is a start.

DeBonis sent a shock wave through the Forest Service two years before, first by publicly condemning his agency's rapid harvest of old-growth trees and then by forming an in-house organization called the Association of Forest Service Employees for Environmental Ethics (AFSEEE). DeBonis did what was long considered taboo by bringing employee discontent out into the open.

He is a symbol of the dissension about ancient forests that, as the decade turned, was tearing asunder the unity of one of the proudest agencies of the federal government. DeBonis subsequently quit the Forest Service to run his rebel group full-time. While he has had some initial successes, he is finding it difficult to convince public employees to move beyond the complaint stage and agitate regularly from within for a more environmental approach to forest management. Some think the rebel has gone from initial thoughtful criticism of forest policy to automatically opposing anything the Forest Service does.

The employee who invited DeBonis to come up from his base in Portland, Oregon, is Stan Betts, a recreation specialist on the north-

161

eastern Olympic Forest. Betts is distressed by the annihilation of old growth and the emphasis on timber receipts. "Some of us are members of the Lake Wobegon National Forest," he told DeBonis.

Another of those present, Kurt Ralston, has come from the Forest Service office in Forks. Agency insiders call employees such as the bearded, ponytailed Ralston, "combat biologists," or wildlife managers who frequently lock horns with the timber sale supervisors they sit next to in the office. Ralston transferred to the Forks Ranger District office from Oregon in order to get a permanent job as a fish biologist, but some of his friends were surprised by his move. "You're going to Forks?" they asked. "You're going back to the 1950s." The same day he got the job an Oregon newspaper painted an unflattering picture of the town. Several colleagues sent him copies of the feature story in the mail. "I looked on it as a challenge," he explained. "I was really committed to change."

DeBonis smiles in understanding as the people in the group are introduced. "I believed a lot of people felt like I did—they were frustrated and wanted to make changes," he begins. DeBonis has the restless zeal of the reformer. At age thirty-nine he is slightly built with short hair, animated eyes and hands, and quickness in both words and thought. His coiled excitement is a bit reminiscent of a kid waiting to spring for recess. Like so many people, DeBonis has been powerfully affected by the trees he works in, and now he has given up his Forest Service career, income, and pension for them. When he quit he used his savings to keep AFSEEE going, and moved to a bare-bones apartment to shave costs.

His organization "is the first time government employees have organized internally for a cause," DeBonis says. "It's a model. If we fail, we set a precedent for this idea failing. We're really under the spotlight."

The whole idea of government employees trying to influence policy strikes some as wayward. The civil service is supposed to carry out policy, not make it, they argue. DeBonis's vision of from-the-grass-roots-up kind of management influence seemed to some as subversive, and far from constructive. Moreover, the Forest Service historically has inspired an institutional loyalty. The agency's first director, Gifford Pinchot, an eastern aristocrat and intimate of President Theodore Roosevelt, created an agency self-image of principled stewardship, a contrast to the cut-and-run practices of the nineteenth-century timber industry. People who loved the forest for its own sake were drawn to the agency. Employees entered a kind of priesthood of conservation. There was at least in image an internal esprit, like the Marine Corps. John Nelson, a Forest Service timber manager for the Olympic National Forest, started in the agency at age eighteen. "I wear green shorts," he said. "We've been in this job of managing resources a long time, and probably do it better than anybody else in the world."

DeBonis believed that, too. He joined after a stint in the Peace Corps; the Forest Service attracted that kind of idealism. "I was so sure the Forest Service was a great organization I didn't believe what my intuition was telling me," he said of his first exposure to clearcutting. "You buy into a bureaucracy and shut out the influences telling you that what you are doing is not right."

DeBonis grew up in Bedford, Massachusetts, where he played and explored in the eastern hardwoods. His idealism and attitude of challenging authority developed early: he criticized his land-developer father when he was fourteen years old. As a teenager, he read environmental classics such as Rachel Carson's *Silent Spring*. He went to Colorado State University in Fort Collins to earn his forestry degree and then joined the Peace Corps, serving two years in El Salvador. In Central America, he saw the severe erosion caused by slash-and-burn agriculture that was converting the jungle to wasteland. Up to 80 percent of the forest cover was gone, with disastrous results. DeBonis also worked briefly for the Agency for International Development in Ecuador's upper Amazon basin. He came back to the United States with a desire to protect the forests here. He joined what he had always assumed was the planet's premiere forest caretaker, the U.S. Forest Service.

What DeBonis expected and what he found were dramatically different. He started in the Kootenai National Forest in Montana and was astounded at the clearcutting and slash burning. It reminded him of El Salvador. When he warned of the threat of erosion, he was told the Forest Service knew what it was doing. Later, DeBonis concluded his first worries had been correct and that the heavy clearcutting was allowing rain and snow melt to wash fertile soil into Montana's trout streams.

Still, any organization stamps its mind-set on its members, and in the 1960s and 1970s the Forest Service had taken on some of the coloration of the timber industry, displaying a Paul Bunyan machismo at punching roads into the wilderness and converting "decadent" older forests. The agency had become alarmed at studies that argued up to three-quarters of the trees in Northwest old-growth forests were decayed, broken, leaning, diseased, or otherwise showing the infirmities of old age. Under the assumptions of the time, the forest would be improved if these trees were cut down. DeBonis succumbed to this atmosphere and pitched into his new career with enthusiasm, in short order becoming what he would later despise, a "timber beast," expert at getting the cut out.

He remembered preparing a timber sale on a mountain that served as the watershed for surrounding ranches and farms. When residents objected, DeBonis assured them that this clearcut on just part of the mountain would be the only one, leaving enough trees to preserve water quality. It was a promise he had no power to keep. DeBonis was transferred and when he called back a couple years later he learned additional sales were being prepared. Though it was unwitting, he felt he had misled the public he was supposed to serve.

DeBonis's enthusiastic swing toward pumping out timber sales ended with a clash with a wildlife biologist named Ernie Garcia. Initially friends, the two became increasingly estranged as Garcia saw the idealistic former Peace Corps member evolve into a timber enthusiast. Their relationship finally blew up in a clash over DeBonis's insistence at cutting a stand of trees used by mule deer as winter habitat. Garcia's bitter words forced DeBonis to take stock of what he stood for. "He startled me out of my brief period of being blinded," he said of his friend. DeBonis began to question the intellectual honesty of his own role as a timber sale planner. While new laws forced planners to consider environmental issues, "The basic job was getting a lot of data to justify timber cutting." DeBonis realized that the agency he loved was not as he had idealized it. He began to speak out for other forest values such as wildlife.

DeBonis transferred to the Nez Perce National Forest in Idaho, where he was impressed by supervisor Tom Kovalicky's ability to strike a balance that satisfied both the area's environmentalists and loggers. Then DeBonis went to Oregon, making the transfer with apprehension. "I knew it was the timber beast capital of the world," he said of the Douglas fir empire west of the Cascade Mountains. Nowhere else in the United States were the timber volumes so high and the public profits so great as in the final forest of the Pacific Northwest. The Willamette National Forest where DeBonis worked was the biggest timber producer in the nation. From the air, its polka-dot pattern of clearcuts made the forest look like a target used for machine gun practice. DeBonis became increasingly critical of his agency. "The Forest Service sees the timber industry as its ally, and environmentalists as its enemies," he said. "Our own scientists were telling us in the mid-1970s that we were in trouble over the spotted owl. We ignored them. We've been totally neglecting our job."

Moreover, the agency seemed to view the general public as a bothersome blob to be kept at bay while the important work of old-growth liquidation and replanting went on. The participation process too often became a time-consuming sham, DeBonis felt. "The way the planning process works is to wear the public down," he said. "There are a lot of hoops people have to jump through. We listen, and then don't pay any attention to them." Many of his colleagues agreed with his criticism but remained loyal to the agency, arguing it was slowly changing.

Impatient for reform, DeBonis decided to take the kind of action that could destroy his career. In September of 1988, during a hike through the Three Sisters Wilderness in Willamette National Forest, DeBonis and a companion hit on the idea of forming an in-house employee organization to push for agency reform. In early 1989 he composed a blistering attack on the Forest Service's record and alleged lack of balance, addressed it to Chief Dale Robertson, and sent it out for general consumption over the agency's computer net. He followed up that summer with the first publication of *Inner Voice*, a newsletter aimed at enlisting members into AFSEEE. In it, he reprinted the letter to Robertson, along with other employee letters, comments, and explanation. "Are you a frustrated Forest Service employee because your resource ethics conflict with your job?" the headline on the newsletter's front page asked. "Are you afraid to speak out for what you know is ecologically right? Do you feel isolated and alone because of your resource ethics? Do you think the Forest Service needs to become a more ecologically sensitive organization? Would you like to help promote this kind of change within the agency?"

An enormous run of 100,000 copies was mailed to every Forest Service employee and ranger district in the nation. The timber industry was upset enough to try to get DeBonis fired, but he had been careful to adhere to civil service rules about political involvement. Still, it became clear he didn't have time to both do his Forest Service job and run his new organization. While he said little direct pressure was applied by his bosses to discourage him, his rebellion drew the attention of the media and he was becoming one of the most widely quoted critics of his employer. "It was harder and harder to live with my split life. Basically, my job was to help liquidate the last ten percent of the temperate rain forest." Early in 1990 he quit his job to devote himself full-time to AFSEEE.

The Forest Service he had criticized did not shun DeBonis or try to forbid his organization. In fact, Chief Robertson assigned a key deputy to head an office spearheading experimentation with "New Perspectives" and advised him to contact DeBonis for advice. Still, DeBonis did not think the Forest Service was institutionally capable of internal reform. It needed a push from the bottom. "I think the Forest Service has made changes," he said, "but not nearly enough fast enough, in my opinion."

So now he has brought his crusade to tiny Chimacum, seeking enlistments with the righteous indignation of the onetime believer who feels he has been betrayed.

"I think the value system for this forest is very much timber industry dominated," DeBonis tells those gathered. "What we basically believe is that the Forest Service has lost the position it historically had in the conservation movement. We want to see the Forest Service become an advocate for the environment."

The personal goals of this Forest Service rebel are dramatic. DeBonis wants to stop all timber harvesting on federal land—period—to give the land time to recover. Failing that—and he is the first to admit an end to logging on the national forests is unlikely—he wants the annual cut to drop by half. That would give foresters the breathing room to try some of Jerry Franklin's New Forestry ideas, he said. "New Forestry, or New Perspectives, is something we should have been doing after passage of the 1976 National Forest Management Act," he said. To do it now, with so few old-growth trees left, "they're going to have to lower the cut by fifty percent to make New Perspectives work. Otherwise, it's all smoke and mirrors."

The night before, DeBonis had drawn about sixty people to the Peninsula town of Sequim to hear him expound on these themes. This second meeting was aimed strictly at employees, to try to get them to form a chapter of his organization. The only way the reformers can ultimately be successful, DeBonis believes, is to be active in every forest, looking over every timber sale. He has just launched a chapter in North Carolina and is now on the Olympic Peninsula, trying to drum up support for another one. Six more are in existence. AFSEEE's newsletter has a circulation of 25,000 and his organization has a membership of 4,500, about 1,600 of them current agency employees. That is about 5 percent of the Forest Service. "They say eight to ten percent is the critical mass to make changes in an organization," he says.

The initial organizational drive has lost a bit of steam and AFSEEE's membership has leveled off. One of DeBonis's problems is that his advice is starting to be taken. The new forest plans recently completed to the dictates of the 1976 National Forest Management Act, coupled with spotted owl habitat conservation areas, are already dropping the cut by up to 50 percent of its historic level in the Pacific Northwest (though Congress set an immediate harvest target that is only about 40 percent lower).

Moreover, the Forest Service is far more diverse than it once was. DeBonis's plea that the agency turn to environmentalists as its natural political constituency, instead of the timber industry, is already a trend, and the agency is awkwardly straddling both camps and pleasing neither.

But DeBonis is still skeptical. The Forest Service has lived so long on the aura of its early years, he says, and has so resolutely burnished its public relations, that even its leaders have difficulty separating the agency's evergreen image from its stump reality. "It has been politicized."

The Forest Service's budget, the number of its personnel, and its employee evaluation and promotion system are all based on harvesting trees, DeBonis notes. The more trees sold and logging roads built, the bigger the agency has to be. The Forest Service tells its critics whatever they want to hear, and then cuts, and cuts, and cuts. Congress becomes caught up in this, authorizing a big cut to court favor with timber communities and bring in federal revenue. The harvest ceiling the agency and Congress agree to—supposedly set as the maximum that can be cut while still ensuring a sustained yield of wood over time—becomes an unspoken floor, the goal every district ranger strives to meet.

"If we had a chief with spine, a risk-taking attitude, he might do it," says DeBonis. "We need a kamikaze chief. We need a chief who believes in the tenet of Gifford Pinchot: 'Go to work every day expecting to be fired.' He says he wants to do the right thing, but he doesn't do the right thing."

Such talk has not endeared DeBonis to either the agency's leadership or the timber industry. DeBonis's critics think he goes overboard. Mark Rey, executive director of the timber industry's American Forest Resource Alliance, told the *Seattle Times* that DeBonis is "a professional disgruntled Forest Service employee, as opposed to a disgruntled professional Forest Service employee."

But employees frustrated by the Forest Service's bureaucratic inertia are responsive. Within two months of DeBonis's visit, three Forest Service employees including Betts were drafting a set of goals for the Olympic National Forest an AFSEEE chapter would pursue. One was to reduce the timber harvest. Another was to guarantee the right of Olympic employees to speak out. The third was to experiment with collecting revenue from forest users besides timbermen. "A lot of mistakes the Forest Service makes comes from its budget structure," said Betts. "Too much of the budget is linked to timber harvesting."

To understand Bett's criticism, one has to understand something about the Forest Service. The United States is a country that started out with nearly all its land in public ownership, and until the frontier closed at the end of the nineteenth century, the government's goal was to encourage homesteaders, railroads, or other private concerns to acquire such land and develop it. Private exploitation of timber in New England, the South, and the Great Lakes had been brutal and shortsighted, however, so in 1891 Congress created the first Forest Reserves from unoccupied land in the West. As the name implied, these forests were reserved to avert the "timber famine" expected when logging of private land was completed. This system evolved over the next fifteen years into the Forest Service.

In the twentieth century, the agency's ability to supply rural, wood-dependent communities with timber gave it a powerful economic, cultural, and political bond with the timber industry. A community's fortune rose and fell with federal timber policy. So much forest land is publicly owned in the West that without federal and state timber sales, a town such as Forks has little economic reason for existence.

Several laws have helped refine the mission of the Forest Service, however, away from unbridled logging. In 1937, for example, Congress directed it to pursue a policy of "sustained yield," in which on average no more wood would be cut each year than could be replaced with growth, ensuring a steady wood supply forever. (Actual calculations of sustained yield produce important but arcane debates among experts that can seem to a layman as convoluted as medieval controversy over how many angels can dance on the head of a pin. Environmentalists have alleged for decades that the Forest Service cooks its numbers to cut timber faster than can be sustained.)

In 1960 Congress directed the Forest Service to follow a policy of "multiple use" in which it managed the forests for multiple goals besides timber, such as recreation or wildlife. In 1964 the Wilderness Act set aside some of the most pristine parts of the national forests into wildernesses protected from logging. In 1969 Congress passed the National Environmental Policy Act requiring the Forest Service to justify its management decisions with hearings and environmental impact statements. In 1973 the Endangered Species Act was passed, and in 1976 the National Forest Management Act reinforced the idea of "multiple use."

As a result the federal government has national parks and wilderness areas, where logging is prohibited, and national forests, where it can occur. To complicate things further, portions of the national forests that are particularly fragile, remote, scenic, or used for recreation can also be protected from logging under forest plans.

Today, the United States has 159 national forests totalling about 187 million acres. The most profitable of these are in Region Six, the Douglas fir empire of Washington and Oregon. The federal forests in the two states make up only 13 pecent of the total system but until the spotted owl restrictions they produced more than 40 percent of the wood cut and more than half the timber revenue. The Pacific Northwest's ancient forest has been the federal government's timber cash cow. Within Region Six, the 627,000-acre Olympic National Forest wrapped around Olympic National Park is the smallest of nineteen forests. It is also one of the most heavily harvested.

In 1989, a Wilderness Society ecologist named Peter Morrison (another former and disillusioned Forest Service employee) began doing computer studies of the remaining old-growth forest in western Washington and Oregon, using Forest Service data. His conclusions about the Olympic Peninsula were stunningly grim. Morrison estimated there were about 2 million acres of old growth on the Peninsula when pioneers arrived. About 318,000 acres are left, he calculated, with 70 percent of what remains already preserved in Olympic National Park. Since World War II, Morrison said, the Forest Service had harvested 76 percent of the ancient trees on Olympic National Forest, leaving just 94,000 acres of old growth on its share of the Peninsula's land. Low-elevation old growth—the truly big trees—have become even rarer. Just 36,700 acres have survived.

Ted Stubblefield, supervisor of the Olympic National Forest at the time, did not like the Wilderness Society study. It defines old growth too narrowly, Stubblefield argued. Still, there is no question that the natural forest on the Peninsula has been dramatically transformed, and transformed so quickly that logging communities such as Forks became artificially bloated by the once-huge harvest and now are lopsidedly desperate. While national forest harvests as a whole in Region Six have fallen by half, since the 1970s the proposed annual harvest on the Olympic National Forest has fallen even faster, plunging an incredible 90 percent. The forest went from a peak harvest of about 400 million board feet to just 40 million. (In 1991, a temporary court injuction issued until the Forest Service completed an owl protection plan reduced the cut further almost to zero, but that reduction was not expected to be permanent.)

It is difficult to claim such a 90 percent decline is a pattern of "sustained yield." However, the Forest Service does its best to try.

The Olympic is an unusual forest. First, the heart was set aside in the 1930s to create Olympic National Park. Logging is prohibited in national parks and, as Morrison's study suggests, that complicates any debate about how much surviving old growth is enough. The 318,000 acres of old growth remaining on the Olympic Peninsula, while only 16 percent of what once existed, is not negligible. If the park has most of that surviving old growth already, does it matter what happens to the fragments outside its boundaries? Owl scientists such as Eric Forsman contend that it does. The Park is high and steep. The birds don't ridge-hop across the alpine terrain from one forested valley to another. To move, mate, and prevent genetic inbreeding, the owls depend on the donut of lower-elevation Forest Service land outside the park for winter range and to migrate. Environmentalists like to turn the question around: *Isn't 84 percent of the original forest already converted to tree farming and development enough? How much does the timber industry need?*

The second oddity is that the southeastern corner of the Olympic National Forest was transformed, by act of Congress, into a kind of private fiefdom for the Simpson Logging Company. On March 29, 1944, a law was passed allowing "sustained yield units" to be created on federal forests. This bizarre, controversial law was designed to give individual companies a monopoly on huge "units" of public timber in return for the companies guaranteeing that they would process the wood locally. The ostensible reason behind the law was that it would assure the stability of nearby timber communities. Simpson applied for a unit two days after the act was passed and, after some stormy public hearings, got one in 1946.

In effect the agreement joined Simpson's private land on the Peninsula with the public forest for the next one hundred years. By the end of World War II, Simpson was nearing the end of logging on its own land, and the purpose of the agreement was to ensure that federal timber could take its place for the next forty to fifty years. By the time the National Forest timber was exhausted, Simpson's should be regrown. Meanwhile, the towns of Shelton and McNary would have stable employment.

It was a cozy arrangement destined to be repeated nowhere else in the United States. It had two controversial consequences: it artificially inflated the harvest of Olympic National Forest old growth beyond normal sustained yield levels, and it gave Simpson a bidding monopoly that probably saved the company a small fortune—although whenever federal forest supervisors suggested this, the company unleashed a flood of statistics that argued the prices it paid were within industry norms. In any event, the 100 million board feet taken out of the Olympic Forest for Simpson alone each year was too much to be sustained. It was designed as a onetime timber bonanza to fill a local "timber gap" and protect the economy of two towns.

The Simpson deal is one reason the forest's annual harvest has fallen so drastically. By the early 1980s the peak harvest of 400 million board feet had already fallen to about 350 million as the timber-rich old-growth groves disappeared, as additions were made to Olympic National Park, and as sustained yield was recalculated. Then came completion of Forest Service harvesting on its Simpson unit. In just forty years, the old growth in the forest's southeastern corner was gone. Almost overnight, the annual federal harvest dropped to 250 million board feet.

The drop in Olympic National Forest harvest continued. In 1984 Congress added 88,000 acres of wilderness that could not be logged to the Olympic Forest, and as a result the timberland base on which the annual allowable cut is calculated declined. Less commercial forest means less can be harvested each year on a sustainable basis. As a result, the annual cut dropped to 185 million board feet.

Then the owl debate began, and that introduced the third oddity of the Olympic National Forest. When it comes to the owl the Olympic Peninsula is a peculiar case: in effect, an ecological island. Elsewhere in the Pacific Northwest, owls forced out of one area by heavy logging could presumably migrate to adjacent forests. The Peninsula was different. To the west and north were the ocean and Strait of Juan de Fuca, to the east was Puget Sound and the state's urban corridor, and to the south were the completely logged Willapa Hills, where virtually no old-growth timber favorable to owls existed at all. The Olympic owls couldn't move. Effectively, they were marooned on the Peninsula. Because of that, and because 84 percent of the Peninsula's old growth was eliminated, the owl was considered in more danger of extinction there than anyplace else.

As a result the Forest Service initially proposed dropping the annual cut on the forest to about 135 million board feet to protect the owl. Appeals by environmentalists drove that down to 111 million board feet. Then the recommendation of Jack Ward Thomas and his committee said even the environmental appeal was inadequate. The Thomas committee pushed it down further to 40 million board feet.

Locals thought somebody must have made a bookkeeping error. For the cut to decline by a third, even half, perhaps they could understand. But 90 percent? They felt dumbfounded and betrayed.

"We don't have anyplace to go" for wood, Stubblefield explained. Most of the forest was either cut over or designated for wilderness and owls. Already, those owls that had been found were discovered to be "packing," or overpopulating, the remaining islands of old growth. An ecosystem had been reduced to an archipelago of remnant survivors.

Yet the obvious question is whether a federal agency that goes from a harvest of 400 million board feet to 40 million in little over a decade has been a good land steward. Did the Forest Service demonstrate foresight? Or did it plan narrowly, focusing on only the single goal of timber and failing to foresee that as old growth shrank, public demand to save the remainder would grow? Stubblefield argued the Olympic Forest is a victim of peculiar circumstance, not bad planning.

Community stability has been one of the fundamental goals of the Forest Service. Back in 1911, George Cecil at Region Six headquarters in Portland wrote that, "Communities will depend upon the National Forests for a steady supply of timber and if we cannot meet this demand, we will have failed in our mission. . . . [It is] doubly important that we regulate national forest cuttings with the greatest consideration for the future welfare of the local communities."

Unfortunately, after World War II the region calculated its annual cut on the assumption that all its prime timberland would be available for harvest for the foreseeable future, completely failing to predict the drive for wilderness and wildlife preserves. As a result, the declining cut came to be seen as a broken promise. Timber manager Nelson remembers hosting meetings around the Peninsula to tell loggers that the 1989 cut was projected to be only half that of the year before because of the owl. "Those were pretty stressful meetings. Up until then, folks weren't paying all that much attention."

Public officials contend that Forks was repeatedly warned what to expect. The federal government's Pacific Northwest Regional Planning Committee, cited earlier, had predicted in 1938 that timber depletion would occur between 1980 and 1990, given the rate of harvest. While that specific study was forgotten by most, the idea that the federal harvest would have to slow was commonplace in Forks by the mid-1970s.

The same trend was inevitable on state timberland, which also had become crucial for Forks's harvest. The state commissioner of Public Lands in the 1970s, Bert Cole, gave a speech in 1979 in Forks warning that the high harvests on state lands would inevitably go down as the old growth disappeared. "We had a meeting [with the chamber of commerce] in Forks," recalled E. C. Gockerel, the manager of the state's Department of Natural Resources regional office there. "We told them, 'Our cut is going down.' " There was little reaction, Gockerel said. "They said thank you for telling us, and left." Cole's successor, Brian Boyle, told them the same thing in the early 1980s.

In 1987, Stubblefield issued his own warning. When Clallam County Commissioner Lawrence Gaydeski, irked at the plunging national forest harvest level, asked that the annual cut be set higher, Stubblefield explained to a group of loggers at Forks that the only way to do this—given the land being set aside for owls and ancient forest preservation—was to cut without any regard for future supply. "You can pay me now, or pay me later, I told them. Are you in this for the short haul or the long haul? All of a sudden the lights went off in the meeting room and everyone left. No one supported the departure alternative" of cutting without regard to sustained yield.

The picture was no better on private land. The Olympic Peninsula's old growth had enormous value and zero net growth, and industry was anxious to get it cut and regrowing. ITT-Rayonier, which cut about 180 million to 200 million board feet around Forks in the 1970s, was down to 80 million board feet per year by 1990 and expected the cut to drop to 40 million or less by the year 2000, with or without the owl. These precipitous declines are hard for some to accept. "There are a lot of people who didn't want change and won't accept it," said Stubblefield. "They are going through the mourning process of denial."

The fact Forest Service harvests are dropping so rapidly throughout the Northwest is evidence to critics that it ignored other forest values for too long. Now the logging industry is paying for the agency's postwar cutting spree, they contend.

Some who have investigated the agency in detail find it pretty much guilty as charged as a "timber beast." In his history *Timber and the Forest Service*, author David Clary argued that the Forest Service's popular image as a conserver of Western forests was subverted almost from the beginning. Early in this century the nation's trees were being cut four times faster than they grew. With such overharvesting proceeding on private land from 1900 to the Great Depression, the national forests were seen almost from the beginning as a backup reservoir. The wood industry would turn to it when its own lands were cut out and regrowing, thus avoiding a "timber famine." Early on, political alliances were forged between the Forest Service and the timber industry and its rural communities dependent on wood production. Once markets and roads created the opportunity following World War II, Clary found, the Forest Service had the institutional and scientific bias for rapid clearcutting in the Pacific Northwest.

In the 1960s and 1970s, Clary argued, the Forest Service's claims of "multiple use" of the nation's forests "were fine words, but as became increasingly apparent over the next two decades, what the Forest Service said and what it really believed were not always the same. Timber remained the agency's principal focus, and 'forestry as propaganda'— now dressed up as 'information and education'—remained its principal way of dealing with the world." Clary quotes a 1965 plan for the Willamette National Forest in Oregon that celebrated logging as a means to encourage recreation via logging roads, and a way to increase game populations via the brush that replaced what had once been forest. The plan doggedly contended that "clearcuts break the monotony of the scene."

In his book, *Reforming the Forest Service*, economic consultant Randall O'Toole took this criticism a step further. O'Toole presented a complicated and exhaustive argument seeking to prove that the Forest Service, like most bureaucracies, is a "budget maximizer": almost unconsciously, it tends to do whatever will sustain and increase its own budget and employees. The means for this, under the system Congress has created, is the sale of timber. The fault, O'Toole argues, is a system that only rewards foresters for the wood they produce, not the arguably equal values of wildlife, tourism, watershed protection, and so on. He proposes, among other things, to charge recreationists user fees to give the agency economic incentive to manage the woods for other purposes. By the beginning of the 1990s, O'Toole was trying to find ten national forests, primarily in the East, to put his ideas into effect on an experimental basis.

Biologist Jack Ward Thomas, a Forest Service employee, believes analyses such as O'Toole's are a little too pat and mechanistic, that agencies and the people who work in them are motivated by more than economic systems. "I've never seen any agency with more people desperately wanting to do right than the Forest Service," he said. What happened, he said, is that for decades, cutting timber was the right thing: the nation needed the wood and there was little alternative use of the forest. Now that has changed. Recreationists crowd trails and wildlife is under increasing human pressure.

"We're confused," said Thomas. "We used to be good guys, and somebody changed the rules. Now the Forest Service is in the process of a great transition." A new generation represented by people such as DeBonis is challenging all the old dogmas. "This myth of the omniscient forester—we don't believe that anymore," Thomas said. "The world has turned out to be more complicated than we thought."

Al Burkhardt, the timber supervisor for the nineteen forests in Region Six, contends that the allegation the Forest Service overcut its lands ignores the way its land base has been modified by Congress.

To explain, he gave a rough acreage inventory of the Pacific Northwest's federal forests. Region Six national forests have 24 million acres in all. Of that, 21 million acres are actually trees, the remainder being alpine meadows, grazed clearings, water, and so forth. Of the 21 million, some 18 million acres have large enough trees and good enough soils to rank as commercial forest land. Finally, the Forest Service designated about two-thirds of this base after World War II as truly harvestable: the rest was too pretty, too steep, too wet, too important to wildlife, too remote, and so on to reasonably assume it could be or should be logged. That remaining 12 million acres—half the total acreage in the forests—could in theory produce 5.2 billion board feet of timber each year forever, under sustained yield calculations. The forest could regrow that much wood each year.

That timbered land base has steadily eroded since then, Burkhardt pointed out, as acreage is subtracted for wilderness areas, new parks and monuments, additional wildlife preserves, and so on. Particularly schizophrenic was Congress, which would please the environmental lobby one day by designating wilderness, and then please the timber lobby the next by setting an artificially high harvest level. Investigation by the Portland *Oregonian*, for example, showed that in 1986 Congress ordered the Forest Service to sell 700 million board feet more than the agency suggested; in 1987 it ordered an extra billion board feet; in 1988 the increase was 300 million, in 1989 200 million. In 1990 1.1 billion board feet were freed from court injunctions obtained to protect the spotted owl, and in 1991 Congress ordered a cut 500 million board feet above what the Forest Service thought it could sustain, given the recommendations for owl protection.

Congress was not entirely cynical. Averaged across the decade, Congressionally mandated timber sales were below Burkhardt's 5.2 billion board foot level. The problem was, the 5.2 billion target was obsolete. The same Northwest politicians pushing for higher harvest levels had backed wilderness withdrawals from the land base. As more land was set aside it became increasingly difficult for the Forest Service to provide the kind of wood supply Northwest communities had become accustomed to. By 1989, Burkhardt's office calculated the annual sustainable cut had fallen to 3.4 billion board feet.

The addition of owl-habitat conservation areas dropped the Forest Service's recommended annual sales even further, to 2.6 billion board feet, or half of what it was before. Congress pegged the goal at 3.1 billion board feet anyway in an attempt to soften the owl's impact on towns such as Forks, again postponing realistic harvest planning.

Meanwhile, Stubblefield tried to explain to his Peninsula constituents that society as a whole is unhappy using the national forests solely as a wood lot. "I told them the interest in this issue is larger than the Northwest," he said. "It was a paradigm shift. Values have changed. The population of the Puget Sound basin has changed. They are no longer dependent on timber at all. It is Forks that hasn't changed."

Stubblefield sees nothing insidious in either the heavy postwar harvest or its sharp braking today. Both reflected what society wanted, he said. The Forest Service was simply following the law at the time. "There's a vortex now. You have laws calling for preservation and laws calling for wood production. You have laws coming together and conflicting. They are all good laws. There is nobody to blame."

11
THE FORESTER

▲▲▲▲▲▲▲

Most careers result only peripherally in three-dimensional, visible achievement. Few give the worker an opportunity to see in a glance the results of a lifetime of work. Engineers can point to their product sometimes. So can architects, or carpenters, or visual artists. These are the exceptions. Few people can do what Jim Bleck can do, which is to come up to a ridgetop on the Clearwater drainage of the western Olympic Mountains and point to a landscape he has helped to utterly transform in the past two decades.

The years of work are laid out across the expansive panorama like the chapters of a story, each chapter marked by the height of its trees. From where Bleck stands, the ridges of the Clearwater Block roll away eastward toward the higher blue mountains of the Olympics, the white dome of glacial Mount Olympus poking up beyond them. Those high mountains are part of the national park, and not much changed from when the sailing ships of explorers coasted offshore. But the foothills in the foreground are owned by the state of Washington. While the national park and the state timberlands are adjacent to each other, they have been managed as if on different planets. The federal park has been left alone but the old growth on state land has been cut and the ground replanted. It is a rumpled carpet of younger, brighter green.

Bleck, a management forester for the state Department of Natural Resources in Forks, had a bit of trouble one day finding a decent vantage point to show me his work. The young conifers grow so fast in their hundred-plus inches of rain that the landscape always seems to be changing, tricking memory. He paused at a junction in the spaghetti of logging roads, trying to remember which spur led to the view he intended. Not only can the fast-changing young forest confuse direction, but it blocks the view from the old logging roads like a planted hedge. Parking Bleck's truck, we jumped a ditch and walked toward an old landing. The former logging platform was thick with conifers, and trying to get a view from it was like trying to see from the middle of a Christmas tree lot. Accordingly, we changed direction, finally coming to a steep bank to get the vista he was looking for. We saw some patches of recent clearcuts and heard the gunning rumble of a logging truck in a draw far below, but most of this land was harvested a decade or more ago and has grown back in hemlock and Douglas fir.

"It isn't all raped, it isn't all barren," Bleck said proudly. "It's a crop that is coming back, and coming back quite fast. Nature heals itself." This view does more than capsulize Bleck's career. It capsulizes Forks's self-image of its forest stewardship.

Bleck came to Forks in 1970, a Port Angeles kid who had tried life in the Air Force and a California railroad repair yard and decided the Peninsula where his Dad had logged wasn't so bad after all.

It didn't seem that way when Bleck was growing up. Dad had been a pulp wood logger out of Port Angeles, the kind of independent who cut for paper the punier trees the big lumber outfits would overlook. It was a hard, economically marginal life. The chainsaw was being developed at the time and a two-man machine came out around World War II. It vibrated and bucked like hell. Bleck's dad and his partner would flip a coin to see who would get the "stinger" end of the machine. The stinger was the end without the motor, and it would jerk the wildest if the saw jammed.

Neither partner liked to climb trees either, which was necessary in the days before steel logging towers. Loggers had to cut the top off a sturdy tree and attach to it the cables and tackle necessary for yarding. Bleck's dad and his partner would flip a coin to see who had to do that, too.

The pair never made much money. Sometimes Bleck's dad, like many loggers of his day, would pile rocks on the bed of his pickup under a heap of cedar shake blocks in hopes of upping his profit when the load was weighed. Logging was a hard profession, he told his son. Cold, wet, and apt to make a man half-deaf and crippled with white finger.

Initially, Bleck followed his father's advice and stayed away from the forest, but he didn't enjoy a stint at repairing railroad freight cars. He decided to return to school; an ambition to be an engineer was discouraged by the mathematics required, so he turned to forestry against some faculty advice. "A counselor told me, 'Forestry is as low as you can go,' " Bleck said. The profession was considered a dumping ground of the sciences, a slow-moving field that didn't lead anywhere. Bleck didn't care. If he wasn't anxious to be physically wrecked by woods work, he was intrigued at the thought of managing the forest. Somehow the dark green woods had gotten under Bleck's skin as a boy, and he wanted to go back to them.

It turned out that forestry didn't prove slow moving or dull at all. Most everything that Bleck was taught in forestry school has since been challenged, one way or another. In the last two decades, he said, "It's been nothing but change." The more old growth disappeared and the further the clearcuts extended, the more changes were proposed to protect the land. "When I came to Forks I was told we want to get all the old growth off in twelve to fifteen years," Bleck recalled. That intention has been reversed. By 1989, the state had agreed to postpone harvest for fifteen years on most of the ancient forest fragments that are left.

The DNR, the oft-derided Department of Nothing Remaining, was different in 1970 when Bleck took his job in Forks. Bert Cole, the onetime Forks schoolteacher and logger turned state Lands Commissioner, did not so much run the department (he had his good old boy deputies to do that) as preside over it. Given the job of converting some of the greatest forest left in the United States to tree farms, Cole became to the timber industry a benevolent baron. No one paid much attention to how the DNR went about its job in the 1960s and early 1970s, so long as the sale of public timber kept filling the state coffers, and it did. The state's Clearwater Block, a region due west of Mount Olympus, was one of the biggest, densest, most untapped forests of old growth left in the state of Washington. Cole would come up during Bleck's first decade in Forks to hunt and play cards and bullshit with the boys who were punching roads into the Block. The DNR measured itself by how much money it could pump into the state budget from timber sales, and the Clearwater was the most lucrative tract of all.

Cole always had some good jokes, and better tales, some of them even true. "Bert knew his people," Bleck recalled. "He was a department politician." The new, more modern regime that followed him was more serious and able, but also more remote and humorless. Bleck approves of most of the changes that have come, but misses the old camaraderie and looseness of the early days. When the autocratic Cole was finally voted out by a state fed up with his stonewalling and contempt of environmentalists, it was a bit like the frontier closing.

Back in Cole's day the push to build roads into the forest produced timber contracts called "campouts." Loggers would be helicoptered or hike into roadless areas and start cutting, only later to be linked up by road. In a sense it was the kind of wilderness trailblazing one could trace all the way back to Daniel Boone marking a path for pioneers across the Cumberland Gap. And what a forest they were opening! Trees grew rank as mushrooms out in the West End, and as tall as towers. The Olympic area, representing just 15 percent of DNR's fiefdom, was supplying 400 million board feet of state timber a year, or forty percent of everything DNR cut. And most of that 40 percent was not coming off all the state lands on the Peninsula but off just the Clearwater Block, southeast of Forks.

Once Cole asked Gockerel if the harvest couldn't be pushed up to 450 million board feet. Gock, as he was called, remembers he had to say no: not just because the forest couldn't take having so much bare ground exposed to the incessant rain, but because his crew simply couldn't process the paperwork for that many sales that fast. "We were trained to produce," he said, "to cut out the old stuff and to grow good new trees fast." Gockerel never pretended the conversion was aesthetically pleasing. "There's nothing more ugly than a clearcut," he said.

In that heyday of the early 1970s, Forks's population doubled. Those were the headiest years. A high school graduate willing to work hard could pull down professional-level wages and still likely look forward to having three or four months of the winter off, drawing unemployment. The woods seemed inexhaustible. In a single year, the Forks DNR office posted a new record by delivering $100 million to the state treasury from the sale of trees. Cole's policy was to get rid of the decadent virgin forest as quickly as possible, even though it meant the cut would probably be only half as great by the year 2000. Hell, he'd be long gone by then, and the loggers could move elsewhere.

This scheme would betray Forks. What the department decided to do was log Washington State on a sustained yield basis, in theory only cutting as much each year as could be maintained for perpetuity. But to calculate sustained yield the agency looked at the growth on all two million acres of its forest land across Washington State, while concentrating much of its harvest around Forks where the old growth was. As a consequence, there was no attempt to keep the harvest to sustained yield levels in the West End itself. "We did overcut, by today's standards," Bleck said. "Private industry overcut. The Forest Service overcut."

"There's no question we overcut," said Brian Boyle, Cole's successor. One study concluded that forest land dedicated to the University of Washington was cut 15 percent faster each year during Cole's reign in the 1970s than a sustained policy would dictate, Boyle said. The policy changed in 1984, when the state created five sustained yield units to halt the concentration of logging in one corner of the state. But by that time, most of the damage to Forks's long-range future had been done.

Larry Suslick, the former cutter and DNR maintenance man who moved to Forks in 1966, said the change on the land has been stupendous. "The trees were so much bigger then," he said. "Here we had everything: peelers, pulp, cedar, lumber, on all kinds of terrain. It was said if you worked the Olympic Peninsula, you could cut timber anywhere on earth because we had such variety."

Fallers like himself knew the forest was being cut too fast to be sustainable, Suslick said, but they were in no position to object. "I've cut thousands and thousands and thousands of trees. I didn't agree with how fast we were doing it. But I was a tool in that process. If I hadn't done it, somebody else would have." There were no laws, and no incentives, to slow down.

Not only was logging at full throttle when Bleck came to Forks in 1970, it also differed in technique. There was so much wood in the forest in those days that buyers only wanted the good stuff. Half-rotted logs, skinny trees, and blocks of salvage cedar that would be snapped up by the end of the 1980s were simply left in the clearcut twenty years before. There was so much of this "slash" on the ground that the cuts were like an obstacle course of crisscrossed tree trunks, limbs, and waste. DNR's tactic was to burn it.

Gockerel had fought some big fires in his career and was determined not to have a runaway natural blaze on his unit. Fire control was the standard on which many foresters were judged in the decades after World War II, and a bad wildfire could break a career. Out in the Forks area DNR deliberately burned an average of five thousand logged acres a year to try to beat nature to the punch. The result would often produce a smoky pall over Forks when an inversion would lock the smoke over the prairie. Store owners used to call Bleck at DNR headquarters all the time to complain soot was getting on their dresses in stores.

Worse than that, many of the slash burns outran their intended boundaries. "We called it, 'Light em and fight em,' " Bleck recalled. "There were few that didn't get away from us. We used to be the biggest creator of our own fires. We caused more than anybody else." When the flames ran into adjacent groves of standing trees, the sheepish foresters called the resulting damage "needle blight." Anyone who complained was ignored. Better these little-bitty fires than some big natural one. The locals and tourists who objected to the smoke were told they didn't know anything about managing forests. After Boyle defeated Cole in 1980 the slash burning began to slow down.

There were other changes as well. DNR started letting logged sites reseed naturally with the hemlock, spruce, and cedar more indigenous to the West End. Herbicide spraying declined drastically. The logs that used to be cleaned out of streams were now, at the advice of fish biologists, left in. Cutters used to take special care to fall every pole and snag on a clearcut to make sure "widow-makers" weren't left to endanger the loggers; now they had to take even more care to leave some behind for wildlife. Every tenet of the 1970s seemed to be turned on its head in the 1980s.

That didn't stop the debate. ITT-Rayonier had a checkerboard pattern of land ownership alongside DNR. On its ground it still burned and planted Douglas fir. On an early autumn evening while I was visiting Forks a ground fog crept into town when the company was burning, and the smoke combined with fog to create a pea-soup haze. Cars crept along the town's streets, barely able to see twenty or more feet ahead of the hood. Private industry defended the burn. Hand planting instead of natural reseeding from airborne seed gave trees a three- to five-year head start, Rayonier supervisor Al Barr said.

The side effects of logging weren't widely acknowledged when the big harvest began. Bleck remembered that it wasn't until 1973 that the DNR began to wonder about the impact logging had on the siltation of streams.

They were logging the Upper Clearwater so quickly in those days that the hillsides started to slump in heavy rains. This was not surprising because half the ground in the West End sometimes seems in liquid motion; Bleck pointed to the leaning power poles along Highway 101 as evidence of how even vegetated ground never seems to stay in place.

Nevertheless, the landslides up in the Clearwater made the department look reckless and the word came down from Olympia. "I don't care what it takes," Cole lieutenant Don Lee Fraser snapped, "we don't want a shovelful of dirt going into the Clearwater River."

Gockerel pondered a bit, then began ordering every roll of plastic visqueen he could find. The DNR crews went out into the rain and began unrolling the stuff across the hillsides. They'd simply deflect the water from the soil. That, and the use of log barriers and temporary flues to help divert the water, worked. The Clearwater stayed clear. Yet this was the ultimate absurdity, men wrapping the land in plastic to shield it from the damage they had done. It showed there were limits to what the land could take.

The heavy harvest of the Clearwater was not something that was hidden in the 1970s. "We had a model area out there," Gockerel recalled. It was a showpiece of how science could convert an old-growth forest to a productive tree farm. A group from President Nixon's Office of Management and Budget came out to see the Clearwater Block. So did Washington Governor Dixy Lee Ray.

Everyone knew this cut was a onetime bonanza. The old-growth stands had far more wood per acre than the smaller, shorter trees replacing them. When it was gone the cut would have to come down. Gockerel, knowing a decline was inevitable, tried to dissuade his sons from going into logging. "There is no question in my mind that they [private industry] overcut," he said. Besides, "the most dangerous job in the world is falling and bucking. I told them to stay away from it. Of course they wouldn't." By 1990 his boys were scrambling for work. One was forced to Alaska. Another got his picture on the front page of the *Bremerton Sun* newspaper, in a feature article about the plight of loggers.

As the old growth disappeared, what remained became more valuable. After twenty years, old-growth trees were selling for twelve to fourteen times the price they had brought in 1970, Bleck calculated. Cedar in particular became scarce. The state began to worry about cedar poachers who would drive or helicopter into an old-growth stand at night, drop trees worth up to tens of thousands of dollars each, and cut out the best of the wood for sale to cedar mills. Cedar blocks used to make shakes and shingles could bring $500 a cord, an amount that could be cut in a couple of hours. Bleck was put in charge of trying to catch the thieves. He began to give the cases names: The Whirlybird Caper, the Moonlight Cedar Caper. It was frustrating because the local judges didn't view it as a serious crime. After one case, the thieves were fined $254. "Hell, they could cut that night and pay for their ticket," Bleck said.

This same old-growth shortage was beginning to rile the environmentalists from Seattle. They'd drive up to the Olympics or Cascades to hike on a favorite trail and find a logging road had taken its place, or that the trail was cut in half by a clearcut. The hikers would grouse about having walked around the devastation of a clearcut for hours, trying to find where the split trail picked up on the other side.

By the 1980s the state harvest was slowing, but even as it did, other trends kept the harvest around Forks artifically high to continue the illusion of inexhaustible supply. The timber recession of the early 1980s and the Wall Street takeover fever that followed led to upheavals in timberland ownership. Weakened timber companies with uncut assets became prime targets for corporate takeovers, and in 1985 the raider Sir James Goldsmith—an English-French financier who was reportedly a model for a character in the movie *Wall Street*—acquired Crown Zellerbach. He paid for his purchase by selling off the company's pulp mills and 257,000 acres of timberland. He retained 700,000 acres more in Washington and Oregon.

Goldsmith acquired the land just before timber prices leaped to new all-time highs. Every threat of reducing the harvest of Pacific Northwest old-growth forests seemed, for a while at least, to add value to what could still be cut. Some of Goldsmith's new land lay north of Forks in the Pysht River basin. He logged it from one end to the other with fervor and haste, triggering landslides that slumped into the basin's salmon streams. So much silt was carried down the Pysht River to the Strait of Juan de Fuca that it injured the saltwater kelp beds offshore. In 1990, having ordered a cut of virtually all his merchantable trees on the Pysht without, to his employees' knowledge, ever having been there, Goldsmith sold his holdings again to Hansen Mining, another British firm.

Goldsmith was not alone. Scott Paper, which had one of the best-managed tree farms in the United States in the forests north of Seattle, sold to a newly created company called Crown Pacific. To service Crown Pacific's debt, rapid tree cutting followed that threw sustained yield to the wind. The same happened to Georgia Pacific land and Burlington Northern railroad land and smaller private patches bought up by domestic or Asian investors. Trillium Corporation bought 16,000 acres from Georgia Pacific in the mid-1980s and harvested half of it in three years. In the state of Washington, applications to log on private land jumped 50 percent in three years, peaking at 12,000. At the same time, the Port of Port Angeles predicted that in the next decade, private timber cutting would decline by nearly two-thirds because of excessive overharvesting.

These multiplying clearcuts were not in mountains far from public view but in foothills that overlooked freeways and cities. Clearcuts seemed to materialize overnight in the late 1980s: zip, zip, zip! Most of the trees being cut were second growth, not old growth, and had only a marginal impact on owls. But they did affect people. The public began to scream. When DNR asked the protesting public to name locations where excessive logging was causing erosion or similar damage, they responded by naming 463 places in 230 different river and creek basins.

Some loggers and mill employees in towns like Forks made their living on that kind of overharvesting. But others were infuriated at a seemingly heedless cut that seemed to give the entire industry a black eye. "That fucking Englishman," mill owner Larry Mason later said of Goldsmith. "People talk about these little national forest clearcuts, well, there's a 3,000-acre clearcut over that ridge! The direct and most immediate response to the court injunctions on the spotted owl was windfall profit to corporate profiteers and increases in the most irresponsible harvest—which in turn fuels the hysteria to protect more land. The environmentalists shut down public timber, and made him a fortune!"

While conceding the need for change, Bleck and Gockerel had little use for the scientists who pushed it. Gockerel talked about, "that nitwit Jerry Franklin." Bleck said the academics seemed remote and arrogant, ignoring the Northwest forests for years until they were at a crisis point, scampering off instead to more exotic landscapes such as Alaska. "They're a cause of a lot of our problem," Bleck said. "They say we're raping and pillaging, and hell, they're a part of the system." It was the ivory tower boys who endorsed clearcut logging and tree plantations in the first place, he said. Then these other scientists came back and said it was wrong, change things.

Interestingly, the scientists agree to a point. "If there is one thing we in the forestry profession should have learned by now it is humility," said Franklin, referring to past prescriptions that today seem disastrous.

Jack Ward Thomas said he has lost the certain assurance with which he began his career as a game manager. "I used to know what I was," he said. "I was a wildlife biologist, and I knew what that meant. I could put game on the range. I don't know what I am now." But that is why they are now urging foresters to step back, to act with caution, to learn from nature.

Today, everything is different. Modern mills are built to handle smaller logs that once would have been dismissed as slash. The equipment is also changing. As the trees shrink in size, so does the machinery. The yarders and cables are getting lighter.

And that, of course, is the other way to see the Clearwater Block vista. It is not only evidence that an ancient forest can be replaced, but that the replacement is far different: shorter, more uniform, cleaner of rotting wood, quieter, less diverse, with fewer kinds of animals, and so dense that in the first decades all underbrush is squeezed out.

By 1990, two decades after Bleck had come to Forks, the DNR estimate of what it could cut annually there on a sustained yield basis had dropped from 400 million board feet to 258 million board feet. Even before the owl it was expected to fall to 190 million board feet by the year 2000. Once more the talk of sustained yield and of community stability—of having cut only as much each year as could be sustained forever—seemed hollow.

Then came the owl habitat areas. Suddenly, in 1990, the cut was down to 180 million board feet and expected to fall further. Even that was stretching things. Two decades before, when Bleck came to Forks, the DNR planned to cut its trees every 110 years: somewhere between one-third and one-fifth the time in which the trees would, on the average, be naturally felled by fire, wind, insects, or disease. But as the logging went on, the statisticians decided that wasn't quick enough. To make the numbers add up the rotation had to be shortened, and shortened, and shortened. Two decades after Bleck started it was down to sixty years on state land; as low as forty years on adjoining private land.

In Port Angeles, a onetime logger turned environmentalist named Ray Koon fumed about this change. He had been one of a herd of candidates vying to replace Bert Cole in 1980. His political career went nowhere but his interest in the issues persisted. Koon's modest home is stacked with plans, documents, and statistics on forest harvests.

"I'm not a typical environmentalist," said the white-bearded Koon.

"All I wanted to do [was to] get sustained yield for the DNR lands on the West End. Those people fifteen years ago knew what was coming. The state got ripped off by Bert Cole and the speculators. DNR went from a biological rotation to an economic rotation."

Koon points to the agency's own figures showing that allowing trees to grow to the former rotation age of 120 years or so would have provided more than twice the wood fiber per year even if only half as many acres annually were cut. The state threw its future away with a onetime binge, Koon argues. If it hadn't overcut, "you'd have grown more wood over the long term and had a higher annual harvest level."

Each winter the traffic on Highway 101 thins. The plodding motor homes disappear first. The hunters go home. Then, as the snows come in the mountains, the logging truck traffic decreases. For Christmas of 1990, as the SEASONS GREETINGS banner went up over the main street of Forks, there were even fewer log trucks than normal. The woods were almost eerily quiet. The owl acreage had been set aside and simultaneously a recession had made timber markets go sour. Log prices had plunged. As Mason put it, you could go broke from not being able to get trees or, not being able to sell them if you had any.

The federal and state timber offices were quiet too. Region Six of the Forest Service had already announced some staff trims that would be made through attrition because its budget was falling from lack of timber sales. The Olympic National Forest budget was expected to plunge from $20 million in 1990 to $12 million by 1993. At the Forks district headquarters of the forest, the staff would shortly be told it could expect to be cut in half. Pat Van Eimeren, the twenty-seven-year-old staff biologist at the Forks office, noted the irony of it: foresters who were applauded for years for meeting the ambitious harvest goals set by Congress were now told they had overcut. "We're looking to be out of a job just as well as the people of Forks," he said.

Kurt Ralston, the fisheries biologist who went to listen to Jeff DeBonis, said that as the economic impact of timber's long plunge on the Olympic Peninsula has hit home in Forks, his own view of the controversy has gotten more complicated.

It was simpler when he graduated from college. "As we came out of school we were all combat biologists, supposed to save the world," he said. The feeling was strengthened in his early years on the Siskiyou National Forest in southern Oregon. It was his job to do surveys both in old-growth forest and the younger, regrown forest of the kind foresters such as Bleck are proud of. "It was the comparison between the two, the difference, that really hit home," Ralston said. "We were losing diversity."

His early decision to work for environmental improvement from within the government was often tested by the sometimes nonsensical zigzags in public policy. "I've thought a million times of quitting," Ralston said. A congressional amendment that forced continued heavy harvest in 1989 despite court injunctions against it "was almost the straw that broke my back. I learned how much influence politics has on land management."

Nor has he changed his fundamental belief that the public's forests have been harvested too far, too fast. "Especially up here [on the Olympic Peninsula] it's way too late," he said. The accumulation of logging roads and clearcuts is catching up, he said. Heavy rains late in 1990 caused landslides and road failures throughout the forest. On Pistol Creek alone, a mile and a half of salmon egg-laying habitat was lost, buried under mud that slid down from failing logging roads. "We're still not protecting our watersheds enough," he said. "We've got to be more in a preservationist mode."

But Ralston also has seen how hard it has been for the Forks area to switch, not just economically but mentally, from the rapid harvest of earlier years. "It's like hitting a wall at high speed," he said. "The old guard that was here was rewarded for getting the cut out." He has come to respect their skill. "These people have been brought up to believe they are here for resource extraction," he said. "But they do value fisheries, they do value aesthetics, it's just in a different way. It's very complicated, and I'm still trying to figure it out. When I got into this I was more of a preservationist. Now I think that the preservationist groups are as far off base as the timber industry. When I started it was a real black-and-white issue. Now you realize it is not black and white, it is all gray, it is all mush."

Bleck said that as much as forest practices have changed around Forks, the foresters have always tried to do the best thing they could with the knowledge of the time. "Every one of us out here are goddamned environmentalists," he said. "We believe in the environment. It's our livelihood too."

189

Larry Mason once pointed to a satellite photograph of the Olympic Peninsula he put up in his office. The poster shows the Puget Sound basin as well. The Peninsula is dotted with brown clearcuts in the image, but the Seattle-Tacoma metropolitan area is a grid-sheet of bright gray. "There's the biggest clearcut in the state," Mason said, jabbing his finger at Seattle. "The difference is, they don't plant *their* clearcut back. They pave it over."

12

THE CANDIDATE

▲▲▲▲▲▲▲▲

The Ides of March of 1990 was a sunny spring day in Portland, the kind that seems especially sweet after the long gray winter. The barren trees along a causeway had taken on a watercolor wash of fuzzy green, and the sky was a scrubbed blue. To the east, the white crumpled cone of Oregon's Mount Hood stood up on the horizon like a marble sculpture. The warm breeze was nature's promise to eventually dry the soggy Northwest out. It was kite weather and hike weather, the kind in which you can just about hear the streams filling with snow-melt—except here, in this place, the primary sound was the roar of jets taking off overhead.

Four visitors to Portland's International Airport were paying little attention to the bright sunshine outside. The directors of the principal land agencies of the United States—the Forest Service, the Bureau of Land Management, the Park Service, and the U.S. Fish and Wildlife Service—were meeting together outside Washington, D.C., for the first time in memory. The gathering was indicative of the seriousness they gave to the threat spotted owl protection posed to the region's biggest industry. Dale Robertson of the Forest Service, James Ridenour of Parks, John Turner of Wildlife and Cy Jamison of BLM closeted themselves in a windowless room at the airport Sheraton to listen to scientists brief them on the likely result of a Fish and Wildlife study. It would determine if the northern spotted owl is a threatened or endangered species under the Endangered Species Act. They also heard about the tentative contents of the still-unpublished report by a committee chaired by Jack Ward Thomas that would recommend designating 7.7 million acres of habitat for the northern spotted owl.

When reporters were invited in at mid-afternoon the assembled bureaucrats declined to discuss directly what they had been told, since nothing had been officially released yet. But they did their best to drop repeated hints that the timber industry should brace for the worst. The clear impression was that the owl would be listed as a threatened species and, as a result, millions of trees would be protected.

Behind the reporters clustered a gloomy knot of timber industry executives, lobbyists, and community representatives. "We're disappointed and fearful," the federal agency directors were told by Valerie Johnson, chairwoman of the Oregon Lands Coalition, a pro-industry group.

Outside in the sunlit parking lot, about two hundred loggers and their wives rallied to protest the portents of the new research. Most were from Oregon towns similar to Forks, such as Mill City, Stayton, and Detroit. The assembly was bright with bobbing yellow signs, looking in this weather like a cluster of yellow daffodils. JOBS AND OWLS— WE CAN HAVE BOTH, read one.

SCIENCE AND RESPONSIBLE ENVIRONMENTALISM EQUALS BALANCE.

MANAGED FORESTS PRODUCE OXYGEN.

OREGON'S FUTURE DEPENDS ON TIMBER.

FARMERS FOR RESPONSIBLE ENVIRONMENTALISM.

The mood was feisty, the crowd hoping against hope that the government scientists would recognize the economic catastrophe their research implied. "We didn't ask for this war," a saw shop owner named John Kunzman told the crowd from the bed of a maroon pickup truck. "But we stood up to it and will continue to stand up to it," the resident of Sweet Home, Oregon, said. "Rural America is what's being attacked. Forks, Washington, is the first casualty."

It was true Forks was already in trouble, but it was probably in better shape this spring than Sweet Home, where twelve stores were boarded up, six mills had shut down, and the population was dropping. Kunzman himself was modifying his inventory to include outboard engines and other marine supplies in hopes of making up in sales to recreationists what he was losing in sales to loggers. Forks's plight was sharper and more immediate, however. Three mills had shut down in December of 1989, putting two hundred people out of work, and the food bank had run out of protein and fruit. To highlight Forks as an example of what could happen to the rest of the rural Northwest, the assembled demonstrators brought cases of food for the Forks food bank.

To present the food, Kunzman leaned over to give a hand to an attractive blonde woman who gamely hitched up her skirt to clamber onto the pickup bed. Incongruously she wore high heels, and she danced a moment to get a firm balance on the corrugated surface. In appearance and presence she stood out sharply at the rally, catching the crowd's eye. This was no kitchen-bound woods wife. Ann Goos flashed a smile that retreated quickly to a more sober expression, managing to express a chins-up greeting and yet underline the seriousness of the loggers' plight at the same time. With her nylons, earrings, and impeccably applied makeup, she gave an unusual snap of style to this logger gathering, a Cinderella polish to their rural complaints. It was as if to say, hey, we are not just a bunch of backwoods hicks or tree-killing barbarians. We're people, damn it. Goos also had the arresting knack of looking directly at her audience with large bright eyes that were both intelligent and kind of startled, as if to convey good-naturedly the improbability of where she found herself.

This executive director of a Forks organization called the Washington Commercial Forest Action Committee had never cut a log in her life. Yet seemingly overnight, she had become one of the most effective voices for loggers in the Pacific Northwest. A former schoolteacher who was raised in the upscale Seattle suburb of Bellevue, she moved to Forks, married a logger, and demonstrated a knack for explaining this wood-harvesting minority to the urbanized majority of her state.

Goos was handed a case of tuna fish to heft, like a homecoming queen given flowers. "One comment that our food bank is in trouble and, geez, do you get food," she told the crowd in appreciation. They applauded in solidarity. But this winter's hardship is only a foretaste of what is to come, Goos warned. The woods are being shut down and as a result, "We're in a social services overload. We need to make our problems heard."

Six months later Ann Goos stood before an audience of about sixty people in a Grange hall at Joyce, a small farming and timber community about an hour from Forks on the Strait of Juan de Fuca. It was the community's candidate night, a time for residents to eye their representatives face to face. The setting could not be more middle American. The speeches were proceeded by a potluck community dinner, the candidates eating elbow-to-elbow with their constituents. Then the gathering moved to the meeting hall with its timbered ceiling, dusty gold curtain, a hardwood floor scuffed by dances, and an American flag. Farm fair ribbons won by Grange members hung on the wall.

Goos felt pretty good as the evening began. The day before was the election primary, and the former schoolteacher stunned the twenty-fourth state legislative district by getting more votes in her race for a state House seat than the Democratic incumbent, Evan Jones. Not bad for a last-minute, first-time candidate running as a Republican in a district that historically elects Democrats.

The primary vote did not count in this race; it was only indicative of how the candidates are doing on their way to the final ballot on November 6. But Jones's poor showing suggested that his seeming reluctance to champion his district's timber communities had put him in serious political trouble. In Forks, Ann got 91 percent of the vote. She couldn't help repeating this to her campaign manager, John Calhoun, as her sporty Ford clung to the curves along the steep shore of Lake Crescent on the way to Joyce. "Ninety-one percent!" This, for an outsider. She was thirty-two years old and had only lived in Forks six years. Her car passed several logging trucks going the other way. All bore a big yellow and blue sign reading "Goos" on their front bumpers.

On the way to the Grange hall, candidate and manager briefly discussed her strategy and speech. Calhoun, whose regular job is managing the state Department of Natural Resources office in Forks, reminded her that her father-in-law, Frank Goos, married one of the eight Thor sisters of Joyce. Mention that. Stress the local ties.

Her opponent came to the Grange hall as well, shaking hands while carrying a ponderously thick state budget summary tucked under one arm. Jones didn't seem to look at the summary all evening but it was an effective prop, a subtle reminder of the experience he has over his opponent. Evan Jones is ten years older than Goos, tall and slim, a part-time legislator and sometimes-writer who seemed a bit too shy and subdued that evening to fit the politician stereotype. He looks more like a librarian, or a high school teacher. Jones knew he lost the Joyce area to Goos the day before two to one. He does not fit easily into timber country, identifying more with his liberal constituents in the Port Townsend area in the eastern part of the striated Twenty-fourth. His is a strange, sprawling district, wrapping halfway around the Olympic Peninsula from Hoquiam in the southwest to Port Townsend in the northeast. It is the second biggest district in the state. Just getting from one end to the other is a four-hour drive.

In conversation Jones himself is friendly, smart, and perceptive, yet he seems an unlikely representative of this area. He lived in Seattle for a while, writing an unfilmed screenplay set in the Belltown area of the central city. He worked on a liberal weekly there, the *Seattle Sun*. He has had a curious political career. He won a job as a Clallam County commissioner in a write-in campaign, was defeated after one term, and then was appointed to fill a vacancy in the state legislature in 1987. Later he won election to the post on his own by 55 percent, but the loggers in his district have never been entirely comfortable with him.

Most of the other candidates were up late the night before, counting their primary vote totals. Many seemed tired and cranky that evening, commenting on the oddity of having a candidates' night the day *after* an election. Newspaper editorials across the United States bemoaned the prevalence of nasty campaign strategies that year, and this corner of Norman Rockwell America did not seem immune to the tendency.

The incumbent sheriff has just been ousted in the primary amidst rumors he struck his wife in a domestic dispute. That seemed to set the tone. As candidate after candidate takes his few minutes before the Grange audience, they seemed to either draw invective, give it, or both. One auditor candidate, for example, was grilled by heckling members of the audience on why he was allegedly fired from three jobs; he responded that one of his inquisitors is an auditor office employee with the worst record for tardiness in the courthouse.

"I will sue you for that!" she retorted angrily. People in the audience had the uncomfortable, furtive, yet curious expression of spectators overhearing an argument in a restaurant. They shifted in their chairs. Candidate and inquisitor looked frustrated and embarrassed.

The mood did not improve. An incumbent was accused of taking time off from his job to build a house. Lawrence Gaydeski, the Clallam County commissioner who hails from Forks, was accused by his tavern-owner opponent of laziness and inattention, something that struck Goos, who knows Gaydeski, as almost laughably unfair. This was democracy gone sour, a display of American political pettiness most of the voters present seemed to view with distaste. Gaydeski tried to steer the discussion to something substantive. In the past decade, he said, taxes on timber harvesting have provided $13 million for Clallam County road construction and $28 million more in general revenues. Most of that is about to disappear, he warned, as timber cutting plummets. "Folks, we are facing the biggest change this area has ever seen."

When Jones's turn came he stressed his experience, identified himself with some recent legislation, and talked about his campaign to install public toilets on Highway 101, which drew some nods from the female members of the audience. Out in the West End it is a long way between bathrooms. He offered little sympathy to the district timber companies facing a plunge in the permitted harvest. "We're not meeting sustained yield goals and haven't been for some time," Jones said bluntly. "Anyone can go out to Forks and see that ITT-Rayonier cut twenty years too early."

Goos has a smoother, more personable style, managing to come across as intelligent, competent, and yet not brassy: she has a feminine, nonthreatening aura as a woman and uses it to her advantage as a speaker.

Goos gave a quick autobiography and dutifully mentioned the Thor sisters, to no visible reaction from this audience. Then she said the western Olympic Peninsula needs help, not condemnation. "We're trying to act as a voice for timber-dependent communities," she told the crowd. "The West End is changing but we can take control of that."

The reaction seemed positive. "She made *me* a better speaker," Jones reflected afterwards. "I'd sit and listen to her and think I'd better turn up the amperage, or I'm going to sound pretty flat." But Jones, who voiced more specifics, drew more questions.

Afterward in the ride back to Forks Goos was downbeat, depressed by the petty backbiting of the night's speeches and in doubt about her appeal. She envied Jones his toilet idea, and an incumbent's ability to take credit for specific legislation. The swings in her mood are hard to avoid. She felt as if she had climbed aboard an emotional roller coaster and couldn't get off until November 6, election day. She has offered her ego to be stomped on. What is she doing here? Does she even *want* to be a state legislator? She is her own harshest critic, her own toughest questioner.

As late as the Fourth of July Goos had no intention of running. But the timber industry was facing a dark future and it seemed to have few strong voices in the state capitol. A week after the holiday, Ted Spoelstra, a port commissioner and former Forks logging company manager, met her to persuade her to file. The timber industry was simply getting outtalked. The people drawn to the woods work were often introverted by nature; it was the relief they got in the forest from having to deal with other humans that made some of them like the job. The environmentalists always seemed to now exactly what to say for the television cameras. The loggers, in contrast, felt inarticulate, ignored, or misquoted. Goos was different. She could talk. State office would give her the kind of visibility and credibility logging communities needed.

It was a poor time to start a late campaign. Goos felt exhausted, out of steam. She has become a kind of lightning rod for her adopted community, the one willing to field the phone calls from the unpredictable media and make the long trek to inconclusive meetings in Washington, D.C., or the state capital in Olympia. The news this year had all been bad. As had been hinted at Portland in March, the owl had been named a threatened species. The impact was expected to be catastrophic, costing up to 100,000 jobs. A recent *Seattle Times* newspaper poll published just before the decision showed a majority in the state wanting to save trees for the owl even if it cost jobs.

Spoelstra, a shrewd small-town businessman who collects antique logging equipment as a hobby, told Goos the community needed better representation in Olympia.

"I don't want to lose," she told him. She didn't like the idea of having to identify with a political party, of having to raise money, of having to take polls on her own appeal.

"I lost my first election and I survived it," Spoelstra assured her. "Win or lose, it's a good learning experience."

That Ann Goos would be courted to represent half the Olympic Peninsula was an improbability, given her suburban Seattle background. She grew up as Ann Watton in Bellevue, which is separated from the city of Seattle by long and broad Lake Washington, a separation sometimes referred to by Bellevue residents as, "The Moat." In recent years Bellevue has grown to be Washington's fourth largest city with all the urban trappings of modest skyscrapers, immodest traffic jams, street gangs, and homelessness. When Goos was growing up there, however, it was firmly suburban, upper middle class, and about as far removed from logging-town culture as you could get in the Evergreen State.

Goos did not have a pampered childhood, since her parents divorced when she was nine and her family lived on child support. But neither was it hard. She was the youngest of the four children and the one closest to her father who had moved out. Despite the divorce he made sure money was there for such things as a swim club, skating lessons, and the like. She saw only a narrow part of the American spectrum. "You didn't see poverty," she recalled. "You saw successful, pretty well-to-do families." Some of her friends were rich. Her father, Ed Watton, became a mayor of Medina, a more exclusive suburb next to Bellevue. Her mother remembers Ann as a girl who was game for most anything and "good at anything she tried." She tried piano, ice-skating, singing. She sang at her junior high talent show and brought down the house. She was the class clown and every guy's best friend. She worked consciously to improve herself. Her mother described her as an ugly duckling who blossomed. In college she studied music and dance and performed in musical comedies. She sang at weddings.

Her first years out of high school were difficult. She drifted a bit, then at a dance met again an older man she had known earlier. She was swept off her feet. He was handsome, mature, both a mate and a bit of the male authority figure she had lacked growing up. They wed after a whirlwind courtship. "He was more of a mentor than he ever was a husband," she would later conclude. He was a teacher and had been a political candidate. Under his encouragement she attended Pacific Lutheran University in Tacoma, graduating with honors and a degree in social science education. But he also had two children from a previous marriage, debts, and the flotsam and jetsam that can be accumulated over a longer life. The young bride felt she had gotten in over her head. In a short time they were separated, and Ann was looking for a teaching job just as the region slipped into recession.

She found a high school post at remote Moclips, a Pacific coastal town bordering the Quinault Indian reservation south of Forks. There was no supermarket, no theater, and certainly no Bellevue Mall. Coming at the end of her marriage, her new job was a complete geographic and cultural break.

"It was a whole new world for her," her mother, Barbara Watton, said, "seeing the poor and the needy. She hadn't even seen Indian kids before."

"My first year of teaching was so disillusioning," Goos recalled. "I didn't know some kids hated teachers like that or parents talked to teachers like that. I had always loved school." Still, she had a knack for teaching. She was a performer, able to inspire her audience of kids.

The recession deepened. Goos, as last hired, became first fired when cutbacks were made at Moclips in 1984. But she had already pleased her superiors enough that they convinced school officials in nearby Forks to hire her. Still, the job loss made an impression she would carry with her when later speaking out for loggers.

In Forks, everything began to improve. The town of three thousand seemed almost cosmopolitan after Moclips, Goos recalled with a laugh, and she was a hit teaching American history at the high school. She was the youngest and one of the most popular teachers there. "She made learning like a game show," recalled Elaine Hurn, who had two children in Goos's class. Goos brought in toys, puppets, and even showed off her own wretched kindergarten art projects to spoof herself and grab the attention of the teenage woods kids. She was game for anything, wearing roller skates to school for Nerd Day and crashing on her behind. Once the boys stuffed her into a garbage can and rolled her down the hallway. Another time they turned the furniture in her room upside down, and still another time, after an overnight school bus trip to a football game, they ran her sleeping bag up the school flagpole. They also learned about history and government with an excitement seldom shown before. She was good enough that the principal sent a representative of a prestigious foundation to her class to see her teaching. As he came in, she was addressing her sixteen-year-olds with hand puppets.

She felt accepted at more than just the school. Forks was a place to which she could belong. Most people who lived there had made a conscious decision to stay there, and the loyalty to the place was infectious. "I owe this town everything," she would say later.

The intense community of an isolated small town can seem suffocating to some, comforting to others. Goos liked the intimacy and the values. These people seemed grounded, somehow, closer to the earth and to reality. They were almost old-fashioned in their respect for hard work, physical skill, family, and friends. Goos in turn brought urban enthusiasm into Forks. The kids were interested in her. She walked different, talked different, was fired up with energy. She didn't seem fixed by fate; with her, alternative futures seemed possible. You could design your own life. She started singing "The Star Spangled Banner" at graduation and came into demand at weddings. She became intrigued with self-improvement and self-esteem; she began to lift weights and run. "I got obsessed with it and thought everybody else should be," she remembered of her fitness craze. And she went on a date with a quiet logger named Randy Goos.

The logger fascinated her. He represented a way of life different from anything she had encountered in Bellevue. His shoulder had been shattered by a tree that kicked back at him as it fell. A chainsaw had cut his thigh to the bone. Another tree had crushed an ankle. After they married, Goos unconsciously adopted the habit of Forks wives who listen to the wail of the hospital ambulance to determine which direction on Highway 101 it is going, mentally checking whether her husband's current logging site is the same way.

Randy was shy about his scars. "I'm really ugly, and I don't want you to be shocked by that," he told her shortly after they met.

When her husband was later thrown out of work by the harvest curtailments, Ann could be implacably furious. "There is a liberal side to this issue that is never addressed," she said. "They are victimizing the logger. I don't understand it. We wouldn't have the industry if people didn't demand the product. This class difference is phenomenal to me. Seattle wants a bigger playground over here. Well, what are they paying for it? Why should *we* have to bear one hundred percent of this, all the upheaval of this?"

After they married, Goos quit teaching in 1988 to start a consulting business giving seminars to children and adults on self-esteem, weight loss, and stress management. "I just felt it was time to grow up," she said of her plunge into self-employment. "The key to being a good high schoolteacher is thinking like a sixteen-year-old. I got real tired of thinking like a sixteen-year-old. I had to mature."

She still felt relatively anonymous in Forks. "No one knew me as anything but a schoolteacher who quit," she said.

To launch her business she asked the Forks Chamber of Commerce for the addresses of local businesses so she could send them mailings. The chamber president agreed, but suggested she pay the $40 membership fee and come to the next meeting to explain her new business. It was October of 1988, the same time Mitch Friedman was laying plans to drive a giant log around the United States.

Feeling a bit out of place, Goos went to meet this new group. "There is a pecking order in town," she said. "The business community functions on a different level. They are their own social stratum." Tentatively she got up to talk on "wellness." The chamber audience was polite, but, "They couldn't wait for me to sit down because on the agenda was another matter, something about a spotted owl. So I stayed to listen. I was shocked." It was just two months before the Forest Service would propose setting aside 374,000 acres of old growth for the owl. Curb logging for a bird? Threaten her husband's occupation? Goos hadn't heard this before. When they asked for a volunteer to help stuff envelopes and investigate the issue, the chamber's newest, most curious member raised her hand.

The following Friday there was a meeting explaining the intentions of a new state commission to set aside some portion of old growth on nearby state lands. About two hundred local residents showed up: angry, frustrated, and afraid. Many were just becoming aware of the spotted owl issue. Up to now, the conventional wisdom was that there was too much old growth in Olympic National Park already. Now the environmentalists and scientists wanted more? The whole notion, and its enormous consequences for the town, seemed slightly absurd. Goos listened from the stairs at the back of the room. No one seemed to know what to do. "People in small towns are powerless because they don't know the system," Goos said later.

Forks's leaders met afterward to discuss starting up an organization to represent the town's loggers. Everyone seemed to have an organization working on the owl and old-growth issue except the logging communities, the folks most affected. Forks decided it was going to start a Washington Forest Action Committee. Something to get *their* side of the story out. John Calhoun spoke up and suggested Washington *Commercial* Forest Action Committee. It was important for folks to realize there was more than one kind of forest. Randy Simpson, the chamber president, suggested Goos become executive secretary. If she was not exactly Joan of Arc, here at least was a woman who had taught American government, was an effective speaker, wasn't already tied down full-time with an existing business, and radiated energy like a kerosene heater. Some were doubtful. Ann who?

She threw herself into the job, immersing herself in forestry textbooks for six months and blitzing the state's politicians and media with contacts. She was good. She urged loggers to "adopt a congressman" somewhere in the United States and start bombarding the representative with letters on the owl issue. She got Governor Booth Gardner, congressman Al Swift, and U.S. Senator Slade Gorton out to Forks. The visiting politicians didn't always bring cheer—Gardner bluntly warned the community to brace for disaster in the future—but they were impressed with Goos. Swift called her "a dynamo." Instead of being shrill, she was thoughtful. Instead of simply being outraged she was persuasive and good-humored. She was somewhat unique: a true believer who could relate to both sides. Come to think of it, she would make a damn good candidate.

Afterward, the long campaign behind her, Goos said, "I should have stayed true to my gut-level feeling. I shouldn't have done it." Yet an instant later she changed her mind, still exhibiting the tumult of conflicting emotions that came out of the campaign. "I've gained experience you can't buy. I will forever be a better public speaker because of it. I better understand issues other than timber."

The world of political campaigning seemed strange to her at first. The professionals who came up from Olympia didn't talk about issues or ideas or principles much at all. Instead, there as a lot of talk about numbers: votes and money and precinct numbers, a kind of bloodless arithmetic. There was also talk of personality. Voter appeal. The professionals flattered Goos and wooed her, but there was a flatness to the courtship. Sometimes the strategists talked in the room as if she wasn't there. It was as if she were an icon, a symbol, instead of a human being.

She ran as a Republican, which was logical given her pro-industry stance on timber and defense of private property rights over government interference. Her instinct was that the best government is that which governs least. Still, it felt peculiar to tack an R after her name, to take on whatever baggage a party label implied. Washington does not require voters to identify themselves by party affiliation and a majority consider themselves independents. Ann Goos the candidate had to be defined in ways that Ann Goos the person was not. "It was assumed that if you were a natural resource advocate, you were right wing, reactionary," she said, and her views were more complicated than that. She had trouble with the conservative fervor and had to keep reminding people she viewed herself as a political moderate.

Part of it was great fun. The leadership of Forks mobilized for her. There were sign-painting parties and campaign-literature conferences and community fund-raisers. The energy people gave and the pressures of campaigning affected her powerfully. She found the election kind of humbling, an experience that made her question her own esteem, her motives, and her purpose in life. She went to a Republican caucus meeting in Olympia and was repelled a bit by the self-centered egotism, this overblown sense of importance, some of the lawmakers seemed to have. She recognized in them something she could become herself if she was not careful. "I had gotten on a kind of fast track," she reflected. "I had started doing things because they put notches in my belt."

The idea of running was flattering and people were encouraging. "Most people respect anyone who has at least tried," she said. But the vehemence with which some people viewed her after she stepped into the political arena surprised her. One person in Port Townsend wrote her a letter calling her a "frosted-haired, overdressed, underqualified, corporate bimbo."

There were other shocks. Candidates in the state are required to file public disclosure forms that list not only who donates to their campaign and how much they gave, but approximate details of the candidate's personal finances. On her form, Ann volunteered that she and Randy had asked for an extension from the Internal Revenue Service to finish paying $7,000 of their 1989 taxes. This is not uncommon in the timber business, where work slows in the winter months and loggers sometimes seek to postpone tax payments until income picks up again in the spring. But someone tipped the newspaper and in the resulting story, Jones was quoted as asking how a couple earning a combined total of at least $70,000 a year (according to the disclosure form) "could not pay their taxes." Randy was furious and Ann appalled as their private life became a campaign issue.

Other moves seemed to backfire on the first-time candidate. The growing timber crisis seemed to give her the perfect issue, and Jones initially was scrambling. The timber industry his district depended on was being shaken to its roots and he had been pretty silent on the issue: partly because he was a state official and it was primarily federal forests being shut down, partly because he himself was critical of what had happened to the Peninsula's forests. "The mismanagement of the forest on the Peninsula was recognized by most people" who lived there, he reflected after the campaign, "but [the timber workers] don't want to hear about it." He said Goos tackled the controversy skillfully. "She dodged the timber industry issue and focused on the timber community issue. That was smart on her part." When Jones came out with a timber relief plan and was appointed to a special timber committee by the House Speaker, Goos called him "a born-again timber advocate. He hasn't been one for the last two years."

But Jones turned Goos's timber affiliation to his advantage by citing the big contributions she was receiving from the wood industry and implying she would be a tool of Big Timber. At candidate forums, people began asking her what the companies wanted in return. He had the astuteness to keep his neophyte opponent on the defensive. "I had to turn the race around," he said.

As the close race became more heated, the excitement of campaigning became a nightmare for Goos. "I'll never go through this again," she wearily told a reporter in an unguarded moment, predicting she would lose. A day later, she scrambled to deny she would lose and correct the impression she was ruling out ever running for office again. Still, the episode hurt. "She gets rattled easily and she bounces back easily," Jones assessed.

"This has been a very emotional campaign," she said at one point. "I cry a lot. My skin is not real thick."

Both candidates' tones changed as they moved around the Twenty-fourth. In the east was the refurbished Victorian community of Port Townsend, a timber capital in pioneer days and now a place of bed and breakfasts, coffee shops, and liberal opinion. This was not Goos's audience. At a forum a week before the election, she looked tired, beaten down by the acrimony of the campaign. By this point the race was bitter enough that each side was worried the other would launch rumors about the failed marriages of both candidates. Jones took Goos aside that evening. She recalled that he bluntly warned her that he had ammunition to use against her if she alluded to his messy divorce. His recollection is that the issue had already been referred to somewhat obliquely in a radio advertisement by the Goos campaign and that he told her, "We both have reason not to let our personal lives become a part of this campaign." In any event, the exchange seemed to further pollute the experience for Goos, and add to the pressure. "I don't think either of the candidates in this race are anything but good people," she said wearily to the group.

With this audience Goos's timber background was almost certain to be viewed with suspicion. A questioner pointed out she had received thousands of dollars in campaign contributions from the timber industry. "What do timber companies expect in return?" she was asked. Goos gamely said the money was simply recognition for the work she has already done on the issue, in contrast to Jones. To try to find a common ground in this group she talked about the promise of Jerry Franklin's New Forestry in forging a middle stance. She said she understood logging's critics. "That's the difference," she said vaguely, "whether you put a dollar value on forests or an amenity value. That's what our society is grappling with."

Jones was blunter to this audience. "What has been going on here [the Peninsula] has been something between tragic and criminal," he said of past logging. He accused Crown Zellerbach Corp.'s takeover by Sir James Goldsmith of devastating the area's timber base and added, "ITT-Rayonier has been doing it in Forks."

The next morning at an appearance before the business-suited Port Angeles Business Association about fifty miles to the west, the messages changed markedly. "Timber is the underpinning of our economy out here," Jones told the business-suited breakfast assembly.

The following day at a chamber meeting in Forks still further west, the tone changed even more. This crowd was solidly pro-timber and Goos looked as much at home as Jones looked uncomfortable. Some showed up in suspenders and hickory shirts. In this setting she talked in a more personal vein. "I learned a lot about what rural school districts go through when there's an economic downturn because I lost my job," she said of her experience in Moclips. "I am not a voice for industry but a voice for people who are impacted." Jones, in contrast, was asked why he never came to Forks to address the timber issue. He retorted that he was never asked.

But Jones kept hammering on Goos's timber support. At one point she erupted. "That takes away my integrity as a person," she said. "I can't tell you how much that offends me. Nobody should be penalized for whom they get support from or don't get support. I really resent the suggestion I'm a bimbo for corporate America—I'm not."

Later she would ponder the campaign. "I was probably the best when I was a little bit angry," she assessed. "But I'm not a good street fighter. I never put him on the defensive."

There was more implied in these timber campaign contribution questions than simply pointing out Goos's natural allies. The issue was a subtle, almost unconscious reminder to voters of just how powerful, and sometimes unresponsive, Big Timber has been in the Pacific Northwest. In living memory was a stockpile of past abuses: massive clearcuts that went unplanted, bitter strikes, ruthless plant closures, cyclic layoffs and buyouts followed by cynical overharvesting. The timber industry seemed a bit to the new urban professionals who dominated the state like a slightly embarrassing ancestor, or a rough-edged, ham-fisted, blue-collar relation. Uncle Timber always seemed a step behind public opinion, dragged to the future instead of envisioning it. The industry was conservative and frequently inarticulate. Because of that, it often came across as unyielding and fossilized. By the late 1980s the biggest timber corporations were scrambling to overcome this image, but public perceptions had not caught up. The industry's own polls showed it was held in low regard.

The contribution issue also reminded voters just how dependent on timber the region was, and perhaps this caused a flicker of the resentment a benefactor almost always secretly receives. Because it was the region's most obvious resource, the tree harvest had become linked not just to the well-being of the industry and its ports, but to government itself. Timber receipts represent a respectable portion of local government revenues in much of the West, and nowhere more so than in Washington and Oregon.

In 1989, the sales of national forest timber pumped $211 million into the two states for roads, schools, and local government. Oregon counties that have Bureau of Land Management timberland—once granted to the Oregon and California railroad and reacquired by the federal government in the Depression—got another $108 million in 1988. In Washington, two million acres of state timberland provided up to $160 million a year for school construction, university budgets, state buildings, and local government. The timber industry not only had its own 130,000-member work force in the two states to fall back on for political support, but a huge supporting constituency: school boards, county commissioners, port districts, university trustees. Timber spokesmen were not shy about using this. Saving old-growth trees, they warned, meant children would have shoddier school buildings.

Yet here was a central irony of Goos's campaign: that such an institutionally entrenched and economically vital practice as the liquidation of old-growth timber had so fallen from grace. The timber industry had been outflanked. As pervasive as King Cotton had once been in the South, timber once seemed to hardly need a voice, so obviously basic was its economic contribution. But it had been out-hustled by the scientists and environmentalists. Now the industry was belatedly scrambling for candidates to tell its side of the story. It was looking for people like Ann Goos, and yet its need for a candidate meant its very support of her had become a kind of leaden handicap that dogged her campaign. "I'm not sure I'm the right candidate," she said once. Unfairly or not, maybe she was too closely identified with timber.

On election night, it seemed at first like the euphoria of the primary might be repeated for Goos. Both sides knew the election would be close, but the Goos campaign workers thought initially they were pulling ahead. The numbers went up on the boards in a mood of cautious hope. Then came the telephone call.

"Election night was awful," Goos recalled. "We had us up by about one hundred votes. Then at one-thirty A.M. the Associated Press called. They wanted to know our reaction to being eighty-three votes down."

Goos and her coworkers were stunned. Down? The tentative joy evaporated. Worriedly, they went back over their count. They had made a mistake, and AP was correct. They were behind, not ahead.

Still, that was a razor-thin margin in an election with 32,000 ballots cast, and many written absentee ballots had yet to be counted. The weary campaign workers went to bed in Forks not knowing the outcome. "It was the campaign that never ended," Goos groaned later. Two months later, reporters would dub it, "The Election from Hell."

In the following days, the counting went on. Jones's lead shrank. And shrank. And shrank. A week after the election it was down to sixteen votes.

It was the worst kind of nightmare for both candidates. Neither had a clear mandate. The district was split evenly. The parts of the Twenty-fourth District in Clallam and Grays Harbor counties, the western part, voted for Goos. She had been endorsed by the biggest newspapers in both counties. The section of the district in Jefferson County, the Port Townsend area, voted heavily for Jones. He had been endorsed by the Port Townsend paper.

Finally, the day before Thanksgiving, the final tally was announced. It was Goos, 16,169 and Jones, 16,174. Evan Jones had kept his office by five votes. It was the closest legislative election in Washington State history.

Goos cried that night, both from relief and bitterness. "I couldn't stop." Than, as the Thanksgiving weekend stretched on, she laughed a bit, too.

"I know those five votes," she said. "I mean I know who they are. I know five people just in this town, Forks, who meant to vote for me and didn't get to the polls. I personally know five votes I could have gotten." The feeling hung there. If only . . .

Jones, of course, had the opposite experience. "Again and again, I had people come up to me who said they voted for me, and their spouse voted for me, and got their neighbors to vote and that they were those five votes. It made people feel they could make a difference."

But the torture wasn't over.

There was a mandatory computer recount of the ballots. Some mistakes had been made. Goos wasn't behind, she was ahead. She had won, officials said, by one vote. Incredible! It was front-page news in Seattle.

The logger-campaigners couldn't resist celebrating. They baked a cake. Bob Tuttle, one of Goos's friends and campaign workers, remembered being in a near daze at her headquarters. "We finally won one," he said. Goos went down to Olympia and was told the committee assignments she would get if the result held.

Jones, however, asked for a hand recount of every ballot. The tabulation began again, stretching another week In Clallam and Crays Harbor Counties, auditors awarded Goos several more votes. But in Jefferson County they found seventy-five votes the computers had missed.

On December 17, 1990, it seemed to finally be over. It was 16,213 to 16,210. As certified by the Secretary of State, Goos had lost by three votes.

Still it did not end. In early January, Clallam County found three uncounted absentee ballots at the bottom of an envelope. Jefferson County checked, and found two more. "This is scandalous," Goos said. "I can't deal with this anymore."

Goos got three more votes, Jones two. He took his seat in Olympia while the Republican Party filed suit to press for still another count, ultimately rejected by the courts.

In Forks the people were subdued. To come that close and lose, it was unbelievable. It was like a malevolent force had cursed the town. Another loss. They were being hammered, again and again and again.

They met each other in the streets and shook their heads. "Can't we win *something?*"

13

A NAME FOR THE TREES

▲▲▲▲▲▲▲▲

In 1988 the leaders of a notoriously unyielding and effective environmental group called the Oregon Natural Resources Council gathered in the Portland office of Andy Kerr, the group's conservation director. Combative and witty, Kerr thrived on controversy and reflected back the heat aimed his way by antagonists as if he were wrapped in aluminum foil. He would practice his one-liners in the shower, honing them for sting and pithiness. "World War III is the war against the environment," Kerr liked to quip. "The bad news is, the humans are winning."

By the time of the meeting, ONRC had made as much noise about the disappearance of old-growth forest as any environmental group in the Pacific Northwest. It would soon threaten to bring a great deal of logging to a temporary halt by filing appeals against 220 U.S. Forest Service timber sales in a single month. The legal tactic was so costly to the timber industry that Kerr was summoned to a special congressional hearing and lambasted by Oregon lawmakers. This, of course, simply guaranteed environmentalists additional exposure of what had been a somewhat obscure, distant environmental issue that revolved around complex, subtle ideas of ecosystem survival and biodiversity.

Kerr loved the notoriety. "Our power and influence was our ability to always get headlines and sound bites," he said later. Despite the periodic threatening telephone calls and bumper stickers that read, KISS MY AX, ANDY, he called his job as environmentalist lightning rod "a great job, and somebody's got to do it." Then he'd grin.

The confrontational tactics drew support. Between 1988 and 1990, ONRC doubled in size to 6,000 dues-paying members, and its annual budget hit $500,000. Nor did the organization worry about enraging the opposition. "I'm glad they're upset about me," Kerr said. "The more they lambaste me, the less time they have to realistically assess their position."

The Natural Resources Council's persistence drew Oregonians into a debate they had long deferred. "ONRC has a reputation as being careless and radical," Kerr would note. "I would prefer bold and in novative. . . . We have been like guerrillas: big enough to start trouble but not to finish it." The ONRC strategists reasoned that in the long run they could win the old-growth fight only through public opinion, not through the courts. The voters, through Congress, ultimately made the law.

The people most likely to be persuaded were those who did not depend on the forests for their income. Thus, environmentalists had to bring the forest issue to national, not just regional, attention. "We knew the battle should not be fought in Oregon and Washington," Kerr said. Timber was Oregon's biggest, most basic industry. As for its northern neighbor, "The massive urbanization of Washington and the fact it was addicted more to Boeing was helpful, but we knew we had to make it a national issue there, too." The environmentalists outside the Pacific Northwest were certain that most Americans had little idea of the scale of logging going on in their national forests. Outside the West, they suspected, many were confused by such basics as the differences between a national forest, where logging is encouraged to produce money for the federal treasury, and a national park.

Still, the question was: how to get people excited about certain kinds of trees in a landscape that had the image of being all trees. The immediate problem was the name.

"Old-growth forest. That's a jargon term," Kerr assessed. It had been coined by forestry scientists but was difficult to explain because old-growth is not simply synonymous with virgin forest, or forest that has never been cut. Not all uncut forest land is old-growth—fire, wind, and terrain ensured that only about 60 to 70 percent of the virgin forest pioneers found would meet the biological definition—and it is possible for regrown forest to develop into old growth, given enough time. In fact, there was no scientific consensus on what old growth even was: how big the trees had to be, and how many, and what kind and shape, and how many snags and logs. The Forest Service changed definitions on two different studies that estimated how much old growth there was and came up with totals more than a million acres apart. "The term *old growth* is imprecise," said Kerr. "Worse, it sounds wrong. We are a youth-worshipping society, and old has a negative conno-

tation. And growth is something you go to the doctor to have removed."
They needed something snappier, sexier, to crystallize in a word the
value of what they wanted to save.

Kerr suggested "primeval forest." He remembered hearing it for the
first time when reading Longfellow's poem about Evangeline in school.
He liked the rolling, majestic sound of the word, suggesting the gran-
deur of the trees. Others were less sure. Did people know what primeval
meant? Besides, it had the same problems as "old-growth." There was
that "evil" sound. The name might backfire.

James Monteith, the organization's executive director, strategist, and
complement to Kerr's storm-the-walls style, suggested "ancient forest."
Technically, the name was inaccurate, if one accepted common dic-
tionary definitions that "ancient" be confined to events or objects dated
before the fall of the Roman Empire. Among living old-growth trees,
only some California redwoods and sequoias could boast that kind of
age. Still, "ancient" had the advantage of identifying one of the aspects
about old-growth trees that made them so fascinating: the considerable
age of these living things, routinely older than the republic and sometimes as old as the Norman Conquest. The trees themselves suggested
the columns of an ancient ruin. Besides, environmentalists wanted to
draw a contrast between the ecosystem that preceded humans and the
more sterile industrial tree farms that were replacing it.

Finally Monteith came up with a clincher argument. "He said
ancient forest should prevail because ancient only has two syllables,"
Kerr recalled. The group shrugged. Ancient it was.

The term was remarkably successfully, catchy but short. With striking speed, *ancient forest* came to be synonymous with old growth in
public discussions.

The careful choice of words is reflective of the thought environmental groups put into galvanizing public opposition to logging. But
their skill at promoting the issue does not mean they manufactured it
out of whole cloth. Many high-profile environmental organizations
came to old-growth late, long after scientists had identified its ecological
uniqueness and scores of grassroots groups in different communities
were already battling clearcuts. Promoting the Grand Canyon or the
Everglades was one thing, but touting the protection of woods for their
own sake seemed much more nebulous. Later, Kerr would argue that
"the issue sells itself. We're talking about trees older than the Republic,
up to a thousand years in age." But the saleability of ancient forests
was not at all apparent in the mid-1980s. Forest Service mapping was

so primitive that no one knew for certain where the surviving old growth *was*, exactly. Unlike a spectacularly scenic area, old growth seemed to require a lot of explaining, and national groups were lukewarm about trying to interest Congress. "I didn't think we could do it," Brock Evans, chief lobbyist for the Audubon Society in Washington, D.C., admitted to a group of environmentalists later. The issue came to the attention of national environmental groups right after a bruising battle over more wilderness areas and in the middle of the Reagan administration. "If ever there was a lost cause, I thought it would be a cause to protect any more ancient forest in 1985," Evans said. "I was wrong about that, and I'm glad."

"The national groups don't do anything unless it is plopped down steaming right on their desk," groused Andy Stahl, the resources analyst at the Sierra Club Legal Defense Fund office in Seattle.

It was the radical fringe of the environmental movement that first drew media and public attention to the old-growth issue, most environmental leaders would later agree. "A significant role was played by Earth First!" Kerr said. "NBC TV was not interested until people started sitting in trees."

From that, the issue built incrementally, hinging on protection of the northern spotted owl. The plight of the owl gave environmentalists ground to file lawsuits against clearcutting.

Turning to the courts had become one of the most effective weapons environmentalists had developed. In the last generation Congress had passed a huge body of ambitious but somewhat vague environmental law, much of it contradictory to the equally ambitious timber harvest levels Congress was requiring to pump money into the federal treasury. Having set up this conflict, Congress then left it to agencies such as the U.S. Forest Service to resolve it. Such agencies, pressured by special interests who had opposed the environmental legislation to begin with, inevitably made compromises in enforcing the laws once the issue moved out of the spotlight in Washington, D.C. Environmentalists then sued the government for not following its own laws, and federal judges frequently backed them up.

Both sides filed exhaustive briefs trying to educate judges on the basics of forest ecology and timber economics. Sometimes issues seemed to hinge on the broadest philosophies, and other times on arcane twists and turns in legal reasoning and argument that could even leave the opposing lawyers confused. But as the cases mounted and the ever-more desperate agencies procrastinated on owl protection, judges became increasingly testy over the foot-dragging. By the spring of 1991, U.S. District Court Judge William Dwyer did not flinch from shutting down 80 percent of proposed federal timber sales west of the Cascade Mountains, stopping logging of 66,000 acres until the Forest Service completed a long-delayed owl management plan. Failure to do so already "exemplifies a deliberate and systematic refusal by the Forest Service and the Fish and Wildlife Service to comply with the laws protecting wildlife," Dwyer wrote in a blistering, eloquent opinion.

"You could see the gloves coming off," in Dwyer's ruling, said Don Barry, a former congressional aide who followed administration of the Endangered Species Act for sixteen years before leaving to work for the World Wildlife Fund. "Once you've hurt your credibility with a judge, as the federal agencies have, it's very difficult to get it back."

Overall, the ponderous proceedings bore down on the industry with the inexorable, frosty might of an iceberg. "The timber industry didn't take it seriously at first, and that's the advantage we had," Kerr later assessed. "Their whole history is of getting their own way. They never thought the owl would be listed [as an endangered species]. What we had to do is force the body politic in the Northwest to confront its own behavior." The lawsuits did that.

Hikes, tours, and flyovers by groups such as Project Lighthawk were initiated to let public officials, the media, and local environmental groups see the scale of clearcutting. Forests were being cut down in Washington, Oregon, and northern California at an estimated average rate of four to five square miles a week, but the arena was so vast that such change was somewhat insidious. Whenever possible, environmentalists made sure policymakers saw the worst of the clearcuts.

Publicity efforts began as well. Mitch Friedman had his log tour. Lou Gold in southern Oregon put together a slide show and talk that became superb environmental theater. Articles were written in the environmental press such as *Audubon Magazine* on the broader ecological issues. Several books were published urging protection of the old-growth ecosystem. These magazines and books in turn encouraged the Northwest's mainstream media to go beyond spot news reporting of the latest lawsuit or press conference and start scrutinizing clearcutting as a whole. Sometimes the local media was too close to the issue to recognize its full significance; Kerr remembers that when the *Times* of London sent a reporter to write about ancient forests it helped prod Oregon's newspapers to cover the issue more aggressively. Eventually, enough noise was made to attract the attention of the national media, from *The New Yorker* to *National Geographic*. "I knew for sure we had won when the owl made the cover of *Time*," said Stahl.

Different environmental groups tended to take different roles. Earth First! and ONRC tended to loudly call attention to the issue. Audubon sponsored some of the earliest seminars, provided informational material, and mounted a legal defense of the owl. The Sierra Club Legal Defense Fund's opening of a Seattle office in 1987 provided the legal expertise for a sustained pattern of lawsuits. The Wilderness Society pumped the most money into quantifying how little old growth was left. The Sierra Club tried to address the economic issues raised. Regional groups, such as Headwaters in southern Oregon, mobilized grassroots support.

All this looked more carefully crafted in retrospect than it did at the time. Kerr said there was coordination between the different environmental groups, but no master strategy. The issue snowballed naturally. Stahl agreed. Mainstream environmentalists decided in 1985 *not* to challenge logging head-on and were swept up in events like everyone else. In retrospect, their only regret was that they had not acted earlier. "All the national organizations tried not to be inflammatory—and a lot of forests were cut down," said Jean Durning, Northwest regional director of the Wilderness Society.

The environmentalists labored under a curious public image. They came across as smart, well-meaning, persistent political underdogs. But they could also at times seem strident, humorless, brutal in their idealism, and even a touch misanthropic.

Andy Kerr can joke about this earnest, righteous, somewhat Puritanical image. "The environmentalist is the kind of person who volunteers to be the designated driver," he says. "The kind who says at a party, 'Well, let's help pay for the keg.' " He laughs. "But they make great ancestors."

In the end, it didn't matter how warm and fuzzy environmentalists were perceived as being. To a majority of the public, the issue was as blatant as a clearcut. "The issue nationalized much faster than I thought it would," Kerr later marveled. "Fortunately, it's a pretty ecosystem. If it was a grassland or a swamp it might have been harder." In the end, thousands of people would rally, write, donate, testify, and otherwise support the old-growth crusade. But the number of key environmentalists who worked almost daily on the issue and turned it in a few years from perennial grumbling about clearcutting to one of the planet's first campaigns for ecosystem protection was surprisingly small: at the estimate of Durning, perhaps fifty people.

Two of those fifty squared off for a debate in 1980. On one side was the bullish, bearded, outrageously provocative Kerr. On the other side was the slightly built Andy Stahl, a mild, sly political and legal tactician who had just taken a job representing the Association of Oregon Loggers. Kerr, with his boxy build, raptor nose, and bushy beard has been suggested to resemble a spotted owl. "That really ruffles my feathers," he told *Time* magazine. He makes no pretense of being an avid backpacker and, outside of a rally or a press conference, he confesses to being a bit of a loner who grew up shy and introverted in his small Oregon town of Creswell, where the timber industry paradigm was a standard part of education. He recalls reading an article in high school explaining "that forests were just a crop and one could start cutting at one end of a forest and by the time they were done at the other end, start over. It was then that I figured out that their plan wasn't to replace the forest, but rather to eliminate it and have plantations instead. It was to be closer to a cornfield than to a forest."

There is nothing complicated about his motivations, Kerr says. At heart he is an idealist, the kind who believes one person can make a difference. "I happen to still think there is good and evil," he says. "There's a right and a wrong. My underlying belief is the belief in the system. You advocate your position, and the system decides. I shouldn't have to compromise—the system is supposed to. The double standard is expecting environmentalists to compromise. Earth First! is considered a radical position, a fringe position. Earth Last is considered a respectable position."

In the 1980 debate with Kerr, Stahl answered the moral condemnations of clearcutting with the traditional reasoned arguments of foresters about its alleged biological and economic necessity. In retrospect, Stahl believed he won the debate on style, since he refused to be rattled by Kerr's attacks. But Kerr remembers that *he* won—and ultimately perhaps he did, given that Stahl was shortly to switch sides and give forestry advice to the National Wildlife Federation and then to Legal Defense Fund lawyers who were seeking to shut old-growth logging down.

While Kerr helped lead the frontal attacks, Stahl developed a different talent in his work for environmental organizations. He ended up probing the timber industry's defenses for weak spots, feeding information to the environmental organizations that employed him. Stahl's skill was being able to analyze and understand both sides, but confidently adhere to one. The commuter bicycle he kept in his Sierra Club Legal Defense Fund office fit the environmentalist stereotype nicely. On the wall, a photograph of starfish glowing in the brilliantly clear water of a wilderness beach reminded him of another hobby, sea kayaking.

Stahl had been introduced to the old-growth issue when he was a forestry student at Oregon State. In 1979 during his final year, he attended a conference at Lewis and Clark College in Portland and heard a prediction there that the recently passed National Forest Management Act would require preservation of old growth. Like Kerr, Stahl too fundamentally believes in the system—and that the correct side will prevail in court. "I have always felt that existing laws were sufficient for saving old growth, and if we could get Congress and the courts to implement the laws we had, that would be adequate."

But Congress didn't, and in fact in 1989 it passed an amendment, called Section 318, that prohibited environmentalist-sought court injunctions against logging for a year. Kerr called the 318 amendment, sponsored by Senators Mark Hatfield of Oregon and Brock Adams of Washington and tagged onto an appropriations bill, "the Rider from Hell." The environmentalist lawsuits had been based on environmental laws Congress had passed; in effect 318 kept its own laws from being enforced by the court. Little wonder that the Ninth Circuit Court of Appeals later declared that 318 trespassed on judicial branch power and was unconstitutional.

Still, before 318 was found unconstitutional it allowed most of the timber sales the courts had enjoined to proceed during fiscal 1990. Congress had responded to the anguished screams of the timber industry, which had seen more than a billion board feet of national forest trees temporarily tied up in the courts. Later some members felt they had been buffaloed by Hatfield into voting for an amendment they did not fully understand. Section 318 is an example of how confusing the timber issue became.

Three months after 318 was found unconstitutional and 1990's share of trees had been sold, the issue was still in U.S. District Court in Seattle. The lawsuit that had prompted 318 had become the Lawsuit That Would Not Die. The Forest Service had not had time to sell a dozen of the disputed timber contracts before the Rider from Hell had been found to impinge on judicial branch powers. The question was whether the original injunction still stood. Typically for this issue, Dwyer's Seattle courtroom was nearly empty of spectators. The lack of interest was testimony to the tedious minutiae of the legal issues.

Sierra Club Legal Defense Fund attorney Todd True produced a new compendium of arguments, distributing copies to the court and opposing attorneys. Mark Rutzick, True's longtime opponent, complained about still more paper. "Well, yes, but it is unbleached," True quipped about the brownish stationery, chosen by the environmental firm because it did not go through a pulp mill bleaching process suspected of producing cancer-causing dioxins. Stahl chuckled appreciatively.

Stahl grew up in Eugene, Oregon, the son of a molecular biologist who taught at the University of Oregon. He did well enough in high school to enter college as a sophomore, but early ambitions to pursue mathematics or biology foundered as he adjusted to college life by spending more time finishing growing up than studying. He got a "C" when he took a biology class from his father. He dropped out of college for a while and then moved up the Willamette Valley to attend Oregon State's forestry school, an experience he called, "three wonderful years" of learning in the woods.

Stahl took graduate courses in forest planning, "the single most important decision I made to influence my career." The training not only got him an early job teaching the Forest Service how to write plans; it also gave him insights that were to prove invaluable in advising environmentalists how to challenge timber planning and harvest levels. That was in the future. In 1980 Stahl was hired by the Association of Oregon Loggers to represent them and in his second week on the job he found himself debating Kerr. "Working for the forest industry was fun, but a little one-dimensional," Stahl later assessed. "They were pretty narrowly focused on cutting trees. There's definitely a culture gap—on both sides."

He moved in 1982 to a better-paying job with the National Wildlife Federation in Portland, one of the nation's largest and most moderate environmental groups. The NWF, originally more of a fish and game organization with a conservative membership, kept a much lower profile than Kerr's group. But it worked persuasively to educate its members and the public about the ecological value of old growth. "James Watt [President Reagan's first, controversial secretary of the interior] turned the Wildlife Federation into an activist organization," Stahl remarked.

From there, Stahl moved on to the Legal Defense Fund when it opened its Seattle office in 1987. His sympathies for old growth matured with the biological arguments during the 1980s. As early as 1979, Kerr's ONRC and the Audubon chapter of Lane County, Oregon, had appealed the U.S. Forest Service's first attempt at writing a spotted owl plan, objecting that the proposal to draw 300-acre circles around owl nests was woefully inadequate. That appeal was a turning point: it marked the environmentalists' break with the government's science, their notice that they would not wait for public agencies to protect the owl. The split would culminate in 1988 and 1989 with the humiliation of the government's sloppy science and weak owl plans in a series of court decisions.

The push for this break came not from environmental leaders but from grassroots members, Stahl noted, people who felt instinctively there *had* to be something wrong with the rapid elimination of old growth in the region. The 1984 appeal had one quick result; in response to it in 1985, the Forest Service was ordered by the Secretary of Agriculture to prepare a full-blown environmental impact statement on its spotted owl program. Still, the ammunition the environmentalists needed to shoot down the government's proposal wasn't quite in hand yet. They didn't have their own experts lined up, and thus weren't ready to file any lawsuits challenging logging head-on. Nor had any groundwork been laid by getting articles in the media or briefing politicians. What they needed were better arguments on the environmental side. Stahl went scientist hunting.

Forsman's work had given environmentalists the basis for concern: the owls were few in number, seemingly dependent on the old-growth forests the environmentalists hoped to save from the chainsaw, and suspected to be declining in number. Depending on who was doing the estimating, critical owl habitat on national forest lands in Washington and Oregon was disappearing at the rate of one to two square miles every week. Still, the government said it would take fifty to one hundred years at current logging rates to wipe out all the remaining old growth, an optimistic estimate environmentalists would not be ready to challenge in detail until 1989.

The argument the Forest Service and the logging industry developed in defense of keeping owl protection to a minimum was fairly simple: since we are not certain the owl is in immediate danger, we should continue logging until we are. In one of the court filings, Dr. Mark Boyce of the University of Wyoming spelled this out: "Although nest sites have been destroyed at a rate of 1.5 percent per year," he wrote, "the ultimate fate of the occupants is unknown. Because of inadequate population surveys and small sample sizes for demographic parameter estimates, there does not appear to be any reliable evidence that spotted owl populations are indeed declining in the Pacific Northwest." The burden of proof, the government suggested, was on the other side to prove the owl *was* in fact endangered by clearcut logging, not on the Forest Service to prove the owl was not.

In many ways this was a safe stance: no one knew for sure how many owls, on how many acres, were needed to sustain the population.

Stahl decided to find out just how firm the Forest Service's assumptions were. The 1984 plan had proposed 300-acre islands for 400 pairs of owls. "I took a look at this and wondered why 400 pairs of spotted owls were enough," said Stahl. "I wondered what the basis of their conclusion was." The Forest Service cited work by Dr. Michael Soule at the University of Michigan, so Stahl called Soule up. "I asked him if he knew his advice had been taken. He said, 'What?' " As it turned out, Soule had done genetic studies on the rate at which bristle hairs would multiply on fruit flies, and had concluded that 400 pairs of flies were sufficient to ensure rapid mutation. He was unaware his study had been cited as supporting evidence in the spotted owl debate. He agreed to question the use of his data on the owl issue.

It was the beginning of a team of scientists the Legal Defense Fund was to assemble that in court records would initially swamp the lineup of the government and timber industry, leaving it scrambling to catch up. Contributing arguments were provided by Dr. Paul Ehrlich, the population and evolution expert at Stanford University, Drs. Gordon Orians and Peter Kareiva at the University of Washington, Dr. Mark Shaffer of the U.S. Fish and Wildlife Service, and Dr. Andre Dobson at the University of Rochester.

One of Stahl's most successful hunts involved Dr. Russell Lande, at that time an associate professor at the University of Chicago. Stahl read an article about animal population dynamics by Lande and decided to ask the statistician to look at the owl specifically.

The problem was, Lande was no longer in Chicago. Stahl started calling around the country to track him down, finally finding Lande doing research on an island off the coast of Georgia where there was only one telephone. Stahl told Lande about an article by Harriet Allen, the biologist who worked for Washington's Department of Wildlife. She had discovered that only about half the owl nests found were being used. It could be that young owls were not surviving long enough, and dispersing far enough, to fill up the habitations of their elders—and thus the owl was on the road to extinction. Lande agreed to read this and similar studies.

Stahl eventually caught up with Lande in a Maine restaurant. Having studied the data, the scientist quickly sketched on a napkin the basis of an argument environmentalists could use. "This guy is now the world's top population geneticist," Stahl described. "His only interest is science. He's a total babe in the woods when it comes to politics or people. He's been in the ivory tower all his life. Heck, I'm amazed he's married. But he's a total genius."

Lande explained how mathematically, science could show an owl population needed a minimum number, on certain sized patches of old growth, at a certain concentration of patches, to ensure the owls could find each other to mate, disperse, and prevent inbreeding. Lande, intrigued by the puzzle, pursued the mathematics and concluded in a paper published in 1988 in the journal *Oecologica* that the Forest Service's 300-acre islands were inadequate. "It is well established that territorial habitat specialists [such as owls] go extinct long before all of their habitat is lost," Lande warned. "At some point, well before the complete loss of territories, the rate of recolonization becomes less than the rate territories are vacated due to the death of the residents, leading to the extinction of the population."

Daniel Doak, a University of Washington zoology graduate student, conducted a similar exercise using a different methodology and concluded the same thing.

Other scientists fired broadsides as well. "The single human activity that most threatens species the world around is the cutting down of forests," warned Paul Ehrlich, best known for authoring *The Population Bomb*.

The legal pressure was steadily applied. The Sierra Club Legal Defense Fund opened its Northwest branch in Seattle in January of 1987; by October it was ready to represent Portland Audubon and a number of other environmental groups in a lawsuit that challenged the Bureau of Land Management's logging of spotted owl habitat in Oregon.

The challenge to the Forest Service's logging took longer to develop. In 1986 the agency issued a draft of an environmental impact statement, and on December 8, 1988, a final EIS, defending its plan to set aside "spotted owl habitat areas." These included circles of protected habitat around owl nests ranging from 1,000 acres in the owl's southern range where game was more plentiful to 3,000 acres on the Olympic Peninsula, where the owl was considered the most threatened. The total acreage proposed was 374,000. Compared to what was to come later—7.7 million acres proposed by the Jack Ward Thomas committee in 1990, and 11.6 million acres of critical habitat proposed by the U.S. Fish and Wildlife Service in 1991—the plan was extremely modest, formally designating just 9 percent of the owl habitat the Forest Service claimed it still possessed. Half the identified owls were not in protected areas at all. The agency projected that, even if its plan was followed, the number of owls would decline 11 percent over the next fifteen years. That was justified as an improvement over doing nothing, in which case the owl's numbers would decline 24 percent.

Neither side liked the proposal. The 1986 draft of the plan had drawn an incredible 41,000 comments from the public, most fostered by a write-in campaign from the timber industry that produced 32,000 objections to setting aside any old growth for owls. The final plan drew 6,300 comments, of which 5,400 objected to more timber set-asides. If the Forest Service's owl plan was followed, the timber industry attorneys said, there would be disaster: the loss of 25,000 jobs in Oregon and Washington, a loss of one billion board feet in annual harvest, and the evaporation of $268 million in timber sale receipts to local government in the two states. Among the hardest hit areas would be the Olympic Peninsula, where the industry predicted (conservatively, it turned out) that national forest timber harvesting would decline by half. All this, industry lawyers complained, for a proposal that had a marginal benefit for the owl.

The timber industry suggested an alternative to the Forest Service: do nothing for five more years, cutting as usual until more studies were done.

The environmentalists had the opposite conclusion. Owl studies dated back to Forsman's efforts in 1973. Biologists such as Charles Meslow argued it was the best-understood threatened species in America. To adopt a plan that guaranteed further owl decline was simply against the law, they argued: it violated the Endangered Species Act, the Migratory Bird Act, and the National Environmental Policy Act.

Two months after the Forest Service issued its proposal, Seattle Audubon and a host of companion environmental organizations filed suit in court challenging both the plan and old-growth logging. In response to initial arguments, Judge Dwyer issued an injunction halting the sale of most federal old-growth timber in the Northwest not already affected by a similar injunction issued in Portland under a similar suit against the federal Bureau of Land Management. While there was no immediate industry shutdown—the Forest Service had already sold about two years' worth of trees that had yet to be harvested—the ultimate impact would be catastrophic.

In response, Congress passed 318, Kerr's "Rider from Hell," in the fall of 1989. Bowing to Congress, Judge Dwyer lifted his injunction in November, and during fiscal 1990—before 318 was found unconstitutional—most of the disputed timber was sold as planned. In an attempt at compromise, 318 shifted some of the harvest away from the most critical owl habitat.

The timber industry argued in retrospect that by using lawsuits, environmentalists had held a gun to loggers' heads. Instead of raising the issue politely in the state legislatures and Congress, they tied up hundreds of planned timber sales with court injunctions. Stahl contends that environmentalists couldn't wait for the slow grinding of the legislative system. "Trees were being cut at an incredible rate and it had to be stopped," he said. Besides, the "media reports conflict better than it reports anything else. Few things are better for conflict than lawsuits. It's a dramatic event. It's through lawsuits we've gotten the message out about old growth."

As if the legal locomotive bearing down on it from the BLM and Forest Service challenges were not enough, the timber industry faced an even more significant locomotive steaming from the opposite direction.

In December of 1987, the U.S. Fish and Wildlife Service, against the advice of its own biologists and under pressure from the Reagan administration, decided that the spotted owl did not meet the criteria of being a threatened or endangered species. Its conclusion was in response to the petition filed by GreenWorld. It took the agency six months after acceptance of the GreenWorld petition to decide to even study the issue, and biologists were actually given only three months to make their evaluation. Even then their conclusions were overthrown by the top brass in Washington, D.C., which was acutely aware that listing the owl would likely reduce national forest harvesting in the most lucrative woods in America by a quarter to one-third.

This controversial decision would, in 1989, receive a blistering General Accounting Office review after Congress asked for a study of Fish and Wildlife's methodology. "Fish and Wildlife Service management substantively changed the body of scientific evidence," GAO charged. "The revisions had the effect of changing the report from one that emphasized the dangers facing the owl to one that could more easily support denying the listing petition." Two of the three scientists making the evaluation, for example, told GAO they had concluded the owl was already endangered on the Olympic Peninsula. They were ignored. Administrators took out from the report a section warning that Forest Service logging would lead to the owl's eventual extinction and excised a twenty-nine-page appendix of work from other scientists supporting this conclusion. Fish and Wildlife put in its place a new report prepared by a forest industry consultant.

Before the GAO report was even ordered, however, environmentalists had taken Fish and Wildlife to court. On November 17, 1988, U.S. District Court Judge Thomas Zilly, in one of his first cases on the federal bench, ruled that the U.S. Fish and Wildlife Service had been "arbitrary and capricious" in its decision not to list the owl. He ordered the agency to start over again with a more honest appraisal.

Federal officials realized they could stonewall the owl issue no more, regardless of the economic consequences. Unless politics overruled the biologists again, few doubted that Fish and Wildlife would come back in 1990 with a decision that the owl was either threatened or endangered. Under the Endangered Species Act, logging that harmed the bird would be prohibited. Federal agency chiefs decided to form a committee made up of representatives of the affected federal agencies and a representative each from the environmentalists and industry. This panel would sift through the rapidly mounting heap of sometimes conflicting owl studies and try to decide once and for all what was needed to protect the owl.

The government gave the group an unlimited budget, told it to find the best owl experts available, and set a deadline of six months. To head the group, they picked a burly elk biologist from La Grande, Oregon. His name was Jack Ward Thomas, and in the following year, after his report was issued, he was able to find his name somewhere on the front page of the Portland *Oregonian* newspaper for thirty-seven straight days.

14

REFUSING TO LOSE

▲▲▲▲▲▲▲▲

In the months after the report of the interagency committee chaired by Jack Ward Thomas had stunned the Pacific Northwest, the burly, gray-haired, thick-armed biologist would say to angry audiences: "I want to stand up here and let you see if I'm as big a sonofabitch as you think I am."

At least three things in what was popularly called the Jack Ward Thomas report were guaranteed to cause popular frustration. First, it asked for a staggering 7.7 million acres to be set aside as habitat areas for the spotted owl, of which about 3.1 million acres was timberland that had been designated for harvest. (The remainder was land already in national park or wilderness areas or otherwise too remote, steep, high, or scenic for cutting.)

Second, it termed this prescription a compromise, warning that even with this preserve, the owl could decline 40 to 50 percent over the next century before its population stabilized.

And third, the 427-page report was so thoroughly argued, so simply written, and so impressively researched that it seemed unassailable, at least given the biological knowledge of the time.

The Bush administration, aware of the hardship that the owl conservation strategy would cause the region's timber industry, asked some government scientists to review the Thomas report and, if possible, discredit it. After review, they announced they couldn't. The Thomas report represented the best owl biology available. The Forest Service declined to adopt the report's proposals for owl conservation areas as formal policy, but did announce its intention to "not be inconsistent with" the report's recommendations. Tree sales halted in the new habitat areas.

The wood industry was deflated. For two decades it had fought, fairly successfully, to confine park and wilderness areas to the high alpine country of little commercial value. Now it had been beaten by a bird. Almost overnight, *A Conservation Strategy for the Northern Spotted Owl* had become a textbook case of how to marshal scientific argument in a political and sociological dispute.

This was a new, uncomfortable role for some of the scientists. Larry Irwin, the forest industry consultant who served on the committee, talked sometimes with Thomas about how wildlife biologists used to feel safer—aloof, omniscient, above the fray—when predicting darkly that society was about to send a species into extinction. The biologists would usually offer no realistic alternative, instead shaking their heads, wisely and impotently, as the critter indeed disappeared. "Wildlife biologists love to lose," Irwin said. "We love crying in our beer, saying we did our best, promising in our next battle we'll fight harder. . . . We do too many studies just to prove problems. We spend too much time identifying the problem and not enough time looking for a solution."

The biologists were not used to issuing prescriptions that could cost thousands of wood industry jobs, Thomas said. "Scientists would rather just do their thing and print the results in the Journal of Esoteric Results. Now they were being thrust center stage." As human population pressure builds on the planet's ecosystem the trend will increase, he predicted—and perhaps that's not a bad thing. To Thomas, it makes more sense to base political land use decisions on scientific facts, the evolving truth, than simply to split the difference between competing interest groups. "I am pleased science is being built more and more into the decision-making process. This will not be the last time."

Thomas is surprised to find wildlife biologists in such a position. He recalled his early days as a game biologist in Texas, and his fury when he felt slighted and misquoted by a sports reporter for the *San Antonio Light* newspaper. Thomas announced to his boss that he was going to storm the newsroom and rip the offending journalist's throat out. His superior told him to calm down. "This guy is a *sports reporter*, Jack," he was told. "What difference does it make? We're insignificant people in an insignificant profession doing insignificant things."

Thomas was in some ways an unlikely leader for the spotted owl report. Best known nationally for his editing of an exhaustive bible called *Elk in America*, he had never dreamed that the spotted owl would occupy center stage in ecosystem politics. He had predicted the old-growth fight, as he watched the big trees disappear, but never guessed the owl would become the tree's designated hitter. When he was named to chair the interagency committee, he had never seen a spotted owl.

He had been born and raised on a farm in Texas far away from ancient forests and owls, graduating from Texas A&M University as a game biologist. He began his career in Texas in 1957, moved to the Forest Service and worked in West Virginia beginning in 1966, and over the years picked up a master's in wildlife ecology and a doctorate in forestry. It was not until 1974 that he came to be stationed at the Forest Service wildlife research station in La Grande, Oregon. Over the years he authored about 250 articles and several books on wildlife, taking leave in the early 1980s to do some research and training work on wildlife and ecology in Pakistan and India.

"My personal career parallels the evolution of the profession," Thomas said, "in that attention to game animals gave way to much broader consideration of other wildlife. When I came in the business it was essentially all male, and predicated around hunting." He still struggles to keep pace with changes in attitudes. He remembered with amusement that in 1989 he taught a seminar to forty young biologists, half of them women. When he remarked casually that like most of them, he had become a wildlife biologist because he liked to hunt and fish, he was met with a chorus of boos. Surprised, Thomas asked how many participated in these sports. Less than a third had ever hunted, less than half had ever fished. "They come into it from a totally different direction than the old-timers," he said.

In another sense, however, Thomas was a natural choice to lead a potentially contentious committee of rival biologists. Like Franklin, he had a knack for seeing the big picture. Wildlife biologists had a tendency to consider one species at a time. In La Grande, Thomas devised an administrative system for how biologists could determine the impact of alternate management plans for all 379 vertebrate species identified in the area. "The great thing lacking in science is synthesis," he said.

Thomas also wasn't afraid to tackle big questions with big investigations. Frustrated by endless debate about how deer, elk, and cattle coexisted and competed on national forest range, he spearheaded a research effort that built a $560,000 fence to corral forty square miles and then got $1.3 million more to radio-tag the animals inside. The intent was to determine the correct balance and habits of the different species: where they feed, how they react to each other, and how they react to human intrusions such as tree harvesting or roads.

Thomas had another credential making him a natural to lead the bird study. He had no emotional stake in the spotted owl, and remained somewhat less than captivated by its personality even after his study came out. "Well, it's incredibly tame," he mused. "It is caught easily, and its nests are found easily. Interesting? It will sit there for thirty minutes watching you and blinking. To me, that's about as exciting as watching paint dry."

Given free rein to come up with a defendable spotted owl plan, Thomas assembled seventeen committee members, thirteen of whom he considered the leading spotted owl biologists in the world. Represented were the key agencies, the states of Washington, Oregon, and California, the timber industry, and environmentalist organizations. Government attorneys immediately advised him to put tight controls on how the committee operated to ensure there were no leaks to industry, environmentalists, or the media. "Leaks?" Thomas replied. "Hell, I've devised this thing to leak." Thomas opened all committee meetings to the public. A few observers watched for a while and left. Once it was clear the committee wasn't hiding anything, its painstaking assembly of a plan became rather dull.

The scientists also decided not to write a kamikaze report that demanded the ultimate for the owl, a position almost certain to be ignored. "If we only wanted to do what was good for the owl, we could have gone home in thirty minutes," Thomas said. "Stop cutting old growth and grow as much back as possible. We could have been heroes to one side. But we knew that wasn't practical. Anyone who thinks you can put forward a conservation strategy that ignores the needs of people is crazy. It will fail. The spotted owl would have ended up with nothing."

Instead, they opted to compromise, realizing the owl's present decline would take time to halt and reverse. "We recognized we would give up 40 to 50 percent of the owls before the population came to equilibrium," Thomas said. After the report came out and Thomas was explaining it in testimony to Congress, several members—assuming the report was a biological wish list—asked how many acres the owl *really* needed. How could the report be compromised? Thomas told them the compromise had already been made. "We are already dooming up to half the owls," he said. "I told them, 'Gentlemen, this is as fine a line as we can cut—there's no more room for a deal to be made.' "

If the scientists seemed too intransigent to some in Congress, the process of proposing some hard numbers that fell short of the ideal for the owl was agonizing to some of the committee members. "Compromise is the essence of the political process," said Thomas, "and some search for truth is the essence of the scientific process." That truth may be elusive. The report noted how primitive human understanding of ecosystem and species protection still is, and how imperfect any strategy would inevitably be. But it added, "Delay in implementing a conservation strategy cannot be justified on the basis of inadequate knowledge."

The committee's central conclusion was that the circular habitat islands the Forest Service had proposed around owl nests were inadequate. "We came to the conclusion it was a prescription for extinction," said Thomas. In effect the agency would be stranding the owls on a fragmented archipelago, making it extremely difficult for them to disperse from the nest or find each other for mating. The owl, used to unbroken forests, simply hadn't evolved with the ability to search effectively for isolated patches. Even if the patches were linked by corridors of trees to serve as hallways, the corridors were likely to be too skinny to let the owl population flourish. What was needed, the Thomas report said, were large blocks of contiguous old growth. On the Olympic Peninsula, there had to be enough to make that donut around the park.

The committee members spent eleven days hiking through the woods to different owl sites to see firsthand the habitat the bird seemed to prefer and then asked just what did one of the "habitat conservation areas" have to contain? At last the long, weary years of finding, tracking, counting, and observing owls begun by Forsman and continued by dozens of other biologists began to pay off.

Based on the years of study, the committee decided a minimum of fifteen owls per habitat area was required to ensure successful mating. Next, the distance between adjoining habitat conservation areas had to be short enough that the birds could disperse from one to the other. How short? They counted up the observed dispersal distances recorded over the years and decided the minimum had to be short enough for two-thirds of dispersing owls to make it: about twelve miles. The conservation areas themselves, the scientists determined, had to have big trees. How big? At least half the trees had to be eleven inches in diameter or larger, they said. Part could be logged or second growth, but about 40 to 50 percent of a habitat area had to be old growth.

These parameters decided, the scientists went to the map and drew their habitat areas. On paper, it looked like an army of amoebas were swarming over the forests of the Pacific Northwest.

Their rationale for the size and spacing of habitat areas is an interesting example of how science works. It was built on basic research that, when done, seemed to have nothing to do with the subject at hand. The committee cited obscure bird studies dating back to 1970. They read about tawny owls near Oxford, England, sea birds on islands off the English coast, hawks in Baja, California, and birds on the Channel Islands off California proper. "Who would have thought all these things had anything to do with each other?" Thomas reflected. Now the studies were being assembled to make a case for an owl that would affect thousands of human jobs.

To make clear their reasoning, the committee wrote its summary report in language aimed at high-school-level readers. In the summary's postscript, they indicated a bit of the discomfort they had to feel in making such a sweeping recommendation. "We were asked to do a scientifically credible job in producing a conservation strategy for the northern spotted owl," the team wrote. "We have done our best and are satisfied with our efforts. We have proposed. It is for others— agency administrators and elected officials and the people whom they serve—to dispose. That is the system prescribed by law. It seems to us a good one. We can live with that."

The Forest Service later estimated that forest industry employment in the Pacific Northwest would fall by about 15 percent, or 20,000 jobs. Of those, only 7,000 were attributed to the new owl areas; the remainder to the decline in cutting caused by the new forest plans that addressed other issues besides timber. The industry said that was an underestimate and initially warned up to 102,000 jobs could be lost. The figure was too high. Even after a further court injunction issued by Judge Dwyer in 1991 the industry revised its total downward, to 93,000 jobs. By that time the government was guessing a total job loss of about 40,000.

Shortly after the Thomas report was released, the timber industry suffered other defeats. The United States was almost the only nation left on the Pacific Rim that permitted export of raw, unprocessed logs from state and private land. (Log exports were already prohibited from federal land.) Late in 1990 Congress extended the ban to all state lands in Oregon and 75 percent of the logs cut from state lands in Washington.

In another move to conserve dwindling timber, Congress moved to protect more of the Tongass National Forest in southeast Alaska, where harvest was so expensive that taxpayers were subsidizing the logging of virgin forests to provide wood fiber for two pulp mills, one Japanese and the other American owned. A million acres of additional trees were set aside and the guarantee that the mills would be supplied with wood at negligible cost was repealed.

Environmentalists were less successful in northern California. Even though an estimated 96 percent of the virgin redwoods outside national and state parks and preserves had already been harvested—and even though Houston-based corporate raider Charles Hurwitz had bought out Pacific Lumber Co. there and doubled the company's annual cut from 175 million board feet to 350 million board feet—voters narrowly turned down in 1990 an initiative to raise $710 million to buy endangered redwood groves and ban clearcutting. Afterwards, some judged that the initiative was tarnished by a crowded ballot and a "Big Green" environmental initiative so overreaching that it went down two to one. A "Redwood Summer" of rambunctious protests by radical environmentalists may also have turned many voters off. After the election, however, California's timber industry announced it was taking some steps to modify clearcutting.

Certainly the overall trend spelled trouble for the timber industry. After several decades of freewheeling cutting, it was reaping a harvest of adverse legislation and public distrust. Poll after poll showed people wanted some trees protected and had low opinions of the credibility and motives of the timber industry.

Thomas found no one to blame for the crisis. "I don't really see any villians," he said of the sharp drop-off in cut. "I just see a set of circumstances that exist": a new concern for other forest values, a burst of rapid harvesting in the late 1980s that could not be sustained, the end of an era. In the supermarket at La Grande, Thomas would look at the loggers and their wives going up and down the aisles with him, realizing his research might be helping to put some of them out of work. "I particularly care about the people who are chewed up that had nothing to do with anything," he said.

One congressman asked Thomas if he had given any thought to the people being harmed by his owl report. "Congressman," he replied, "every night from one to five in the morning."

Implicit in the owl debate was the larger issue protecting the bird's remaining old-growth habitat. "This issue was never just about a bird," said Thomas. "The owl was a surrogate." There was general agreement that about 17 to 19 million acres of old-growth forest and owl habitat existed when pioneers came to the Pacific Northwest, but estimates of how much survived ranged from 30 to only 8 percent, depending in part on definitions. By the end of the 1980s it was clear old growth was nearly exhausted from private lands. For example, ITT-Rayonier near Forks had none left; Weyerhaeuser had charts showing that its harvest would change from virtually all old growth in 1980 to zero old growth by the year 2000, and that the average diameter of its typically harvested tree would fall from twenty inches in 1980 to half that by the turn of the century. The bulk of the old growth was gone from state-owned lands as well.

About 86 percent of the surviving owl habitat—in essence, old growth—was on federal forest land managed by the Forest Service or Bureau of Land Management, the Thomas report estimated. Another 8 percent was on national park land. Knowing precisely how much old growth was left seemed basic. Yet the federal agencies had no accounting system in place to do just that. "The Forest Service has been trying to ignore the old-growth issue for years, hoping the whole thing would blow away," said the Wilderness Society's Peter Morrison. "They figured: Why find out anything more about forests we're going to cut down in twenty years anyway?"

Moreover, the new owl habitat areas were not synonymous with surviving old growth, the Wilderness Society found. When Morrison analyzed the Thomas report, he found 42 percent of the surviving old growth in the Mount Baker-Snoqualmie National Forest in Washington's Cascade Mountains would not be protected by the proposed owl preserves.

More disturbing were a series of studies the Wilderness Society conducted that concluded there was about half as much old-growth forest left as the Forest Service claimed.

Some of the differences between the Wilderness Society results and those of the Forest Service hinged on the difference in definitions of old growth: the environmental group looked for biological characteristics while the agency simply defined it as mature timber. But some were apparent errors. In its 1990 report on the Mount Baker-Snoqualmie Forest, the Wilderness Society included photographs of a glacier-clad rock peak, an alpine meadow, and a replanted clearcut that the Forest Service had cited as old growth. The figures for that forest were as gloomy as those for the Olympic: out of 1.7 million acres of land total, only one-third was virgin "ancient" forest, only 17 percent met biological old-growth characteristics important to species such as owls, and only 2 percent, or 38,400 acres, was the biggest old growth below the 2,000-foot elevation.

Much of the work that went into these calculations was old-fashioned visual surveys and analysis of aerial photographs. But one of the keys to the Wilderness Society studies, said Morrison, was the computer. It made possible the quantification and storage of data. "There is incredible interpretative power in personal computers at this time," he said. "This type of project would not have been even possible five years ago."

It is possible to argue, in fact, that without the computer the old-growth forest debate might never have developed at all, or at least would not have developed to the degree of sophistication it did. It was the computer that enabled Weyerhaeuser to develop a detailed plan of intensive forestry in the 1960s that led to the tree plantation known today. It was the computer that allowed timber-selling agencies to speed up their processing of sale permits. It was the computer that gave forest ecologists such as Jerry Franklin the ability to sort and analyze the rich detail of ecosystems that demonstrated their complexity, their graceful feedback loops of nourishment and decay, and their value. The whole science of ecology bounded forward with computers, said Thomas. "Lo and behold, we have number crunchers, in the form of computers, to handle ecosystems." Before the machines, the natural systems were too tediously complex for humans to statistically analyze.

Jean Durning of the Wilderness Society said the message of the numbers was obvious: annihilating the surviving big trees to prolong logging jobs a decade or two was the worst kind of societal shortsightedness. Both the Wilderness Society and Sierra Club urged a comprehensive government program to help timber communities such as Forks ease out of dependence on the harvest of old-growth timber, including encouraging loggers to find new jobs in the region's urban core. Such proposals provoked fury in Forks. The loggers resented environmentalist arguments that they were becoming as obsolete as buffalo hunters or whalers and complained that the aid environmentalists suggested was patronizing, coming from people who had put them out of work. "If we wanted to live in Seattle, we'd move to Seattle," growled Ann Goos.

But Durning was adamant that the time had come to draw the line. "We're at the last ten percent of what was once virgin forest," she said. "It is not appropriate to settle for half of what is left."

Months after his committee's report came out, Thomas himself still seemed a bit surprised at the enormity of its scope and conclusions. He compared it to the controversy over Tellico Dam in Tennessee, where completion of the dam was delayed because of concern over a rare minnow called the snail darter. Congress eventually made an exception to the Endangered Species Act to allow the dam to proceed. "The Tellico Dam was a minor blip compared to this," he said.

What his committee had recommended was unprecedented in the United States and probably in the world. Never had it been urged to set aside so much land, at such apparent economic cost, for so few birds. "Am I going to tell you I feel vindicated, exalted?" Thomas asked. "I don't. I just feel tired. All I can claim is we did a damn good job in what we were asked to do." Scientists were calling the Thomas report perhaps the best of its kind ever written.

The true significance of the spotted owl battle is not just its impact on old growth or jobs, Thomas said. While it is possible of course that society may retreat from the Thomas committee's recommendations on the owl as it did on Tellico Dam, widespread national concern over the loss of old-growth forest made that seem unlikely, at least immediately. There appeared to be a recognition in Congress and federal agencies—sometimes grudging—of the dangers of bending all the natural world to a less-intricate human design. In both the mind and heart, mentally and instinctively, people seemed to recognize a value to preserving biodiversity.

Thomas could joke about the practical difficulty of this: "Dealing with biodiversity is like eating jello with chopsticks—the intent is very clear but there is something lacking in the execution." Still, he recognizes its importance. "I don't think the world's going to be the same place," says Thomas. "We are actually seeing the evolution of the land-use ethic." Ecologists were boldly looking at the entire landscape now, drawing their blobs of critical habitat across the map. "It's been a mind-boggling change in scale. We have a tendency to know a hell of a lot about individual species" and very little about how they fit into an overall picture, Thomas said. "This is a relatively recent discovery, that the world doesn't come one thing at a time."

This business of drawing huge preserves for individual species such as the owl is unlikely to continue, however, said Thomas. "If we consider one species at a time, we are going to drive anybody trying to manage the land absolutely bonkers." In the spring of 1991, the U.S. Fish and Wildlife declared endangered or threatened four subspecies of salmon that migrate from the ocean to Idaho to spawn. That opened the door for a string of likely salmon listings that could ultimately eclipse the land-use impact of the spotted owl. Salmon have even a vaster range than owls, roaming from the sea to the tiny tributaries where they spawn. Protecting them means managing the dammed rivers that the salmon use for fish as well as for people. That could restrict hydroelectric generation, irrigation, drinking water, logging in stream watersheds, cattle grazing, development: in short, virtually any land use activity in the sprawling Columbia River Basin.

Other species are waiting in the wings too. The marbled murrelet seabird uses old-growth forests to nest in. The grizzly bear and gray wolf are apparently becoming reestablished in the North Cascades and some environmentalists were urging wolf reintroduction on the Olympic Peninsula. The Pacific yew tree that grows in ancient forests is, while not endangered, in too short supply to fill the likely future demand for its bark to make taxol, a drug that shows promise in battling ovarian and lung cancer. All these species, salmon included, to some extent benefit from old-growth forest. The next logical step, said Thomas, is not designating individual parks or wildernesses or endangered species, but recognizing entire ecosystems and figuring out how human society can coexist with them.

Is such coexistence necessary? What is wrong with transforming the planet to human needs: to turning forests to tree farms, prairies to cornfields, deserts to irrigation works, and the seas to aquaculture?

Environmentalists offer three reasons.

The first is practical. Species driven to extinction now may prove useful to humans in the future if left to survive. Present-day examples are the Pacific yew or the rosy periwinkle of Madagascar, both used to treat cancer and both threatened by logging. From one-quarter to one-third of drugs on the market today are not synthetic. They still come from plants. Wild salmon are more vigorous and disease resistant than their hatchery-bred cousins. Wild strains of corn and wheat have been tapped to develop new hybrids more resistant to crop diseases.

The second reason is aesthetic. While it might be possible to subsist on a planet with only domesticated plants and animals, it would be a bleak and spiritually barren place, without the charm and wonder and terror of the natural world.

The third is moral. Humans, some contend, simply have no right to drive another species such as the spotted owl to extinction if they can choose another course. At the cutting and controversial edge of environmentalism is "deep ecology," the belief that other species have as valid a claim to the earth as do humans.

Thomas, who has spent his lifetime trying to understand the natural world people inherited, had to muse about the need for preserving it only for a moment. "I am a person a bit more humble about bending managed ecosystems to our whim," he said. "I will never see a passenger pigeon, or a free-roaming buffalo on the great plains. I sure wish I had. Those people who hunted them didn't preserve my option. They settled that before I had the chance."

Well, what about a state such as Iowa? What's wrong with making it all cornfields and cows? "Did all of Iowa have to be cornfields and cows, or could a third have been left in free-roaming prairie?" Thomas asked. "I'd hope for options in the future—not all one way, not all another."

15

THE EMPTY MILL

▲▲▲▲▲▲▲▲

In a chill dusk of the winter that followed issuance of the Jack Ward Thomas report, the million-dollar sawmill completed by Larry Mason is still. Its muddy yard is mostly empty of stacked logs now, depressions in the mud marking where the trees once lay. The few fat cedars left behind are like fossil remnants of Mason's hopes for the future. Their girth is a remarkable contrast to the wall of dense, pencil-like second growth surrounding Mason's mill. It is as if the two kinds of trees came from different worlds.

No one was in more direct competition with the spotted owl than Larry Mason. He had starting building his mill in 1987 specifically to take advantage of the fine-grained old growth the Forks area boasted. "Virgin Timber from the Heart of the Olympic Peninsula," the company slogan on a truck door read. Mason bet a lifetime of work on Forest Service promises that he could get a sustained supply of old-growth timber from Olympic National Forest. He helped log the clearing next to Highway 101 for the mill site himself. He designed from scratch the architecture for its machinery, salvaging some of the equipment and setting it up with a straight-line simplicity and a minimum of walls and roof, to prevent the twists and turns and cramping of production lines often forced on older mills by their enclosing buildings. He poured everything he earned and learned over twenty years into that mill. Then scientists said the trees Mason needed were the same ones the bird preferred.

"It's over," Mason says by way of weary greeting. With his salt-and-pepper beard he looks older than his forty years. As usual he is wearing a billed cap, dirt-stained jeans, hickory shirt and suspenders; missing this evening is the button he sometimes wears that reads, PEOPLE COUNT

TOO. He explains that the banks have already forced the auction of one fork lift for half its real value and Mason has signed up for unemployment. "We're shut down. I've lost the mill."

Two years ago, Mason employed forty people. He sat down once to calculate how much wood a single 3,500-acre spotted owl preserve— the type proposed by the Forest Service that was later declared inadequate by the Thomas Committee—could provide on a sustained basis. Mason figured that single circle for owls could have produced enough trees to keep those forty people employed at his mill forever.

The crazy thing was, before the owl battle began he was making money. He was selling finished wood products to foreigners around the world. He cut wood for boat lumber, ladder rails, door and window frames, molding, stair treads, transmission pole crossarms, scaffolding planks, and veneers for Japanese construction. He was providing work, paying taxes, and lowering the trade deficit. Larry Mason was doing all the things the government had claimed it wanted Americans to do. Then the government took his wood supply away.

"For us to lose everything, that's not what is really the worst," Mason said. "To have a whole way of life destroyed, that's the worst."

It is not that Mason cannot find work elsewhere. He is smart, articulate, tireless, and inventive. Larry will shortly find temporary employment as a consultant to other mills and ultimately direct the Washington Commercial Forest Action Committee.

It is rather that the creation he poured his heart into is stilled, and that the one thing he thought he could do as well or better than anyone in the world—carefully turn premier wood into premier products—is lost to him. He drove three thousand miles before he found Forks. He made something fundamental from the earth. The people who shut him down don't understand the satisfaction, the sheer naturalness, of that. "You take this raw product of nature—this huge, immense tree that could kill you at any moment—and you cut it down, and you yard it, and you truck it, and you get it into the mill, and you make something out of it—there's a real feeling of accomplishment," he says in his half-empty office. Mason shakes his head. The room is cold. The pictures and plaques are down and the wood stove out.

The mill builder is puzzled at the direction the United States economy seems to be taking. Sometimes it seems like everyone is becoming either a stockbroker or a hamburger fry cook. "I cannot for the life of me understand that if somebody doesn't make anything, how can you have an economic system that works?" he asks. He believes people such as those in Forks were once the keystone of American productivity, and yet their plight seems to be regarded with indifference.

"My family really personifies the ludicrous nature of this situation," Mason says. "It's really hard to teach your children to be honest and hardworking when all they see is honest and hardworking people being fucked over. It's really hard to teach them to respect the environment when the environmentalists have taken your livelihood away. It is difficult for kids to understand the complexity of this."

In Forks, they call Larry Mason their Connecticut Yankee, though he was born in Maine and spent his childhood in Massachusetts. He describes himself two decades before as a hippie, the first male in his family to decide to drop out of college. Instead he got in a van and drove west to escape what he called "the pollution and chaos" of the East Coast. He went first to California, then drifted north to Washington. Like so many others of his generation in rebellion against postwar conformity, he was looking to get back to something basic. He wanted to get back to the land.

"I had the most amazing experience when I rounded the corner at Port Angeles to come out here," he remembered. Highway 101 crests a hill just east of Lake Crescent and then descends to the water, the gate to the West End. When the weather and the light is right—the water ruffled by the wind, the walls of mountains surmounted by towers of cloud, the sun throwing beams of energy like lasers to pick out details of the landscape with a lens of gold—the introduction is breathtaking. "I got to the edge of Lake Crescent and it was like déjà vu— I had this sense I was home," Mason said. His odyssey was over.

That was an era when there was routine conflict between the longhairs like Mason and the rednecks in rural towns like Forks. But it was also the time when Forks's reputation as a logging capital was being established. There was a lot of work available for anyone willing to do it, and plenty of chances for any man to prove himself, whatever the length of his ponytail or beard. "I loved it here," Mason said. "No matter what your views you were respected if you worked hard. It's not like in the city, where if you work hard, if you do physical work, you are thought too dumb to make money an easier way." There was a simple honesty about the values on the West End. He adopted its culture, and in turn the Forks community adopted him.

It might seem peculiar for a back-to-the-land hippie to adopt the

Logging Capital of the World as his home, but Mason does not see the conflict. Because people do depend on the land for their livelihood, they replant it and monitor it, he said. "A lot of people in Forks are more in tune with the land. That's historically the way they've lived. They grow a garden, they recycle, they use compost to make fertilizer. People out here fix their own cars. They do their own plumbing."

His wife Liz, an Ohio arts graduate, still recalls the seeming bleakness of the place when she arrived there on New Year's Day in 1975. "It was nighttime, it was pouring rain, and I felt like I was at the end of the world," she said. But the land pulled at her, too. She met Larry, this hippie living in a van, about a year after her arrival. They began living together and started their own business in the least-capital-intensive way they knew, contracting to plant seedlings in recent clearcuts. There was no mechanical equipment needed. Just a shovel, a bag of seedlings that cost pennies each, and a strong back.

"When you plant trees, you can get days like this morning," Mason said on a soft and sunny autumn day, the brush heavy with dew and the trees seeming relaxed and sleepy in the stillness before winter. "You get out there, and the mist is rising, and it's just you and those trees." The seedlings would be in a bag slung over the shoulder—a bit like Johnny Appleseed, perhaps, but heavier—and the couple would move across the steep slopes, prying apart a wedge in the soil, stooping to drop in a seedling, closing the wedge with their feet. Sometimes it was raining, and sometimes it was too hot. But often consciousness of the weather would be overtaken by the rhythm of the work. "Your body goes on automatic after a while and you dwell on whatever you want to dwell on. I used to think about how I would build my house."

He liked the fact that most tree planting occurred during the winter, when the soil was wet with moisture. Working through the darkest months like that, studying the ground, the Masons would get the first glimpses of spring. "You see all the colors that start to occur on the forest floor," he said. "It was like our spring was longer than anyone else's."

They also saw areas of windfallen timber left to rot. In those days when the cut of live trees was so high that no one wanted to bother with windfall, the Masons broke into the timber business by salvaging what others saw as waste. The couple couldn't afford yarding machinery to drag the logs up to the road, so they used hand winches and muscle. "It was taking something no one else would," said Mason.

They applied the same ingenuity to building a house. The Masons heard about a garage being torn down in Port Angeles and were able to cart off the lumber for free, pulling out the rusted nails to reuse the wood. They cleared part of a fifteen-acre patch of dense second growth up against a ridge and started building a home. They dug a well and used wood for heat. Electricity didn't come until 1988. Their ingenuity with wood shows up in their home. It is a cozy, modest place of gables and open beams and multipaned windows, with a big cast-iron stove inside. Deer wander through their yard.

Liz grew up in the Cleveland suburbs. The lush fertility of the land still astounds her. A tree in the Mason's front yard that was shrub height when they started their house sixteen years ago has grown forty to fifty feet high. The heavy rain does that. When Liz drives her children out the gravel road through the trees to the school bus stop each morning, frequently they pass and recognize a local doe with two fawns. It is like knowing another neighbor.

The ridge behind their house was logged about the time Larry's youngest son was born, twelve years before his mill was shut down. Every birthday since then the father has taken his boy up to see the replanted trees there, now high above their heads. "It gives you perspective on what farming trees is all about," Mason said.

By the end of 1990 Liz was worn down by the rancor of the old-growth debate. "In the past two years it's been constant limbo," she sighed. "Is this business going to make it? Your nerves get fried." Looking at the dense flush of evergreens sprouting all around her home, she does not understand what seems like urban hysteria. "I really feel like we've been the environmentalists," she said.

After they settled in their Forks home, the Masons continued finding opportunities in the nooks and crannies of the local wood industry: selling cedar blocks to shake mills, going partners with a small mill, surviving when the other owners failed. Larry was a good businessman. Each year he made money. One thing he noticed was that Forks was a bit like a Third World country, shipping out its wealth of timber for others to process. Federal law banned the direct export overseas of trees from the national forests—it had to have at least a minimal pass through U.S. saws—but the highest-grade Douglas fir coming off the Olympic National Forest near Forks was being trucked all the way to Oregon for milling. It didn't make sense.

"We went to the Forest Service and asked them about wood supply," he said. Forest Service projections showed that the agency was cutting on a sustained-yield basis and that the three to four million board feet of old growth per year that Mason needed should continue to be available for years, probably decades. "The Forest Service said they were supposed to harvest the same volume every year in perpetuity," Mason recalled.

He saw an economic opening. The increasing rarity of old growth was swelling its value. Its clear knotless grain and high strength made it the top choice for scores of finished products. A modern mill designed to handle the huge old trees could be built to process the wood where it came from, near Forks. By the time the last of it was cut out, Mason figured, he would have had time and income to convert his mill machinery to handle smaller second-growth trees. To get the million dollars necessary Mason put up his home, his land, and all his possessions. Mill construction started in 1987 and was fully completed in 1989, "just in time for the court injunctions to take our wood supply away."

"Up until this conflict, I loved my job," Mason said. "This business is everything we've made in twenty years. I liked the independence of it. There was no time clock, no foreman, no drug test, no bullshit. The same people who work here are the same people I drink beer with. This is more a way of life than an investment for a fiscal return. We aren't in this because it gives big paychecks—we're in this business because we love it and we think we do it right. All I want to do is continue my goddamn job and keep people working."

As night falls Rick Hurn comes in the office. Both men pop a beer, Mason collapsing each can as it is emptied and putting it in a recycling box. Rick is built like a wrestler and has the direct, blunt manner so common around Forks. He is a logging contractor who specializes in salvage sales on national forest land. He was the one who bought the tangled mess that Russ Poppe cut.

Rick is in economic trouble this winter too. About two weeks earlier, five to six inches of rain fell in a single night, cutting the roads that led to two sales he had bought and washing half of what Poppe harvested down into the rivers. Hurn figures he lost about one hundred truckloads of cut logs in a single night, or half of what he has already paid the Forest Service for. Below Poppe's cut, he and a Forest Service employee picked their way down the creek bank for a couple of miles, looking vainly for his logs.

Hurn said he has employed about twenty loggers. Now he doesn't know if he'll be able to purchase logs at all.

In September of 1990 Mason and Hurn were among several Forks residents who went back to Washington, D.C., to lobby Congress. Both men hated the city. Rick was initially intimidated by the capital's subway system, but he soon felt more comfortable in its tunnels than in congressional offices. He remembered one Washington congressman jabbing his finger at a group from Forks, heatedly lecturing them on overcutting. Rick, who has a reputation for a quick temper, shouted back, but it did no good. The congressman took pause for breath and then went back to lecturing, jabbing that finger. Everyone in D.C. seemed to want to save the trees and no one seemed to have any idea what would happen to the people who had been cutting them.

"What you see there is just ludicrous," said Mason, with a note of wonder in his voice. "It's a let-them-eat-cake psychology back there. Nobody in the place makes *anything*. They're all working for government, and they all seem to lead this extravagant life-style."

Their mood toward government didn't improve when representatives of the governor's office showed up in Forks to announce the state had no money to help the town. Later, on the telephone, Mason got so testy with the governor's office that the aide hung up on him.

Mason is a dinosaur, urban environmentalists would argue. Magnificent in the way he works hard, noble in his ingenuity, but doomed by changes in the economic climate. The United States has entered a postindustrial era. We are in the information age. Production is measured in electrons that blip through wires. The era of the big trees is over, a nineteenth-century occupation trying to carry itself over into the twenty-first. People like Mason need to adapt, environmentalists argue. The future of Forks is in catching up to the present.

"They lecture us about economic diversification," said Ann Goos sourly once. "When you ask them just what they've got in mind, it's eco-tourism." She almost spits out the word. "That's their solution for our future!" She shook her head in contempt. Make all the Peninsula a playground. Cater to the urban tourist on the intermittent weekends when the sun shines. Make their beds, cook their food, carry their high-tech yuppie outdoor gear into the forest for them, dawdle along behind their motor-homes. Yes, Bwana. It turns her stomach.

Rick Hurn feels as if lunatics have seized control of forest management. Jerry Franklin's New Forestry will prove a colossal failure, he predicts. The trees left behind for wildlife will topple and the clearcuts will be reclaimed by brush, or trees diseased with mistletoe and insects. Everything that has been learned in the last half century about the sometimes brutal necessities of managing a tangled and unruly forest is being thrown out. "Twenty years from now, people will look back on this and think this one of the biggest scams ever pulled on the American public," Hurn said.

Rick is the eldest son of Dean Hurn, arguably the most important businessman in Forks. Dean runs timber-purchasing and milling companies that employ about one hundred people directly and probably a couple hundred more indirectly, and is often one of the most generous donors to both community projects and timber-issue lobbying efforts.

Dean Hurn and his wife Elaine grew up in the Cascade Mountain town of Concrete, Dean's father running a shingle mill so remote it had to generate its own power. The couple married in 1958 and by the early 1960s the family began looking for a new source of wood. "We came here in 1964 because cedar was getting scarce in Skagit County," Elaine explained in the kitchen of her expansive, sunlit home on the Sol Duc River near Forks.

She had much the same reaction to the remote West End as Liz Mason. "When we first came out it was February, and it was snowing. I thought, 'My God, this is the end of the world.' " For the first six months the couple and their four children crammed into a two-bedroom trailer.

The western Peninsula seemed dark to Elaine because of the trees that gripped the highways, keeping them icy because no sunlight could reach the pavement. "It was just like going through a tunnel. I hated it. You'd never see daylight." But Elaine has grown to love the place. "When we finally cut the trees from here to Beaver, you could finally see some mountains. I couldn't believe it, it was so pretty." She even enjoys how the clearcuts bloom with foxglove and fireweed and blackberries. She also has more sun now: their present home is on a sixty-acre cattle spread with expansive views across rolling green fields.

On paper, at least, Dean Hurn is a millionaire in business assets. He has the build of a longshoreman, the blunt manner of a crew boss, and the habits of a laborer. He typically goes to work at six A.M. and comes back thirteen hours later. He spends as much time as he can out-of-doors. After going through the mail and returning telephone calls he will devote a good part of the day to sorting logs by driving a fat-tired log loader across the mud of his log yard. Evenings he often spends on the telephone.

"There's a lot of people depending on Dean," noted Ingrid Dahl-gren, whose family is the Hurn's primary logging subcontractor. His purchases of federal or state timber are what logging firms such as the Dahlgrens' depend on to harvest.

Hurn's operation fuels the economy in other ways. Of $2.9 million he paid for 128 acres of timber in Olympic National Forest, $875,320 went for state and local taxes.

In a business where many go broke, Hurn has survived a quarter century. The battle over old growth and owls is making it far tougher, however, causing prices to fluctuate unpredictably. In September of 1990, Hurn was so desperate to ensure a future wood supply that he bid $1.6 million on the sale of 6.3 million board feet of timber on the Olympic National Forest that the Forest Service had conservatively appraised at only $353,900. The next closest bid was only $828,144. In effect, Hurn had bid nearly $800,000 more for the wood than he had to, but he had expected ferocious competition for that kind of volume. Ironically, wood prices plunged shortly after the sale was made.

There are other costs as well. Hurn noted that he spent $250,000 in campaign contributions and lobbying costs in the past year fighting the lockup of the woods. The owl controversy was simply eating him alive.

Elaine is frustrated at the squeeze this puts on her family. "We don't know who these people are," she said of environmentalists who file lawsuits in Seattle and Portland. "They are just 'They.' We have to follow all these rules, but then they change the rules, so that whatever we've done is always wrong. What I want to know, if they tie up all the trees what are they going to use for all this stuff?" she said, rapping her wooden kitchen table and the newsprint and stationery heaped upon it.

It is not that couples like the Hurns could not foresee the danger and sorrow and uncertainty of their trade. Like E. C. Gockerel they tried, unsuccessfully, to interest their children in a safer kind of future. "I kept telling the kids, 'Can't you get into something else?' " Elaine said. "They wouldn't listen." All three of the Hurns' surviving sons have gone into logging—two work directly for their father and Rick has his own firm—and both daughters have also worked for the company. "That's the problem," she said, gesturing to the green rolling hills outside her kitchen window and the gray, rushing Sol Duc River.

"They were raised in an environment that's so nice. They want to stay out here in it."

While the Hurns have been economically successful in the woods, the trees have extracted a bitter price. Everyone in Forks, it seems, knows someone who has lost someone to the forest. Part of what links the community together is the web of shared tragedy that living on the edge of a wild place seems to weave. In February 1976, one of the couple's sons, fourteen-year-old Roger, got lost hunting on Dead Man's Hill, a ridge north of Forks. He died of hypothermia shortly after being found.

The following year (the same year the Hurns learned their youngest daughter had leukemia, from which she later recovered) a log fell on Dean as it was being loaded onto a truck. The log flattened him, stretching out his body as if it were hit with an iron. Hurn's eye was torn out of its socket, his cheek was crushed, and a key nerve in his leg was elongated, temporarily destroying the use of the limb. He was back at work as soon as he could limp, but the leg still pains him.

The tragedies went on. Two daughters of one of Hurn's partners were killed by a logging truck on their way to school. Two friends of another son were also killed by a truck.

Elaine Hurn likes to take long, morning walks with Vicky Queen, a young widow whose husband Wayne—the third son of his family to die in the forest—was killed by a falling tree while working for the Hurns. A network television show featured the Queen family in a story about the terrible odds loggers face. When Vicky was asked about her own sorrow, she spoke of the peculiar bond to the forest that persists in the West End. "I don't have any hate for the woods," she told the cameras.

The reality was, the loggers had paid, and paid dearly, for their life in the wild. That was one reason the old-growth fight hurt so much. The work that their friends died for seemed itself to be dying.

Larry Mason is more outspoken about his rage and frustration with environmentalists than most people in Forks. Perhaps it is because he identifies more closely with them. He came to Forks to escape pollution and get back to the land. He lived in a van, he built his house of recycled lumber, and he started in the timber business planting trees. "I came out to live in the land with harmony," he said. "That perspective has never changed."

"People don't understand the dynamic nature of the forest," he said. He regards the heavy dark green of the older trees as a sign of their declining vigor, compared to the brighter green of replanted growth. "It's decadent—it's in the dying phase of its cycle," Mason said. "This concept of groves of eternal sentinels is just not true. The forest is always changing."

Mason believes he has the environmentalists' number. One year he put a float in Forks's Fourth of July parade that featured an enormous old-growth stump with a Volkswagen van spiked to it, a visual raspberry to every ecotage enthusiast who had ever thought of spiking a tree. *"Get the point?"* the banner on the side slyly asked.

"My feeling is that the endangered species act was written with good intent, but quite naively," he explained. "It is being misused for a land grab." He doesn't understand why an owl with a range across three states necessarily has to be saved on the isolated Olympic Peninsula, where it requires huge ranges to survive. He thinks the Olympic National Forest should be designated for *more* wood production, not less, because Olympic National Park already provides a huge old-growth preserve. Instead, the opposite has occurred. The park has been used to help justify more preservation. Wilderness buffer zones line the park boundaries. Some environmentalists urge buffers in front of those buffers.

What hurts as much as anything is that all the change seems to have come from outside, Mason said. It is as if Forks was a name on a map, not a place with history and old families and a store of local knowledge. All the important decisions about Forks have seemingly been made without consultation with those who lived there.

"When you go around the U.S. and systematically discard people, people like my wife and myself—we who combined a lot of our own financial resources with integrity and hard work . . ." He looks quizzically, exasperation in his eyes, as if still dumbstruck that people can't see the obviousness of his tragedy. "What happens when America discards that population?"

Mason said he understands the origins of the old-growth conflict. "For the first time, Americans are aware resources are finite," he said. "I agree it is very appropriate that areas be set aside."

"But on the other hand, it is also very appropriate some of the land be farmed. An inappropriate way is to file a court injunction and make a town die." Mason shook his head. "There are three and four generations of people here who haven't done anything wrong."

The world will cut just as many trees, Mason predicted. They will just cut them elsewhere and probably in places that recover more poorly, such as the tropical rain forest or the slow-growing taiga of the north. Since 1960, worldwide wood consumption has nearly tripled.

Mason simply isn't convinced by the environmentalists' arguments. He thinks they have a manipulative leadership and a naive rank and file. "They've got this sense of guilt that it is wrong their life-style is gobbling up the earth," he said. "The way they address this guilt is instead of curbing their consumer use and conserving resources they continue their life-style and send a check to the Audubon Society. That's the tragedy of this whole thing. What they're doing doesn't curb world demand. All it does is restrict supply."

16

SANCTUARY, I

▲▲▲▲▲▲▲

The self-built home of recycled wood where Bonnie Phillips-Howard lives nestles on the six-acre site of a former logging camp, some forty miles north of Seattle.

There is irony in her homesite's history: first, because Phillips-Howard has become one of the most implacable foes of freewheeling logging, a quintessential example of the citizen activist who has bit into the vulnerable heel of the timber industry and, like some determined terrier, won't be shaken off; second, because her yard could serve as an example of the earth's potential for recovery after logging.

The former logging camp is so lush with trees and shrubs that it is easy to miss her driveway. Even when it is found, the visitor wonders if the tire-wide gravel strips that lead away through the grass into a tunnel of trees go to a place presently inhabited, or a place once used and now abandoned and overgrown. There is a purposeful wildness about the home, a garden that is the antithesis of a mown lawn.

The environmentalist has made her yard an experiment in living in harmony with nature. There are old-growth stumps on the site with their springboard holes, memorials to that first logging. There are second-growth conifers up to a century old that seeded into the old clearcut and are now more than one hundred feet high. There are also scores of planted fruit, ornamental, and conifer trees and hundreds of shrubs, including more than one hundred varieties of rhododendron. The Phillips-Howard yard is a mini-arboretum, a pleasant thicket of winding paths and hidden openings and secret orchards such as a child would delight in. The variety of the vegetation—planned in part as a deliberate contrast to the timber industry's single-species tree farm— draws so many birds that Bonnie once counted twenty-three species in her yard at one time. The raccoons got the corn in the vegetable garden this year, but the Phillips-Howards don't seem to mind. Their yard has been designated by the state as a Wildlife Sanctuary.

The timber industry recognizes in Bonnie Phillips-Howard the kind of earnest, insistent watchdog they have come to dread. Childless, highly educated, and with no outside career, she has the time and persistence to monitor the industry's performance. While privately recognizing the issue's complexities, in public she can summon an expression of certainty and outrage when she insists that logging the last of America's greatest trees is simply wrong. Phillips-Howard found one clearcut she might support, however, a controversial one proposed to be on the doorstep of the logging town of Darrington. "Why shouldn't they have to look at what they do?" she asked when the town's residents complained about the cut.

Ann Goos recalls with distaste running into Bonnie outside the legislative chambers in Olympia, Phillips-Howard poking into a huddle of timber-industry lobbyists and proposing they share what their position was on a technical issue. "She just butted in," Goos complained. Phillips-Howard has also tirelessly badgered the Darrington Ranger District office where Jerry Franklin lectured on Gold Mountain, urging that old-line Forest Service employees there recognize other forest values besides timber.

Fred Harnisch, the Darrington district ranger who came in December of 1987, was the first to cautiously welcome the environmentalists. He opened his headquarters to both sides. But building a constructive relationship has not been easy. The Pilchuck Audubon chapter headed by Phillips-Howard, named for a prominent local mountain peak, "didn't understand the complexities" when they first tried to monitor forest planning, Harnisch said. The ranger watched his district's annual cut plummet from 80 million board feet when he came to 18 million by 1991, and witnessed the resulting economic dislocation this caused in Darrington. Trying to work with both the increasingly desperate loggers and the environmentalists who urged such a drop is hardly easy.

Yet slowly, "The chips on their shoulders kinda fell off, and the chips on our shoulders kinda fell off," Harnisch said. "We needed the public's help, actually. Within the organization, a lot of us knew a change was needed for more balanced management, but we had to have a push from outside."

If fate in the form of physical disability had not intervened, few might have heard of Bonnie Phillips-Howard. In 1984 she was stricken with a severe arthritis that made it impossible for her to continue her passion for hiking, mountain climbing, and running. After two fruitless years looking for relief, "I decided I wasn't going to spend my life looking for a magic cure," she said. She elected to devote herself to environmental activism. "There should be something you are doing besides just living," she said. "There should be something you *do* with your life." The restless shifts of her slight body curled on a couch gave hints of both her pain and her energy.

Phillips-Howard had never seen a spotted owl. She could not go more than a few hundred feet into the forest without a wheelchair. She had no background in forestry. None of this proved to matter. So intensely did she plunge into the old-growth forest battle that she soon was the Pilchuck chapter's president.

Her life has made a kind of parabolic curve: from antiwar activism in the 1960s, to retreating from society to her six-acre homesite in the 1970s, to old-growth activism again in the late 1980s. When she began participation in the forest debate, she started from simple conviction that the ugly brown mange of clearcuts in her beloved Cascades and Olympics was wrong. Only slowly did she learn about the new ecological discoveries that backed up her instinct, seizing on new studies like someone discovering coins in the sand. Despite her lay status, she demanded change in the technical forest practices of Forest Service bureaucrats, of career loggers, and of landowners whose families had held their deeds for generations. Depending on your point of view, it was either presumptuous and arrogant or gutsy and necessary.

"Sometimes something has to happen in your life for you to say, this is it. I don't have any more time to know this issue. I have to speak up."

Since she often felt over her head in debate with forest professionals, she began reading voraciously and seeking advice. She got Jerry Franklin to spend five hours explaining old growth and new forestry to her Audubon group. She came to accept as normal that loggers would call her up on the telephone, sometimes to quietly agree, sometimes to debate, and sometimes to call her names or issue threats. Once she went to a rousing pro-timber speech by Washington Senator Slade Gorton that was attended by an angry crowd of loggers. "I was the only one in the audience without a yellow ribbon," she recalled. The only time she had ever felt that much hostility was when she marched with blacks in Milwaukee after Martin Luther King was killed.

Another time she challenged a Forest Service timber sale in the

Darrington district and learned the buyer who had won the bid was Lawrence Hornbeck, a longtime logger who was still climbing trees at age seventy-two. Hornbeck was counting on this one last sale so that he could retire a year earlier than he had planned. Phillips-Howard's appeal was eventually rejected, but it bothered her to think of Hornbeck all the way home, of how big fights about the survival of a magnificent ecosystem boiled down, in the details, to a tiny tract of timber and one man's plans for retirement.

The uncertainty was worse because the battle for biodiversity was so new. The statistics were elusive and the proposals for new forestry were controversial. "The uncertainty was true for everybody," Phillips-Howard said. "We're breaking new ground." After a typically hard day of arguments and contention she would lie awake in bed at nights, replaying what she had said and done and imagining how she might have said it better, or considering the arguments used against her. "To lead environmentalists you have to be willing to let people not like you," she said. "If there are two hundred versions of reality out there you can't promote two hundred different versions. You say what you think is right."

One of the interesting things about the Phillips-Howard house is that it is so reminiscent of mill owner Larry Mason's. Both homes were built by their owners over a number of years. Both exhibit a love of wood and craftsmanship. Both were made out of recycled materials, the Phillips-Howard residence taking wood from an abandoned tavern and two old houses that were torn down. (Bonnie enjoys the fact that one of the houses they recycled was on property owned by the Buse family, a timber clan that owns a large lumber mill in nearby Everett and clearcut the woods in the rear of her property.) Both houses have a wood kitchen stove. And both owners are from the East: Bonnie from Wisconsin.

The Phillips-Howard house has a recycled hardwood floor, massive wood beams, a door with a wooden bar like a castle entry, and huge skylights that let the pearly illumination of a Pacific Northwest overcast filter into the living room. The cedar on the roof was taken from shake bolts salvaged by Bonnie and Curt from old clearcuts. The slate underneath the wood stove is from a rockslide in the Cascade Mountains. Having built the house in the 1970s when bumper stickers read, SPLIT WOOD, NOT ATOMS—and when Northwest wood seemed as plentiful to the counterculture as it did to loggers—they heated it with a wood

251

stove. More recently, as the Puget Sound basin has filled with people, air pollution agencies have raised alarms about carcinogenic pollution from smoking chimneys. Accordingly, the couple is switching to electricity.

Trying to match the ideal to the real is a constant struggle, Bonnie said. "The thing that gets me is all the gasoline we use trying to save the world," she admitted, recounting the countless drives up and down the freeway to environmental and government meetings. "All the gas, and all the paper."

When the couple moved to this site in the Seven Lakes region between the Cascade Mountains and Puget Sound, it seemed fairly remote, safely removed from the metropolitan sprawl of Seattle and Everett. In the sixteen years since, however, it has filled with people who commute from five- or ten-acre lots or live on the lakes.

Recently the Buse family clearcut the property in back of their home, the clearcut visible through a line of alder. Bonnie does not object. Better they cut second growth on flat land than old growth on a steep mountain slope, she said. Better to see a clearcut that by state law must be reforested than see the land cut up into asphalt roads and five-acre housing lots.

She grew up in the 1950s in Wisconsin and, as long as she can remember, she has been enchanted with trees. As a little girl she used to give personal names to the trees in her neighborhood.

As a student she was a perfectionist. "If I got a B, I'd be crushed," she said. She seemed likely to spend life as an academic on a college campus, and when she finally rebelled against her own relentless intellectualism and dropped out of graduate school, it was like coming up for air. "It took me a year or so before I could read a novel and not feel guilty," she said.

Maturing in the '60s, she argued so fiercely against the Vietnam War with her father that the two had to declare a yearlong truce on the subject during the period her brother served there. She married, followed her first husband to Seattle, and worked to help support them while he obtained a doctorate in psychology at the University of Washington. In about 1967, she joined Students for a Democratic Society, the radical antiwar group, and became a regular in marches against the war. Meanwhile, her marriage broke up and she tired of being an academic overachiever. Some friends had a commune in Vermont. She went there for three months to think things over.

It wasn't long before she returned to the Pacific Northwest. "I decided I was going to move back to Washington State and climb mountains," she said. She got a job at the University of Washington Medical School and began taking classes on mountain climbing. Curt was an instructor who invited her to share his tent on a climb. Eventually, they married.

Climbing absorbed her. Like many athletic pursuits it demanded a single-minded devotion in order to maintain the physical conditioning and skills required to do it well. The couple climbed every possible weekend. Old-growth forests were simply something the pair passed through on the way to the peaks. "In order to be a serious climber your only goal was to get to the top," she recalled. "You didn't have time to look around."

It was only when age began to slow the pace of such climbs that she began to study more deeply the fabric of the landscape around her. Her environmental interest came in part from simple observation. The difference in a man-made and natural forest was obvious. So was the growing checkerboard of clearcuts that sometimes wiped out familiar trails. Her impressions were reinforced by science. "The science started showing us more and more how important low-elevation forests were," she said, "even if they were fragmented, even if they were no longer pretty."

In 1974, when news of the Arab oil embargo was filling people with uncertainty about the future, Phillips-Howard woke up in a hotel room with the conviction that if she didn't buy land soon, she might not be able to afford it. She and Curt considered northern New Mexico where he was contracting a house, but it seemed too arid to welcome more people. They considered Washington's Skagit County, but there were tentative plans to locate a nuclear plant there. They finally settled on as much land as they could afford in cut over, second-growth land near the Stillaguamish River. It was big enough and rural enough for a couple to live in a teepee the first years without raising neighbors' eyebrows, and there was soil enough to grow some of their own food. They led a counterculture existence that fit the stereotype of the time: flexible employment, rambling travel, a low income that required them to buy clothes at rummage sales and use recycled wood for their house. They had an old Volkswagen van for a decade, the type Larry Mason spiked to a stump in protest. To make friends in their new area, they joined the Pilchuck Audubon chapter. Both would eventually become president.

When the rheumatism hit Phillips-Howard, it made the mountains and trees she could no longer easily get to more precious, not less. She was joining a crusade to save one of the grandest ecosystems on the planet, arguably the most beautiful forest on earth, and it was both challenging and self-flattering.

"I don't think this is a pace a person could take for too many years," she said, "but it almost becomes addictive when you're hooked on it. It is not just because of the issue but because of the people. It is so intellectually challenging. And there is no other social life. People joke about having to be resocialized, to join mainstream life when it's over." She worked elbow-to-elbow with environmental activists from other organizations, and yet the conversations were so focused on the forest that she would realize that although she had spent dozens or even hundreds of hours with them, she wasn't sure if they were married, or had children, or had any kind of life outside the environmental arena.

The frequent target of these obsessed activists became the increasingly beleaguered U.S. Forest Service. Bonnie's interest in the federal agency began about 1987 when an Audubon group found a bear in a snare trap. Subsequent investigation showed the bear had been captured by agency biologists to be radio collared and monitored. Audubon members who poked into the project thought that the study's aims were murky and its methods careless. The collars had been fitted so tightly on growing bears that as the animals matured they had difficulty breathing, the organization complained. The incident encouraged the environmentalists in the North Cascades area to suspect that on many land-management issues, the government could be wrong. If its study of wildlife was poorly designed, what about its management of timber? Pilchuck Audubon decided to start mapping the surrounding national forests to see how much old growth was left, since the government seemed to have no idea. Then Phillips-Howard decided the chapter should "adopt" the Darrington Ranger District in order to monitor it.

A month later the Audubon chapter sued the agency to block a timber sale. The Forest Service's response was to try to lock Audubon out of the disputed area by closing the gates on roads. The *Everett Herald* newspaper did a story on the dispute and Congressman John Miller of Seattle interceded for the environmentalists. When the courts responded to an Audubon appeal by deciding to block a 166-acre clearcut because of inadequate environmental study, the Forest Service pulled back all its planned sales to redo its environmental assessments.

Meanwhile, Phillips-Howard worked to enlist the Tulalip and Stillaguamish Indian tribes in the old-growth fight. The Northwest tribes had treaty rights that had been used with considerable effectiveness to protect salmon and modify tree harvesting. They also used old-growth forest for religious retreats and sanctuaries.

Into this battleground came Harnisch, transferred and promoted with orders to try to repair relations with both sides. As a youth, he might have seemed an unlikely forest ranger. He was raised in the steel mill area south of Chicago, a railroad track on one side of his house and a ship canal on the other. "I got my interest in forestry from Weyerhaeuser drawings in Life magazine," he recalled. He decided to major in forestry at Purdue University and during summers while at college, he got a job as a forest-fire fighter in Idaho's national forests. The camp where the fire crew was based was fifty miles from the nearest town. It was the first time Harnisch had been in a wilderness. He had never even slept in a sleeping bag. Feigning an expertise he didn't have, he watched his companions out of the corner of his eye to observe how they managed to roll the bags up so tightly.

Harnisch found he loved everything about the forest and fighting forest fires, even the bugs and the dirt and the danger. "I loved the adventure of it," he said. "We loved getting dirty. We didn't even wash after fires. The blacker we were, the better. The more dangerous it was, the better."

Upon hiring onto the Forest Service in 1963, he went first to Idaho and then Alaska. "I arrived in Ketchikan with the wind blowing forty to fifty knots, the rain pouring down, and I felt I'd come home," he said. Unlike some foresters, Harnisch had a knack for dealing with people. He was picked to explain wildlife and the forest to tourists on the Alaska state ferry system. Later he was assigned to the Chugach National Forest near Anchorage, the one with the most public use in the state.

Harnisch came back down in the mid-1980s to work first in Oregon and then was promoted to the district ranger post in Darrington. He was the right person at the right time, adept at working with frustrated people on both sides of a difficult issue. He realized that people like himself no longer enjoyed the public presumption of being a benevolent Ranger Rick.

"All of a sudden people were hollering and screaming," he said. "All of a sudden we were no longer just Smokey Bear, we had public involvement." He developed a newsletter called *Forest Winds* to explain to the public what the agency was up to. He commissioned the building of a big WELCOME sign outside the office. He oversaw development of a display of Playmobile toy people in the lobby to illustrate good and bad camping habits. He enlisted sixth graders to replant a clearcut, bringing them back each year to see how their trees were doing. He organized a Forest Service–Darrington picnic that drew four hundred people from both sides who, for once, socialized instead of bickering. Still it was a struggle, helping people cope with the drastic decline in harvest levels and the new emphasis on more obscure forms of wildlife such as owls and salamanders and insects and mice.

The funny thing was, the more the Forest Service worked to accommodate the new environmental concerns about old growth, the more Phillips-Howard understood the pressures the agency got from the other side. "A lot of it has to do with the communities the rangers live in," she said. If one's neighbors are loggers, a forester almost inevitably reflects their attitudes. Moreover, historically, "They got promoted for getting the cut out." Doug MacWilliams, Harnisch's boss, cautioned Phillips-Howard once about the time it takes to turn a large bureaucracy around. "It's going to take a while before the troops know we mean it," he said of the agency's new commitment to nursing the ecosystem.

Phillips-Howard also developed some understanding, if not agreement, with the loggers and their families who were being put out of work. "I have no doubt most of them love the woods," she said. "Maybe they see them differently. They truly believe they can clearcut areas and the sites can grow up productively. I think they're wrong" (she believes the new forest will be a pale, sterile, shrunken imitation of the old), "but I don't think they're evil."

She recognized in many of them a life-style closer to her own than that of some of her political allies in Seattle and Portland. "I feel more of a cultural gap going into Seattle," she said. A fellow environmentalist named Pam Crocker-Davis warned her early on that, "The hardest thing for you will be when you find more in common with someone in the timber industry and those who work in the forests than with urban environmentalists."

In September of 1990, Bonnie Phillips-Howard went back to Washington, D.C.—at the same time as Larry Mason and Dean Hurn—to lobby Congress. Like them, she hated it there.

"It is so much easier back in D.C. to look at the issue as polarized, as black and white," she said. "For us it is much more complicated, both politically and biologically." In the capital, she said, everyone talked of compromise, of just taking the disagreement and splitting the difference. It was Solomon chopping the baby in two all over again. Such proposals satisfied neither side.

Sometimes the pressure was great enough that Bonnie had to remind herself why she had plunged into the colossal fight. When that happened, she would go down to the Stillaguamish River in the rains when it flooded, and watch the brown tide of eroded topsoil run by.

"At the grassroots level, it is harder to understand why compromise must be made," she said. In the real forest, loggers love their jobs and the loss of it chokes off not only their income, but their pride and their self-identity. In the real forest, the rivers run brown with the blood of the mountains, the dirt washed off from the casual and ill-planned clearcuts and logging roads.

In the spring of 1991, Phillips-Howard maneuvered her wheelchair into the Seattle courtroom of U.S. District Judge William Dwyer. She was there to watch part of an eight-day hearing, requested by the timber industry and Forest Service, to debate whether Dwyer should halt all new timber sales on spotted owl habitat in national forests until the agency completed a long-delayed owl protection plan.

Dwyer had ruled a few weeks before that the plan was necessary; now came the question of whether the planned sale and logging of 66,000 acres of owl habitat could proceed for the one or two or three years it would take for the owl plan to be completed. The timber industry argued that selling those trees represented less than two percent of remaining owl habitat and that the bird would survive while humans once more debated the fate of its forest. Its attorneys were delighted when Dwyer agreed to give them time to make their case in court about the human cost of owl-protection laws. But the attorneys representing suing environmental groups were disappointed there was a hearing at all; to them the law was clear that a plan and environmental impact statement was required *before* logging took place. The Forest Service was asking to be rewarded for delaying its observance of the law.

The court hearing had become a kind of reunion—or, in some cases, a first introduction—for many of the people embroiled in the spotted owl fight. Eric Forsman came to testify. So did Jack Ward Thomas, and sociologist and timber-community sympathizer Robert Lee. Biologist Larry Irwin came to testify for the industry, Gordon

Orians for the environmentalists. Andy Stahl, wearing earth shoes, sat at the plaintiff's table to advise Sierra Club Legal Defense Fund attorneys, Todd True and Vic Sher. Jean Durning of the Wilderness Society dropped in to listen for a while. Ann Goos and Larry Mason of Forks were two of several hundred loggers who rallied on the courthouse steps midway through the hearing, protesting once more the threat to forest jobs. Many of the loggers crowded into the courtroom afterward to curiously watch the proceedings.

There was little drama to the methodical hearing. Dwyer kept things on track by interrupting witnesses with incisive questions and enforcing a punctuality like a Swiss watchmaker, breaking for lunch precisely at noon even if it meant cutting someone off almost at midsentence.

Mark Rutzick, the lawyer for the timber industry, cross-examined the environmentalists' few witnesses with aggressive fervor, seeking to undermine their professional credibility. The industry was looking for any wedge of doubt it could pry into the need for spotted owl protection. While Audubon and its allies called just three witnesses, the industry and government called dozens. Here at last seemed a chance to reverse environmental victories, to persuade and make cautious a judge who up until now had been sympathetic to the owl. As the hearing ground on, however, it began to seem that too much ammunition was being fired off, obscuring instead of clarifying the central arguments. So many competing statistics were thrown out that their effectiveness was lost.

Still, the Dwyer court hearing became a rare opportunity to address the fundamental arguments of the ancient-forest issue. "I don't think man has ever struggled so much between his ecological conscience and the need to get goods and services from the land," testified Gene Wood, a professor of wildlife ecology at the University of South Carolina.

Dueling economists disagreed wildly. Bruce Lippke of the University of Washington testified that Dwyer's injunction alone could cost up to 25,000 jobs. Financial disaster was predicted by a Forks school board member, a county commissioner from Washington's rural Skamania County, and a mill owner. But economist Ed Whitelaw of the University of Oregon contended the impact on the Pacific Northwest's economy would be negligible. The industy already had up to a two-year stockpile of purchased federal timber it had not yet cut, Whitelaw pointed out, and besides, Big Timber was no longer driving the regional economy. In the same ten-year-period that the industry has lost 30,000 jobs in Oregon and Washington because of mechanization, the two states overall had gained 932,000 jobs.

The industry and administration were particularly hurt when George Leonard, assistant chief of the Forest Service, admitted his agency abandoned an effort to complete an owl-protection plan in mid-1991 without telling anyone, apparently because of disarray in the Bush administration on how to deal with owl restrictions.

In effect, Leonard admitted under questioning by the judge, the Forest Service wasted a year of planning time that might have made the present injunction unnecessary.

There was rich irony to this court hearing. The industry, which had so bitterly condemned the Jack Ward Thomas committee proposal to set aside 7.7 million acres for the owl the year before, found itself in the odd position of *defending* the Thomas plan before Judge Dwyer. Its position was that the Forest Service, in deciding not to log in a manner inconsistent with the Thomas plan, had in effect adopted the Thomas report as its owl plan and thus was already in compliance with the law. Under this line of reasoning, no new plan—and no injunction against the planned timber sales—was necessary. Thomas found this hugely amusing. "It's been interesting to watch our committee slide from being environmental crazies to patsies of the timber industry," he said wryly.

The timber industry's willingness to support the Jack Ward Thomas proposal in this court hearing came in part because the Thomas report was beginning to look mild compared to the alternative proposed by the U.S. Fish and Wildlife Service early in 1991. Another Seattle federal judge, Thomas Zilly, had ordered Fish and Wildlife to belatedly designate critical habitat for the spotted owl, in his opinion castigating the agency for not having done so a year earlier when it named the owl a threatened species.

To comply with the deadline for compliance that Zilly set, Fish and Wildlife gave four of its employees just a few weeks to map critical habitat across three states. The result was a proposal for 11.6 million acres, 3 million acres of it on private land, that included not only existing old growth but land where old growth might be grown in the future to link up owl habitat areas. Industry was flabbergasted. The acreage the government announced did not even include the land already set aside in parks and wilderness areas. Add that in and the industry calculated land earmarked for the owl came to more than 14 million acres, an area about the size of Vermont, New Hampshire,

Rhode Island, and Delaware combined. Nothing so sweeping had ever been proposed in American history. The closest previous proposal had been an abortive 10-million-acre habitat in Montana for the grizzly bear that was dismissed by Congress in the 1970s as absurd.

It didn't help that no one seemed quite clear what "critical habitat" meant. Clearly, *government* land within critical habitat had to be managed to protect the owl, but other sections of the Endangered Species Act required that anyway. Much murkier was the situation on private land, where owners would have to conduct surveys at their own cost to determine if owls were present and then consult with federal officials to determine what, if anything, the birds' presence or absence meant. Nor was the 11.6-million-acre figure firm: the designation was expected to be adjusted after about six months of public comment, economic analysis, and revision.

To make matters even more complicated, Fish and Wildlife had set up a separate Owl Recovery Team, as required by law, to draw up a recovery plan for the owl.

The resulting regulatory scheme was so confusing that Washington's exasperated governor, Booth Gardner, complained that the Bush administration had made a mess of the entire process. Owl protection had become like a collection of disjointed railroad cars all rumbling in roughly the same direction but on different tracks: the Forest Service drawing up its own plan, the Fish and Wildlife Service drawing up two different schemes applicable to all agencies, the Bureau of Land Management with still another set of guidelines, the National Park Service with owl surveys of its own, and state land agencies trying to mesh their management with the federal government. The locomotive pushing the process was the impatient federal court; appearing some-what hapless was Congress as the caboose, trying to round up the various cars into a single train with legislation that the polarized timber and environmental lobbies were nowhere close to agreeing on.

In Forks, critical habitat proved to be like throwing gasoline on the smoldering fury of the loggers. The boundaries of the critical habitat areas were published only in the *Federal Register*, a daily publication of new federal regulations read by few outside the bureaucracy. Ann Goos, however, looked at the obscure lines and numbers and decided to see how the proposed boundary might affect Forks.

In their haste to get the mapping done, she discovered, Fish and Wildlife officials had followed existing township boundaries, the square grid laid on the American landscape when it was first surveyed. The advantage of following these straight lines on a map was that a legal description was readily available that, as the law required, could be published in the *Federal Register* in time to meet the court deadline. The disadvantage was that the lines had only the roughest relationship to the irregular forest. In the case of Forks, the critical habitat boundary zigzagged through the outskirts of town. It was ludicrously crude: the owl's supposed critical habitat included part of the town's airstrip, Jerry Leppell's saw shop, three mobile home parks, parts of two subdivisions, and thousands of acres that had long since been logged and were either raw clearcuts or regrowing second growth owls didn't use.

Goos took me up to see some of those puny trees proposed for the owl, incensed that owl protection seemed to be getting steadily more extreme and most of the nation didn't seem to care. On a Forest Service sign by the side of a gravel road, someone had scrawled, "Let the logger go extinct."

"That's the kind of attitude we're facing here," she complained.

For many in town, the critical-habitat boundary was the last straw. The community's frustration had been building throughout the winter. By spring, four spotted owls had been found shot and nailed to national park or national forest signs on the Olympic Peninsula, with no one claiming responsibility. Someone had also torched two entry-guard stations into Olympic National Park. A frustrated Goos said a revolutionary mood was building. "Government has become the enemy," she said.

Russ Thomas, seventy, the owner of the Forks Pay-N-Save grocery and cafe, had remained pretty much on the sidelines until the map came out. When he saw that his own cow pasture had been tentatively designated critical habitat for the spotted owl, however, Thomas decided that government had finally gone too far. "This is ridiculous," he fumed.

He helped organize a campaign to shut nearly every business in town on May 23, 1991, and send nearly a thousand residents in school buses to a protest rally in Olympia. It was there that Fish and Wildlife was holding the last of a series of hearings in the Northwest on its critical-habitat proposal.

No other community in the Pacific Northwest duplicated Forks's feat. The town's grocery stores closed. So did its gas stations. The schools locked their doors. The restaurants shut. The *Forks Forum* newspaper, the video stores, even the Hang-up Tavern went dark. Forks became a ghost town as people mustered at dawn in the parking lots to make the three- and four-hour ride to the state capitol. On the readerboard outside Bert Paul's Thriftway, the sign read, FORKS WILL BE CLOSED THURSDAY, MAY 23, TO OBSERVE GOVERNMENT STUPIDITY IN OLYMPIA.

The organizers' initial hope—that 10,000 or even 15,000 of Washington's 55,000 or so woods workers would turn out for the rally to protest this final insult of critical habitat—was not realized. Police estimated 2,000 to 3,000 loggers and family members mustered for the rally: enough to demonstrate concern but not enough to prove a menacing potential voting block of political power. Governor Gardner did show up to cast blame on his federal counterparts. Several state legislators spoke sympathetically, though Evan Jones, Goos's electoral opponent, was not offered an opportunity to speak and hung on the sidelines, looking as uncomfortable in this crowd as ever. Goos was applauded enthusiastically as she harangued the crowd. Honking logging trucks circled the small downtown Olympia park where the rally was held and yellow signs bobbed. THEY'VE GONE TOO FAR, a banner proclaimed. One demonstrator held up a spotted owl with a target on its stomach and an arrow through its head.

Inside a performing arts theater where the Fish and Wildlife hearing was held, few had much good to say about the critical-habitat proposal. Even Jim Pissot, representing the Audubon Society, drew loggers' applause when he complained it was hastily drawn and clumsily vague, arousing unnecessary fear and confusion. Mitch Friedman showed up to testify and theorized darkly that the Bush administration was deliberately giving government biologists free rein to draw lines across the map, hoping to engineer a "train wreck" of preservation so extreme that conservatives would win support to amend the Endangered Species Act. Only a few brave witnesses, such as Wilderness Society attorney Melanie Rowland, suggested even 11.6 million acres might not be enough to fully protect the old-growth ecosystem and its species. But most environmentalists stayed away. "This is their show," Rowland said, gesturing to the loggers in the lobby.

Initially the contingent from Forks felt good at this rally. It was less lonely, going to this park in Olympia and seeing there all their colleagues from Morton and Packwood and Darrington and Buckley and Enumclaw and Aberdeen and Raymond. On this day, at least, they had gotten some attention, by god. They had shut down their whole damn town, a prophecy of what runamuck environmentalism could mean.

The hearing droned on from one in the afternoon to nine at night. Hundreds signed up to testify and protest. Yet the top officials of Fish and Wildlife did not attend the hearings, despite the unprecedented scope of the owl proposal. There was a pro forma air about the proceedings, as if public sentiment on both sides was already obvious and this was an exercise to vent steam, not to reconsider society's new direction.

Certainly the timber industry had fallen a long ways from its position of a few years before. At best it hoped to shrink and modify critical habitat, not eliminate it. Back in Washington, D.C., legislation the industry had crafted for Congress was introduced the same day as the Olympia rally by Representative Jerry Huckaby, D-La. The Louisiana lawmaker's sponsorship was evidence that the industry still hoped to reverse species protection in the national arena—Huckaby said he feared black bear and red cockaded woodpecker protection would affect his own state—but even the industry bill proposed setting some of the remaining old growth aside for the owl. It was seen as irrelevant by most observers anyway, doing little more than staking out one extreme.

Also indicative of how industry had come to recognize the inevitability of some owl protection, a Washington State mill owners group, Northwest Independent Forest Manufacturers, had proposed the same week that old-growth harvesting be allowed to continue but the rotation time between cutting be as much as doubled to 150 to 200 years to let regrowing stands develop old-growth characteristics satisfactory to owls. The prevailing assumption had become that something, somehow, was going to be done for the owl. The question was how much.

An answer came that same eventful afternoon. Sixty miles away in Seattle, at five-thirty P.M. as the Fish and Wildlife hearing was going on, Judge Dwyer issued the decision he had made as a result of the eight-day court hearing that had concluded three weeks before. The injunction sought by the environmentalists against national forest timber sales was granted, Dwyer announced, until the Forest Service came up with an approved owl plan. It was like a blow to the stomach of the rallying loggers. Once more the wind of hope had been knocked away.

Dwyer set a deadline ten months away for completion of the new plan, but industry officials predicted it would take the agency up to three years to complete the public hearings and environmental impact statement necessary under the law. In the meantime he ordered that federal timber sales on all owl and old-growth habitat must cease.

About 80 percent of the remaining timber the reeling industry had been counting on from the national forests was now off limits. On the Olympic National Forest around Forks, the harvest was no longer even 10 percent of what it had been at its peak. It was virtually zero.

In his thirty-five-page opinion, Dwyer put forth succinctly much of the argument used for years by the environmental forces. He called the long years of foot-dragging by federal agencies toward protecting the owl, "a remarkable series of violations of the environmenal laws."

Dwyer rejected the industry's economic case. "Over the past decade many timber jobs have been lost and mills closed in the Pacific Northwest," he wrote. "The main reasons have been modernization of physical plants, changes in product demand, and competition from elsewhere. . . . Job losses in the wood products industry will continue regardless of whether the northern spotted owl is protected. A credible estimate is that over the next twenty years more than 30,000 jobs will be lost to worker-productivity increases alone. . . . The timber industry no longer drives the Pacific Northwest economy. The wood products industry now employs about four percent of all workers in western Oregon, two percent in western Washington and six percent in northern California. Even if some jobs in woods products were affected by protecting owl habitat in the short term, any effect on the regional economy would be small. The remaining wilderness contributes to the desirability of this region as a site for new industries and their employees. The resulting economic gains, while hard to measure, are genuine and substantial."

The dozens of witnesses the industry and Forest Service had mustered had simply not persuaded Dwyer. "To bypass environmental laws," he wrote, "either briefly or permanently, would not fend off the changes transforming the timber industry. The argument that the mightiest economy on earth cannot afford to preserve old growth forests for a short time, while it reaches an overdue decision on how to manage them, is not convincing today."

In newspaper stories and television broadcasts, Dwyer's decision overshadowed the timber rally. The owl, which Ann Goos had come to call with exasperated respect "Spotty," had won again.

17

SANCTUARY, II

▲▲▲▲▲▲▲▲

Many of those who are most deeply affected by the final forest originally come from someplace else. The stolid trees are mute, inanimate, and yet they have a power to draw people, to promise sanctuary. Bonnie Phillips-Howard came from Wisconsin, and Larry Mason from Massachusetts. Mitch Friedman and ranger Fred Harnisch and Lou Gold, an aging activist who was drawn to an Earth First! demonstration near Oregon's Bald Mountain, are from Chicago. Karen Hobbs of Forks is from Texas.

Hobbs is a businesswoman and exporter. She doesn't send truckloads of raw logs thundering down Highway 101, but she ships more from Forks via the United Parcel Service than any other merchant in town. Her steel-and-wood warehouse is crammed like a queer squirrel's nest, stuffed with mosses and reeds and fungus and stalks, the shadowy flowerings of the temperate rain forest. There are papery hornets' nests, bundles of dried yellow yarrow, twisted driftwood and dried kelp strands wound around on themselves. There are pine and fir and spruce cones, lichens, dried bear grass, horsetail reeds, and river roots. All this is shipped to florists across the United States who use the novel material in floral arrangements.

Accordingly, Hobbs prefers the natural forest over a managed tree farm, where the clumsy and reforming hand of man often eliminates the woods' most beautiful products. She reads the trees, maps in her mind the likely locations of different plants, and hires retirees, transients, or the unemployed at low wages to reap their bounty. She teaches her workers how to take only enough so that the source plants remain.

Hobbs, who had worked in the floral business, came to the Olympic Peninsula as a tourist in 1979. She arrived with friends at the ocean beaches of Kalaloch in a night fog. Their intention was to drive the next morning to the Hoh rainforest about thirty miles to the northeast, but when Hobbs woke to fog drip, she was stunned by the lush, riotous green on the coast. "I was just going gaga that things that were shipped on a regular basis to floral shops were here just growing by the side of the road. I'd never seen more than one or two varieties of moss in my life. Here I was seeing all these varieties. I could hardly even register all the textures I was seeing."

She followed a trail that led into the big trees up from the beach. The ground was a sponge squirting mushrooms, fungus, huckleberry, and sorrel. Vales were a carpet of ferns. Logs were moss-shrouded nurseries, baby trees sprouting out of the decaying wood flesh of their ancestors. Alder and maple trailed rags of moss. "I fell in love with the flora though I couldn't name any of it," Hobbs recalled. "By three P.M. I sat on a log and I was about ready to max out. We went to Ruby Beach and stared at the sunset. My head was hurting. I hadn't been that excited for a long time."

She returned to Texas but the following year came back for a month, taking a job at the Kalaloch Resort near the campground. She picked some of the foliage and sent it to florists to test the market. After a while, a check came in the mail. Opening it, next to the rumble of the ocean, Hobbs thought, "This is a way for me to make enough money to stay out here." By the end of 1980 she had bought a small house and four acres in the forest and was asking people if she could pick on their land. They agreed, but were puzzled. Hobbs wanted things that grew like weeds.

"It has helped me to be from somewhere else," she reflected. "People who live in this environment don't see the uniqueness of the product." Brush pickers had harvested evergreens for floral design and Christmas decorations for a long time on the Peninsula, but Hobbs was the first to look not just at the obvious plants but to appreciate the sculpture of the unlikely, such as a twisted root or a sun-dried strip of kelp. "There's no question in my mind that there's nothing else like it on the market," she said.

She doesn't suggest her kind of business, with its low-paying picking jobs, is an economic replacement for logging. Karen Hobbs does suspect that the natural forest, if left uncut, could offer opportunities for business as yet uninvented. "I see that Forks is already really changing," she said. "This could become the backpacking capital of the world as easily as the logging capital." The slogan stamped on her boxes expresses this: "We have a forest full of fresh ideas." And so she stayed. . . .

Lou Gold was on probation. Under its terms, he could not return to the Siskiyou National Forest for a year.

It was 1983, and Gold and a dozen other people had been arrested the day before for blocking a bulldozer seeking to extend a Forest Service road toward Bald Mountain, a ridge that runs for six miles above the Illinois River on the edge of Oregon's Kalmiopsis Wilderness. The intent of the road was to open another section of the Siskiyou Mountains and put loggers within reach of up to 500 million board feet of additional timber.

After spending the night in jail, the protesters had been fined by District Court Judge Lloyd O'Neal a total of $900 in restitution to pay the contractor for the delay. They had also been ordered to stay out of the public forest. Although he was no lawyer, Gold suspected such a prohibition was unconstitutional. If not, it seemed simply wrong. Americans should be able to visit their own forests. "I said, 'Judge, put me in jail right now because I'm going to break that term of my probation.' He just ignored me. The gavel came down."

The prohibition had the opposite of its intended effect on Gold. It gave him a new goal. He went to the counterculture community of Takilma, Oregon, and asked for supplies for a vigil on Bald Mountain. After he stuffed his backpack he issued a press release in the customary manner of late-twentieth-century Americans (apparently ignored by the media) and began the steep, twelve-mile hike to the mountain.

The natural world speaks to individuals through the experiences and prejudices they bring to it. Gold, a one-time university political science professor, brought to Bald Mountain a search for purpose and an outrage against society's intention to take the trees that had provided spiritual refuge. The forest had spoken to him, given life meaning. As a result, Gold had the fervor of a convert, and eventually he would use the tale of his meeting this place as the centerpiece of a popular lecture on old growth. It helped persuade audiences across the United States that freewheeling logging was wrong.

By his own assessment, Gold is an unlikely champion of ancient forests. Short, narrow shouldered, a bit overweight, and a chain-smoker, his favorite haunt in Portland is Sam's, a windowless, red-tinted bar and pool hall with some of the ambience of his native Chicago. Until his late forties Gold had never spent any significant time in old-growth forest. But he is a teacher and a talker, what he likes to call "a motor mouth," and his glibness is tempered with thoughtfulness. With his gray beard and ponytail, headband, weathered smile lines, and impish, gap-toothed grin, he looks a bit like a forest gnome.

Gold taught a radical brand of political science at the University of Illinois as the '60s began to boil, dropped out, sampled the hippie counterculture, and then became a carpenter, the kind who could kitchen-philosophize between hammer swings. As the economy tightened in the early 1980s, he came west, first to California and then north into Oregon.

Gold was looking for answers. "Like so many people, I had simply been an accumulator of experiences," he said. "I had been a consumer of personal and interpersonal novelties. They no more led to happiness than a closet full of fancy clothes and toys." He had hoped experience by itself might lead to wholeness. It didn't. "I was collecting endless new data. I wanted to touch fundamental ground."

He set out to visit friends on Oregon's Illinois River, which flowed from Chicago Peak, and when he got there Gold felt he had come home. "I thought everything you could be interested in, or ever wonder about, could be found between one end of the Illinois Valley and the other." He took up an offer to move in with the family he had visited. In 1983, about six months after Gold had arrived, Dave Foreman and Mike Roselle of Earth First! came by with news of some new road the Forest Service wanted to build into a place called Bald Mountain, on the edge of what would become the Kalmiopsis Wilderness.

The more he learned about the Forest Service's plans, the more alarmed Gold became. The intention seemed not just to harvest the old-growth forest but to replace it, to erect a human-designed wood farm. "The very thing I had run away from—intensely managed Midwest cornfields, academic conformity, the urban life-style of boxes—that was what was happening to the trees," he said. Gold had found sanctuary, and now it was going to be lost. In a very short time, after blocking a bulldozer on the Bald Mountain Road, he found himself in jail. Then he was forbidden to return to the forest, a prohibition it seemed imperative to ignore.

The hike for his resulting vigil was a hot, difficult trek for the neophyte backpacker. His feet and back and lungs were soon sore. "I had never been twelve miles back in the wilderness, alone," Gold would later recall. "This was another step towards vulnerability. Now

I wasn't yielding to people around me, I was yielding to the natural world."

What he found at the trail's end was not a particularly extraordinary place, at least topographically. The older Siskiyous near the California border do not rear up into glaciered battlements like the Olympics. Instead they roll away under their cloak of huge old trees like the blue swell of the ocean. His destination was a modest 3,800 feet high. At the peak's top was the broken glass, rusting nails, and other debris of an abandoned Forest Service fire lookout that had been deliberately burned. Gold had walked twelve miles to take his stand in a minor dump.

But the profusion of plants was enchanting. Fire has hopscotched across the Kalmiopsis area countless times, giving rise to a tabulated 1,400 species. The plants seize opportunity at a latitude in which the trees and flowers of the Pacific Northwest collide with those of northern California. The ecosystem is old; it was never interrupted by the glaciation that sculpted the Olympic Peninsula. The effect is as if a landscape architect had sketched in arboreal variety. There was oak and fir, cedar and pine, madrona and spruce, rhododendron and violets. Gold felt as if he were walking back into some kind of Eden. Bald Mountain might be junk laden on top, but the idea of staying and bearing witness to any harvest of this land seized the Chicago native powerfully. He was a bit stunned by the majesty of the trees downslope and the peopleless panorama from the top.

The crest of Bald Mountain was indeed bald: "like Friar Tuck's head," Gold would later write, "a round, flat, barren area about thirty feet in diameter. From here I can see the great expanse of the untouched North Kalmiopsis, from Chinaman's Hat past Silver Peak to Indigo drainage. It is a holy place: good for seeing the four directions, for touching the four winds, for sleeping under the stars, and for talking to God."

He camped near the crest by a spring that bubbled out from a rock, pitching his tent under a Douglas fir ten feet in diameter that would shelter him from storms. Animals grew accustomed to his presence. Deer moved through his camp in day; at night a family of mice that lived in a nearby stump would scamper across his feet. "One afternoon, as I basked in the warm sun, a hummingbird lighted on my shoulder," Gold wrote. "I knew then I had arrived at some type of harmony." For his dinner greens, he picked some of the ferns and violets and "miner's salad" that grew near the spring.

Gold did not feel entirely comfortable in this wild country. Camping reminds us of how little of what we make is absolutely necessary, but it also reminds us of civilization's comforts. Gold was high enough to experience rapid swings between heat and cold, sunshine and storm. He was far enough from any road to feel exposed to accident, sickness, or lost supplies.

Yet he was captivated by this place. What he felt as he rambled along the ridgetop through its series of meadows and groves was an instinctual sense of wonder, and an eerie experience of recognition.

In Illinois Gold had had what might seem an improbable dream, given his Jewish background. In it, a woman he recognized as the Virgin Mary was coming down a path that ran from some evergreen trees out into a meadow. The extraordinary thing about the scene was that her gaze elicited a response from nature. When she looked at plants or animals, they reacted: the flowers opening, the deer cocking their ears, the trees nodding. It was corny in a way, like something from a Disney animated film, but in the dream's reality it was fascinating as well. Then the woman looked at Gold, who was watching from a rise above the meadow. He experienced what the meadow had experienced: he felt what he later called a feminine, generational force, "the look of devotion that creates God." Then he woke up.

The hypnotic memory of the dream had never left him. And here, skirting the slopes of Bald Mountain, he finally came to a point overlooking a meadow and trail. He was startled by recognition. It was the place from his dream.

"Everything about it was magical," Gold said of those first few weeks on Bald Mountain. "It has an aura of wildness about it. It's not just the natural world. It feels prehistoric." It occurred to him that very few people anymore experience what he was experiencing: the sensations of living alone for a time in a single, wild place, undistracted by civilization, letting the mind empty and refill like a waterwheel under a drizzle of clear water.

Not certain exactly how to care for this place he had adopted, Gold began trying to clean up the wreckage of the old fire lookout. He heaped up the broken glass that was scattered on the mountain crest and piled up the rusty nails. The simple physical work occupied him and became a kind of meditation. A hiker came by and inquired what he was doing, and Gold explained about the protest and the probation and the vigil and his decision to try to care for the mountain a bit. He would shortly have to hike back down, Gold said, because he was almost out of food. The hiker thought a bit, then told Gold to stay where he was. He would bring back food to maintain the vigil. Not only did the stranger from Ashland keep his word by bringing back two weeks of provisions, but word spread. Other backpackers began to leave off what food they could spare. Friends brought food, mail, clean clothes, and news of environmental politics.

"It was like a magic wand," Gold said. "I ended up staying fifty-six days. I lost thirteen pounds, and I have never felt healthier in my life. I felt simultaneously vulnerable and content. I had found a power spot in my own life. And so I committed my life to this place."

When Gold came back down the mountain, he was jailed by Judge O'Neal for five days for ignoring the terms of his probation, but the judge also lifted the remaining prohibition. Gold returned later that summer for a briefer visit, and then again the following year.

In the years that were to follow, Gold was to talk frequently of the importance of place, of finding a piece of the earth that one cherished and identified with and felt compelled to defend. This idea of focusing on a particular piece of ground instead of global problems or national legislation became a common theme of environmental conferences in the late 1980s. It was given the name "bioregionalism," and in one sense was a philosophic underpinning of the back-to-the-land movement that had flourished in the 1970s. Its proponents saw themselves anchoring to a place, caring for it, and influencing by example the environment of the wider world. It was a reaction against the migratory urge and short-term exploitations that marked American history.

Gold invented his own means of support to stay in southwestern Oregon. Recognizing the significance of the final forest and the scale of the logging that was liquidating it, he went back to teaching in the winter. But instead of going to a classroom, he decided to travel the country and speak to groups. After the first two years on Bald Mountain he began giving lectures on his experiences up there and the values of the old-growth forest. At the end he would pass a hat. The money he raised was enough so that each summer he could afford to trek back to Bald Mountain.

At first, none of the forest administrators and timber executives in the Grants Pass area knew quite how to react to this graying wood sprite of a hippie who studied the teachings of Native Americans and built a medicine wheel up on the mountaintop. Gold's circle of rocks and sticks was oriented to the four directions, which were marked by short flagpoles. Sometimes the people who found their way up the mountaintop would watch sunsets or thunderstorms or the rising of a full moon from the medicine wheel and it seemed indeed to have magic. At other times Gold and his visitors felt they were playing Indians and they'd laugh at themselves—and conclude that laughter could be a prayer, too. Once a logging company helicopter landed on the brow of the hill and someone kicked Gold's medicine wheel apart, an action that took him all of two hours to repair. He'd joke about that later in his lectures, the notion of someone ordering a tactical air strike on rocks and sticks.

In staying on Bald Mountain Gold not only flouted the terms of his initial probation, he ignored normal Forest Service regulations to limit camping in one place to fourteen days. After the first year, he worked out a wary agreement with the Forest Service to exceed the limit in return for doing maintenance work on the Bald Mountain Loop Trail.

In winter, when weather conditions kept him away, he used slides to help weave a tale about Bald Mountain and this final forest and the need to save it. By 1990 he had made more than 500 presentations, including talks to the Yale School of Forestry, Harvard Divinity School, and the Missouri State Penitentiary. The prisoners were among his most fascinated listeners, particularly when he described the ancient-forest protests and arrests. "The notion of someone getting arrested on purpose was a new one to them," he remarked.

The irony of this dichotomy of life-styles between summer and winter has not escaped Gold. His basement office in Portland, across from a McDonald's restaurant, has a computer, a teddy bear, three jangling telephones, and an administrative assistant. He has a sheathed walking stick he uses as a prop during his lectures, and a joke poster done by a friend depicting "The Compleet Radical Environmentalist" including waffle stompers, headband, six-pack of beer, and buzzing flies.

"I'm doing all the grinding things I ran away from," Gold said of his often hectic schedule of speaking engagements, interviews, and writing. "Except there is one difference. I'm not saying, 'Why on earth am I doing this?'"

If life was as satisfactorily structured as literature, Gold would have saved Bald Mountain. Or, in a tragedy, he would have been imprisoned, driven away, or otherwise martyred. Neither happened and the battle over the Siskiyous dragged on year after year. Finally nature, which has its own ideas about continuity and renewal, intervened with fire.

The Siskiyous are far drier than the western Olympics, and in 1987 the Silver Fire broke out. It burned 150 square miles, including 53,600 acres inside the Kalmiopsis Wilderness. It ravaged part of Gold's Eden. The blaze raced up one side of Bald Mountain, the tree canopy exploding into flame like gasolined cotton, the fire throwing out such heat that Gold's camp cooking implements twisted and blackened. Gold fled. He ran south from the smoke and flames for three days, crossing creeks and scrambling up cliffs, until he finally ran into another camp and trail.

In the aftermath of the fire, a bitter fight broke out over whether to salvage-log the dead trees or allow them to decompose and the forest to grow back naturally. To the timber industry it was ludicrous to leave behind already-dead trees. To environmentalists, taking the fiber would be mining the forest of nutrients, and the network of roads and disruption would worsen erosion and destroy the wilderness. The Forest Service ultimately decided, after stormy public hearings, to log 9,000 of the burned acres and build twenty miles of new logging roads, including a one-mile extension of the long-disputed Bald Mountain Road.

All this dramatically altered part of Gold's Bald Mountain vista. His views evolved as well.

"During those early days on the mountain," he later wrote, "perhaps as a reaction to aloneness, my mind often got terribly busy. I found myself concocting great dramas. I'd conduct heavy arguments with the logging industry or deliver self-righteous lectures to the Josephine County court. But this is not why I had come to the mountain. My purpose was 'peaceful and religious,' but these mental debates were making me feel furious and angry. I watched my own thoughts come and go like the clouds. I saw that I had no perfect solutions to offer . . . the future of the planet is not going to turn on our ability to produce the 'right solution' as much as upon our fundamental values towards life."

In a 1989 conference in Eugene in which he reflected on his experience with the Silver Fire, Gold talked further of these fundamental values; of accepting the naturalness of death, for example. People need to recognize that nature moves in a cyclic pattern that includes decay and dying as well as birth and renewal, he said. But while loggers took one lesson from this observation, Gold took another: that the "decadent" parts of a forest are as instructive and valuable as its young and growing parts. If there is wisdom in the forest, he reasoned, perhaps it is the pitiless yet hopeful nature of this cycle that, using the dead to nourish the young, provides an immortality.

Civilization "made an exception for us to the general laws of nature," Gold said. Humans strove to gain immunity from natural calamities such as forest fires. Agriculture promised an end to famine. Science promised an end to cold and hard work and disease. Religion promised eternal life, an escape clause from death itself. Gold said his experience in the forest made him question whether something essential in life's experience had been lost in civilization's growing immunity from natural hazard. In beating nature we had beaten not just dread but joy: we had lost our membership in part of a greater fabric, something that could terrify, yes, but also give reassurance. "The story we need now probably comes from Job," Gold said. "No matter what good a man does, God can dump on him. God is something bigger than a human being. What science needs to do is not make an exception for us from the laws of nature, but help us to accept nature. Science needs to teach people they *can't* make a deal."

The practical application of this is more difficult. Acceptance, surrender, and recognition is not the way America has defined itself. One of the appealing things about America was its triumph over the wilderness, and the chance its inhabitants had to surmount customary limits. Gold's idea of the lesson of the forest was antithetical to everything loggers believed in.

Gold does not propose everyone pick a mountain peak to live on, of course. He himself does not winter on Bald Mountain. He is still struggling to find that proper balance, and his only certainty is that he is more likely to find it in groves of huge, age-old trees than in a city. His vigil was magical for him, but it did not alter reality. It did not prevent the Silver Fire that burned some of his favorite places. It did not prevent salvage-logging.

Even before the fire struck, Gold asked himself what he would do if his vigil failed to influence human events. What happens if the road is built anyway, the forest is clearcut, and the proposals that have been made for a national park in the Kalmiopsis area are dashed? "My answer was, I want to win, but it wasn't my deepest objective," Gold said. "My objective was to have my relationship to this place. As an analogy, suppose you have a grandmother who is terminally ill. Do you abandon her? No, you care for her. Not because you can change the situation, but because it is the good and honorable thing to do."

"Humans are supposed to have a choice," he said. "No civilization has made the right choice yet. Nevertheless, as a matter of the heart, you can't let go of the possibility. Somebody asked Krishnamurti (an Indian religious philosopher) if his teachings had changed the world. He said no. So they asked him, 'Why do you teach?' He replied, 'Why does the bird sing?'"

Newcomers such as Hobbs and Gold discovered they had come home in the forest. But there is also a sense of place that comes not from fresh discovery, but from accumulated time. The road to Bob Tuttle's 400-acre family farm near Forks is called Maxfield because it is named for the great-grandfather on his mother's side who first staked a claim on Shuwah Creek. Tuttle's parents, Bob Sr. and Anita Daisy Maxfield, live on the farm, as does his uncle. With Bob's children, that makes three generations on the place right now and five in memory.

The Tuttles have boxes of fading photographs showing old fields and tractors and hay wagons, the huge trees that are now stumps, and saplings that are now huge trees. The family's real album, however, is the land that composes their view. Bob Jr. can point from his property to a ridge line, bright green with nearly mature second-growth fir, and say, "My Dad logged Gunderson Mountain." They have seen the old forest cut down and change irrevocably, and yet they have also seen it persist by coming back. They resent any implication that by harvesting Forks's virgin generation of trees, the've let something valuable and rare in the world's natural system nearly slip away.

Maxfield road skirts a recent 150-acre ITT-Rayonier clearcut of second-growth trees before it gets to the Tuttles' new house. The Rayonier seedlings planted among the stumps for the third rotation are easy to see because they dot the brushy clearcut with bits of glossy white, the color of the plastic cones that cover the tree tips to discourage browsing deer. The corporation is planning to extend the clearcut even further to bend around the Tuttle property but Bob accepts that; it is part of what he sees as the natural cycle of the forest.

The trees start again on Tuttle's side of the road, and his dirt and gravel driveway leads into them. The lane soon forks. Downhill and to the right it leads to his parents' and uncle's homes. Uphill and to the left it leads to the big new house Tuttle is building with his own hands, on his family's land, much of it with wood he cut and milled himself on his property. I first met him when he was sawing decking for a wraparound porch. The roofed porch makes the house look like it belongs here, giving the inhabitants a place to sit outdoors during the incessant Peninsula rains.

Tuttle is big, bearded, and beefy, and would be a bit intimidating if he didn't smile so much; in the Vietnam era he was a Green Beret. His house reflects his own physical strength. The building code called for two-by-ten floor joists spaced twenty-four inches apart, but Tuttle decided to use two-by-twelves every sixteen inches for greater strength.

"This is a house I want to pass on to my children," he said.

By the autumn of 1990 Tuttle had been working on his house for four years. It is a bit like a wood museum. It has spruce siding, cedar trim, fir and hemlock structural members, alder and cedar accents, and oak cabinets. What he didn't mill himself he paid for by logging.

At one time the homestead was farmed for oats, rhubarb, potatoes, and hops. There were chickens and turkeys and dairy cows. Now the farm is limited to beef cattle that wander on sixty acres of fields and browse the recent clearcuts. All thirty-one of the animals have names. One bovine, Gingerbread, is so tame and pampered that it, "doesn't know if it's a dog or a human," said Tuttle. Names or no names, the cattle are slaughtered when age or financial need make it appropriate, and Tuttle's three young daughters grow up to understand this. One can love animals—or trees, or gardens—and still use them, the lesson implies.

If the people in Forks have an image of what they would like to be, the Maxfield-Tuttle homestead would likely fit their dream of self-sufficiency that comes from owning one's own land. Almost no one in town—including Bob Tuttle Jr. himself—could afford today to acquire 400 acres of wooded land with two and a half miles of river and creekfront. The timber alone is probably worth $1 million dollars today from the right buyer or buyers. The one thing the family has done, however, is hang on to this land for more than a century, and Tuttle intends to do the same. "I don't want to divide this up," he said. "What would I have? A lot of money in the bank." He shrugged, dismissing such an asset as so much dross.

Some see in people such as Bob Tuttle a partial solution to the Pacific Northwest's forest fight. Thousands of small woodlot owners such as Tuttle together own more than a fifth of the commercial timberland in Washington State. Much of what they own is in the lowlands, the best tree-growing area. Taken as a whole, however, a lot of this prime land is managed haphazardly. Some has been harvested or cleared and has grown back as tight, pole-like second growth that has never been thinned. Other parcels have grown back as brushy alder groves of little commercial value. Harvesting is often poorly paced. An owner may cut it all on retirement or when his children enter college, shocking his neighbors. Some subdivide their land into five or ten acre mini-homesites, permanently removing the land from wood production. Some cut in panic.

"Basically, a lot of people around here are logging their land before more regulations come in," said Tuttle. It became a vicious circle. As the 1980s drew to a close, the more the public screamed for logging regulation the more frantically landowners cut, prompting yet more demand for reform. Neither side felt they could count on the future. "Sustained yield would work if they made forest land forestry land," Tuttle argued. "You've got to have that land base."

The amount of land managed by individuals is shrinking as they sell to the big timber companies or developers. It has declined from just over a quarter of Washington's forest land in 1962 to just over a fifth today. Still, if they could be given the incentives to invest in tree management the way a Weyerhaeuser can afford to, the wood they could produce would eventually go a long way toward replacing the remnant old growth set aside for the spotted owl and other species.

Tuttle is one of the woodlot owners who could be a model for what is possible. He has a plan. He has calculated he could harvest an average of about nine acres of trees per year on his land into eternity, replanting what he cuts and harvesting again on a forty-two year rotation. The net income, after deducting for logging and hauling and replanting and taxes, should equal a decent middle-class wage. The resulting homestead would not be tidy in the storybook sense of rolling fields and towering groves. Rather, it would be a patchwork of different-aged trees, thinned and pruned and harvested and regrown, with a few groves of epic cedar left untouched for sentimental and ecological reasons. The farm would not be old growth but it would be green and infinitely productive, a habitat for many species of wildlife, and cared for by a family that would know every acre, that had stooped to plant every tree.

In 1989, Tuttle hand planted 43,000 seedlings on his own land and on the acreage of his neighbors that he logged for them, stooping 43,000 times. The seedlings cost 16 to 26.5 cents each. Tuttle couldn't really justify the more expensive ones as an investment, but they have a stronger root structure to make them grow faster and he couldn't resist giving them a try. Tuttle delights in fast-growing trees. He enjoys taking visitors down winding cow paths through the prickly grove of spruce "super trees" he planted that have shot up as if in a White House Christmas Tree competition. To demonstrate the richness of this land for tree growth, Tuttle takes out a steel tape to measure a spiky leader, the vertical top of the tree that pokes above the highest horizontal branches and that marks how much the tree grew this season. "Forty-two inches!" he crows. That's what more than one hundred inches of rain on valley bottom soil can do for you. Tuttle cut one fifty-year-old tree that was six-and-a-half feet around. Some of its annual growth rings were two inches thick.

Tuttle is a man who can sit on his porch and view the best and worst of what he does. He has thinned the second-growth wood that his driveway traverses on the way to his new house, leaving an entry of young, fast-growing trees and bigger stumps. Tuttle and his oldest daughter, Anne, planted the clearcut bank above his new parking area with fir seedlings. Now, a couple of years later, the trees are one and two feet high. Anne also brought a young Douglas fir seedling home from kindergarten and planted it alongside their driveway. When it is not raining she waters it every day. She named the tree Crystal.

"I am not a preservationist but I am an environmentalist," Tuttle said. "I didn't pave over my swamp. There's no drain tile in it. I didn't cut every one of the trees." Small clearcuts of a few acres are scattered here and there on the homestead, but the pace of cutting demonstrates a measured reluctance far different from the corporate and government harvesting nearby. His land is given time to recover. What was a pasture in his grandfather's day is now a grove of fat spruce in need of thinning. As a boy, Tuttle used to play in a field head high in bracken fern; it was planted by his father and now boasts forty-foot-high spruce. "I replant everything I cut," the forty-three-year-old Tuttle said. "Trees grow back." It is the mantra of Forks.

Tuttle has the easygoing, generous nature of a man who has found peace with his schoolteacher wife, April, his three daughters, and his new home in this wet corner of America. He grew up hunting and hiking and as a youth joined the Special Forces in 1966, just when the book and movie about the Green Berets were making the elite commando group famous. The army gave Tuttle the whole world to compare to Forks. He circled the globe twice. He ate on gold plates with Ethiopian Emperor Haile Selassie. President Richard Nixon pinned a silver star on Tuttle at the White House. He served three tours in Vietnam. The last time he was shot up and almost killed.

He came back from Vietnam to heal in the woods. He cut shake bolts for a while, then worked for a house construction company, then worked with his father constructing logging roads for Crown Zellerbach, and then logged some more. Like many people in Forks he has had economic ups and downs in pursuing the cyclic vagaries of the wood business. More recently it has been up. The one son in a family with six sisters, he elected to stay on the family land.

This is home. Tuttle likes the spirit of places like Forks, the independence interwoven with camaraderie. He recalled fondly how the community pulled together to create a "Forestry Fair" at the Fourth of July to try to explain, in twenty-nine different booths, what they did and how they did it. He helped prefabricate the booth walls and roofs and then sketched out a pattern on the ground for their placement. From the air, the pattern would spell out the word "LOGS." Half the town turned out to help and the booths went up in an hour and a half. It was like a barn raising, and it gave people a feeling of competence, of not being impotent victims of distant political whims.

The lush appeal of this land is in Tuttle's bones, and the drum of rain on his new skylit breakfast nook is the sound of nature's continuity. "Sometimes it's neat to put your rain gear on, hop on a tractor, and go down to trim some trees," Tuttle explained, walking through a dark spruce grove. "It's not necessarily a way of life, so much—it's a place of life. These are roots that most people never get to know. If we sold it, we'd be rich on paper. But the truth is, we'd be poor. How could I come back here and know someone else had it?"

When I met Tuttle he was wearing black work suspenders that on one side said, SHOOT AN OWL, and on the other, SAVE A LOGGER. Tuttle was a bit sheepish about the extremity of the sentiment when I asked about that. To his knowledge he has never seen a spotted owl despite a lifetime in the woods, and says he would never shoot one if he did. It would be stupid to do so, first because such violence would only make the bird more endangered than ever, and second it would be the innocent victim of a human quarrel.

The suspenders simply express the community's frustration, Tuttle said. "It's a stupid saying, but it's no more stupid than the preservationists saying, 'Lock it all up,'" Tuttle contends. "If they are going to lock it up, it would be prudent for me to clearcut the whole thing right now."

The truth is, Tuttle lives where he does in part for the wildlife. He talks about the animals all the time. Eagles roost in snags near his house. Elk drift by his new dining area windows. In the fall, Shuwah Creek fills with spawning salmon.

The one thing Tuttle does not want to do is give up his land. He figures the 400 acres are about the minimum necessary to provide a sustained living for a family, so his tentative plan is to leave the place someday to his oldest daughter, Anne. He realizes his girls will face some hard choices, however, and he wants them to attend college to give them as much opportunity as possible. So as each is born Tuttle has developed a ritual. He picks five acres of trees—enough to yield at least 200,000 board feet by the time they graduate from high school—and dedicates it to them as their "college grove." Those trees are their assurance they will have the money to go to a university.

Before each of his daughters is a year old Tuttle bundles her up, snugs her against his shoulder, and walks her down to introduce the child to "her" trees. He explains how important trees are, and how his girls' futures are tied to the forest.

In the fall of 1990 he did this with Caitlin, his youngest, whom he had nicknamed Squeak. He walked her down, and showed her the grove, and thought again of how lucky it is for migratory Americans to find a piece of land to love and call home. And Caitlin?

Tuttle laughed. "Mostly," he said, "she just drooled on my shoulder. But she'll grow up. And the trees will be there."

EPILOGUE
THE FINAL FOREST

▲▲▲▲▲▲▲▲

The final forest, that last magnificent remnant of what stood in America before European discovery, was quieter in 1991. It was as if all sides, exhausted by the acrimony and the worry, had paused to take breath.

On the Olympic National Forest around Forks, the federal government's timber sale program was at an almost complete halt. Half the staff in its district office there, the people who had been applauded for years for achieving the heady harvest goals set by Congress, had been warned their jobs were likely to disappear. Washington State's Department of Natural Resources had also slowed letting any new contracts, while it considered the impact of protecting the bird.

Logging had slowed anyway due to the winter's recession and war with Iraq. The timber industry was in the downward swing of an economic cycle it regarded as inevitable as the seasons. By mid-year lumber prices were rising again, but the pause was a good time to take stock. Compromise was still elusive.

Most Pacific Northwest congressmen, not anxious to carry the feud into the 1992 election, wanted the issue resolved. The 1990 election had not proved to be a clear referendum on the timber issue. Ann Goos's narrow loss was symptomatic of the confusing mix of wins and losses for both sides. Most incumbents prevailed. Oregon Senator Mark Hatfield, one of the firmest defenders of the timber industry, got the scare of his political life when polls showed him trailing his liberal challenger, but he hurried home to campaign and won election to a fifth term. In Washington, a Democratic liberal named Jolene Unsoeld easily held on to the timber district congressional seat she first had narrowly won two years before, but only after appealing to the gun lobby and dancing around the tree issue. The only thing the voters seemed to confirm was the wisdom of the politicians' cautious wariness of the no-win old-growth controversy.

Earlier predictions that the 1990s would be the "Decade of the Environment" had yet to be proven. Despite polls showing strong public support for environmental protection, environmental initiatives across the nation were pummeled less than six months after the twentieth anniversary of Earth Day. The most ambitious timber proposal, California's "Forests Forever" initiative to buy up old-growth forests, was defeated. In Washington State, a measure for statewide growth controls and planning was trounced two to one. An attempt to forge a compromise on logging of private lands in Washington, called the Sustained Forestry Roundtable, broke down in disagreement between environmentalists and the timber industry. By the end of 1991 the acrimony was so strong that environmentalists once more turned to the courts, this time suing the state Forest Practices Board for not imposing stricter regulations on logging.

In Washington, D.C., the desire of Northwest congressional representatives to put the issue behind them was stymied by a hardening of positions on both sides. Environmentalists, having nearly shut down national forest logging in the final forest through the courts, had little incentive for making concessions. The industry, meanwhile, was a temporary political victim of its own economic prudence. Having routinely purchased timber it did not intend to harvest for two or three seasons, it was still cutting wood from this backlog despite the court prohibition on more timber sales, meaning the economic disaster it repeatedly predicted was slow to develop. A persistent recession also dampened national demand for lumber. Some industry strategists counseled waiting until the wood shortage became so apparent there might be support for amending the source of its trouble, the Endangered Species Act. While half a dozen competing ancient-forest bills had been introduced and more were expected from committee chairmen, it remained uncertain whether agreement would be reached before the 1992 elections, and whether a solution would be a temporary truce or permanent protection.

The bureaucracy's plans for owl protection, meanwhile, plodded onward. The U.S. Fish and Wildlife Service did not expect to arrive at a final map of "critical habitat" and finish its owl recovery until 1992. The Forest Service hoped to end the Judge Dwyer injunction by adopting the Jack Ward Thomas recommendations as its owl protection plan in 1992, but fierce fighting was expected over whether that was adequate.

That something as sweeping as the 7.7 million acres for owls proposed by Thomas would come to be grudgingly defended by the industry and government and regarded as a bare minimum by environmentalists showed how stunningly swift had been the change in attitudes in just a few years. By the fall of 1991, environmentalists were already looking ahead to even more ambitious campaigns: to shift the fight from specific trees or forests to a call for protecting biodiversity across urban, rural, and wilderness landscapes. They want to preserve not just one species like the owl but all native species, to invent a new kind of harmony in which economic development is sustainable and accommodates the natural world. "There is a lesson of boldness in all this," Mitch Friedman said in a speech to an environmental powwow in Seattle. Logging had been curtailed far more swiftly than most had dared dream five years before, and the public was seemingly more receptive to ecological arguments than environmentalists had dared hope. "We must dare to state our case," Friedman said. "If not us, then who? Who will speak for biodiversity?"

Still lacking was agreement on how many jobs would be lost to the owl and how much old growth was left. Estimates of the number of jobs lost through adoption of the Thomas and the Fish and Wildlife recommendations ranged from nearly zero by the environmentalists' economic consultants to the timber industry's latest forecast of 93,000. The mapping of old growth had gotten more precise, but deciding whether the ancient forest glass was 90 percent empty, as environmentalists calculated, or up to 30 percent full, as the industry argued, continued to hinge on what was counted as old growth and how much high-altitude land was included in the estimates. Many preservationists suggested that rather than worry about numbers, people wondering should fly over the Pacific Northwest and judge for themselves.

If there was any certainty, it was that the region could expect continued change. The Pacific Northwest, accounting for just 15 percent of U.S. lumber and plywood production by 1991, had been at least temporarily eclipsed by the South's tree plantations as the nation's foremost lumber and paper producer. Its competitive edge—quality lumber, provided though the harvest of tight-grained, knotless ancient trees that take centuries to grow—continues to erode with or without the owl. Modernization is expected to cut the timber work force by

25 percent in the next two decades. Urban and suburban growth, not tree preservation, is removing an average of 75,000 acres of timberland from the forest base each year in Washington and Oregon. Timber's share of the economy, and its political clout, is fading.

Yet for all its woes, economists predicted that the timber industry will persist. The final forest remains the best place in the world to grow merchantable trees. Darius Adams, a Seattle-based consultant, told congressional aides that even with owl restrictions, the second growth of trees coming of age east of the Cascades should keep the region's overall timber harvest at about the same level in the future as it was in the 1960s and 1970s. "I don't see an enormous crash in the future here," he said. He also predicted that worldwide wood demand, and prices, will continue to rise.

Ed Whitelaw of the University of Oregon contends that timber communities near the urban corridor that stretches along Interstate 5 in Washington and Oregon can expect to survive but also to change, as they are gentrified with urban commuters and tourism. Many believe there is enormous, long-overdue work to be done in the forest besides cutting it down. Chad Oliver, the forestry expert at the University of Washington who clashed with Jerry Franklin, estimated that 800 unemployed loggers could be put to work to thin and prune trees just in western Washington at a net profit to the industry, since the thinned stands produce more and better wood. Brian Gerber, an economist at Oregon State University, said property values were rising, not falling, in timber regions and that schools and local governments overall were getting more tax revenue, not less. Meanwhile, fewer and fewer urbanites in the Northwest feel any direct connection to their onetime bedrock industry. And for the rest of the nation, the cost of setting aside old growth will likely be slight. The Portland *Oregonian* newspaper cited economist calculations that the kind of restricted harvest called for in the Thomas report would add only about $200 to the price of a new house and $12 per year to the price of household consumption of wood and paper.

Unresolved, however, was the fate of individual communities and woods workers. Whitelaw was far less optimistic about remote communities such as Forks, outside of the I-5 corridor. He talked bluntly about "triage," of the fact there may be no *reason* for a place like Forks if it could not mine timber. He said the dichotomy between urban growth and rural calamity was an extension of a trend going on in the United States since the start of the industrial revolution.

When economists spoke of tourism and gentrification, they talked about the potential of places such as Zigzag, Oregon, on the road to a popular ski area. "How many places are there like Zigzag and how many like Forks?" asked sociologist Richard Gale of the University of Oregon, to illustrate the two extremes. Forks, he added, is caught up in technological and economic change that is both national and global. "We're at the end of an era," he said, "of high-paying jobs which require little education and allow their workers to live in a low-cost community."

Sociologist Robert Lee complained that the glibness with which economists promised the Northwest would continue to have both old growth and a net gain of employment ignored specific tragedies. "These labor markets do not work efficiently," Lee argued. "Some people do retrain and some do move, but others don't. There's a lot of stickiness." He predicted that for scores of communities such as Forks, a dark era was beginning of unemployment, despair, alcoholism, and abuse.

At the core of such a tragedy will be a loss of self-esteem and purpose among woods workers. Forks has largely felt excluded from the philosophic shift toward the forest. Many loggers feel they have been condemned without being notified their way of life was on trial. The result is wounded dignity. "People don't adapt very well when they perceive themselves as being oppressed," noted sociologist Matthew Carroll.

Forks was already trying to grapple with change. The town set up committees in 1990 to look at everything from promoting local milling of logs to beautifying Highway 101 to entice tourists visiting Olympic National Park to stay longer. There was talk of trying to revive a moribund industrial park on the edge of town that is now just a weed-grown field. As always, the town's remoteness from markets, supplies, and educational institutions made attracting investment difficult. Balancing this was a never-give-an-inch determination and self-sufficient creativity.

There were signs that even remote Forks will be sucked into the orbit of Washington State development. Washington gained an average of 70,000 new people per year in the 1980s. Even as logging slumped in Forks, housing was still difficult to find. Its biggest motel was building an addition. A new state prison at Clallam Bay had brought new residents, and retirees were discovering that if they could put up with the rain, housing in the West End was as cheap as anything in western Washington. If some fear Forks will die, others wonder if its "discovery" by a new wave of immigrants will put pressure on the landscape no less serious than logging.

While the humans grappled for answers, the trees that survived abided with nature's patience, rooted with a solidity that suggested longer cycles and a different perspective.

The forest is represented most eloquently when it speaks for itself. No book can sing the message the wind does as it riffles through the cottonwood and alder along the Peninsula's green rivers, a luxuriant carpet of dark conifers climbing the ridges behind. No photograph can capture the complex smell of fir needles and wood dust and moist, yeasty decay. A visitor hardly needs a boundary sign to sense when he or she has entered Olympic National Park, so obvious is the difference between the natural ecosystem and its man-made replacement. Cross into the park and the forest changes in its scale, its complexity, and its promise of discovery. It seems to whisper that here, in these protected groves, are secret answers to questions you have not yet dreamed of asking. A child senses the difference.

The gigantic spruce and cedar and fir of the Olympic Peninsula are in a sense dinosaur trees, descendants of the conifers that developed in that prehistoric era before the evolution of the more advanced but smaller broadleafs. I don't know why humans are so fascinated by creatures that are big, such as dinosaurs and elephants and whales, but that instinctual awe certainly extends to these forests. The idea that something that big is alive, pumping water more than twenty stories high, grasping the sun with seventy million needles, and showering the ground with up to eight million seeds per acre each year reminds us how unbelievable the planet is. To ramble along the mossy mat of a big old-growth log—using it as a sidewalk to look down at the garden of fern and wood sorrel and salal and skunk cabbage and mushroom and salmon berry and fairy bells and lady's slipper and huckleberry—to do that is to walk across the breast of a giant, sleeping mother. So fiercely do plants compete in the wet of these forests that tree seed can have difficulty getting a start below. Accordingly, these logs become nurseries, the body of these prone leviathans sprouting with the seedlings of the young.

The three-dimensional complexity of this world is what sets it apart. Trying to see its top is like peering through veils of green gauze: the lacy weave of vine maple and yew, the drooping tips of young hemlock straining to grow up under their seniors, the thick catwalks of the first boughs, and the light-speckled lattice of the higher limbs. Much of the wildlife in this vast apartment house remains out of sight to the casual observer, but you may find yourself scolded by a Douglas squirrel: eying you judiciously as she picks apart a spruce cone for seed and then leaving a midden of flakes at the butt of an enormous trunk, like a brown doormat signing welcome.

When the sun shines through this puzzle of green, the forest becomes a temple, speaking of greater powers and further worlds. And when a storm comes and the wood darkens and the trees rock with ominous creaks and thunder rumbles in the valley, the forest becomes threatening and spooky—and it is beautiful in that guise, too.

How much of this world should be preserved? First, consider the peculiarity of that question, so reflective of the history of American settlement and the way we measure wealth. Our civilization arrived assuming it would consume all of whatever resource it found, except for whatever bits it might set aside for wonder and memory. In hindsight one can't help conclude that this approach was backward. Perhaps we should have started from the assumption that all the natural ecosystem was valuable and the question was not how much to leave alone, but how much we truly needed to convert. With that approach, the question of "what should be left" would be as old as Pacific Northwest settlement itself, and the implications of preservation would be apparent before, not after, people had staked their lives and dreams on the virgin forest's complete replacement.

What is most astounding about the old-growth debate is that we don't even know for sure how much we've already taken, as if we were brainless consumers who never bothered to total the withdrawals in our checkbook. We simply spent, until some people began crying "Too much!" and others, who depended on those checks to survive, felt betrayed that no one had warned them what the balance is.

Eric Forsman sounded warnings about the spotted owl as early as 1973. Congress ordered a change in direction and values in national forest management in 1976. It took fourteen additional years for federal officials in the Pacific Northwest to adopt plans that reflected that new direction. Had leadership been exercised in the mid-1970s to determine what was going to be done to preserve both the majestic ecosystem and the dignity and self-reliance of logging communities, there would have been more than a half-million acres of additional old growth to compromise with. The leadership was not there.

A political realist might say of course not, that any resource must reach scarcity before society can be expected to grapple with conserving or preserving it. Perhaps. The delays in decision making won timber communities an extra ten or fifteen years, but it also ensured that any compromise after that would be hard fought and bitter.

Similarly disheartening is the failure of our society to look at the forest as a whole. Divided between federal, state, and private owners, each part is jealously managed with little regard to what is happening to the trees next door. It is past time not only to ask how much old growth we need, but what kind of a forest we need: What kind of overall ecosystem and landscape and productive forest do we really want to pass to future generations? How much for wood, how much for habitation, how much for developed recreation, and how much for contemplation? If the old-growth forest fight does nothing else, it may encourage us to lose our myopia and look at the final forest as a single great piece.

As salmon joined owls on the threatened species list in 1991 and the consequences of the Endangered Species Act became ever more apparent, scientists and congressmen in the Pacific Northwest began talking seriously about this. The world's population had doubled since 1950. So had the population of Washington State. Both were projected to as much as double again by the middle of the twenty-first century. With this kind of development pressure, a casual approach to landscape planning based only on private property rights seemed increasingly doomed. Being proposed by Franklin and Thomas and other scientists was not species protection or preserves of plots of wilderness, but ecosystem management across the human landscape. Envisioned for the final forest was a complex scheme. Its backbone would be the parks and wilderness areas along the region's mountain ranges. Its skeleton, or veins, would be riparian zones along rivers and streams that stretched from mountain to tidewater. These riparian zones were the richest regions biologically. Urban areas would be given some geographic limit, and the surviving forest would be managed in a variety of ways: some of it set aside as permanent old-growth groves, some of it managed as tree farms for wood, and some of it harvested on much longer rotations, two centuries that allowed second-growth trees enough time to become habitat for owls and other species. Clear-cutting would fade, replaced with the complex pattern suggested by Franklin.

The scientists said this kind of complexity would require a new kind of forester, one trained to look at the entire landscape. In order that foresters might acquire the expertise to do so, they suggested, America might want to copy European systems in which each forester spent his or her entire career in one place, apprenticed to a senior forester who would pass on his or her local knowledge.

It it precisely this kind of local knowledge that people in Forks argue they can offer. People there feel they have been vilified out of urban ignorance: that their skill, their expertise, their work ethic, and their replanting has drawn no respect. They argue they love the forest most deeply of all. It is the love that comes from living in the forest in all its moods, of depending on it for sustenance, and of not running from it even when it tries to kill you. Ranger Fred Harnisch talked of a similar kind of feeling once. He discussed his simultaneous love of wildlife and love of hunting, how eating the meat of his kill months after the hunt did not exploit the spirit of the animal but paid homage and respect to it. Such a meal can be a bow to the interdependency of life. To use the meat was to reimagine the hunt and the landscape and the magnificence of the animal itself, it was a sacrament to put some of the wild country inside you.

It is probably difficult for people accustomed to getting their meat in foam and plastic containers to comprehend this kind of bond, but it is nevertheless real. The twin tragedy in the Pacific Northwest is not just the loss of the trees, but the destruction of self-esteem in people producing goods that society demanded, doing it in the best way they knew how. If their skill could be coupled to the kind of long-range ecosystem management that ecologists are dreaming about, the region could set an example for the world.

To the inhabitants of the Pacific Northwest, big trees are so familiar that one fully recognizes their uniqueness only by traveling elsewhere. In the summer of 1990, I had the opportunity while on assignment for the *Seattle Times* newspaper to look at trees around the world. I saw the tightly managed, heavily pressured forests of Japan, still recovering from disastrous overharvesting in the years during and after World War II. I saw the eucalyptus plantations in Thailand that are replacing the logged-off teak jungles: bleak new fields where pole-like saplings about thirty feet high, planted in monotonous rows, are cut after only three to five years to keep pace with the nation's pressing demand for lumber and firewood. I saw shaven Himalayan foothills in India, the oak replaced with seedlings of faster-growing pine and the weakened hillsides sheering off in monsoon rains to fill valleys with glacial rock. I saw parched plains in Pakistan, where pathetic seedlings planted in a brown pan of land are hand-watered with five-gallon cans, a tree-by-tree attempt to slow growing desertification. I saw the scrubby maquis of the Mediterranean, the product of thousands of years of overgrazing and resulting erosion, with grand acacia trees preserved for centuries in a Turkish village giving some notion of what the forests there must once have been like. I saw the forests of Germany, so weakened by acid rain that heavy winds toppled in one month what normally would have been harvested in five years.

"We have downsized our vegetation, and are living in a pygmy world," I wrote after that trip. I was sobered by the contrast between these foreign woods and what still survives in America's final great forest: one of the last in which the design of something greater than ourselves can clearly be seen.

This book is, of course, written on a tree. You hold its fibers in your fingers. I am grateful for the skill and sweat and ingenuity that went into providing the paper it is printed on.

I hope you read it for whatever understanding it provides. Then, when you get a chance, go and read the living things that it came from.

INDEX

▲▲▲▲▲▲▲

INDEX